Cover Image:
"Dump Culture" by Marie D. Moldovan

Editing, Layout and Design
Marie D. Moldovan

Published by

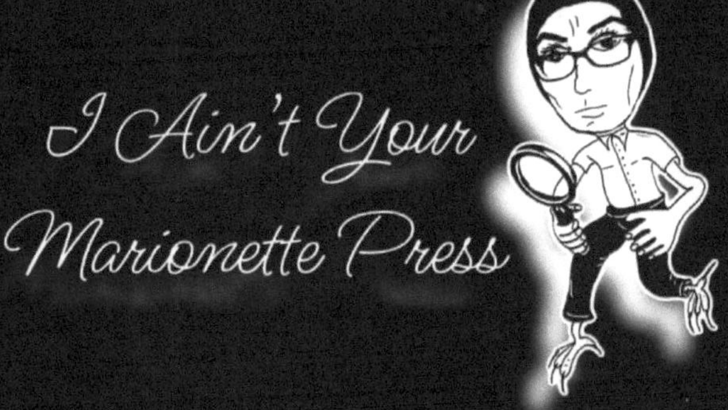

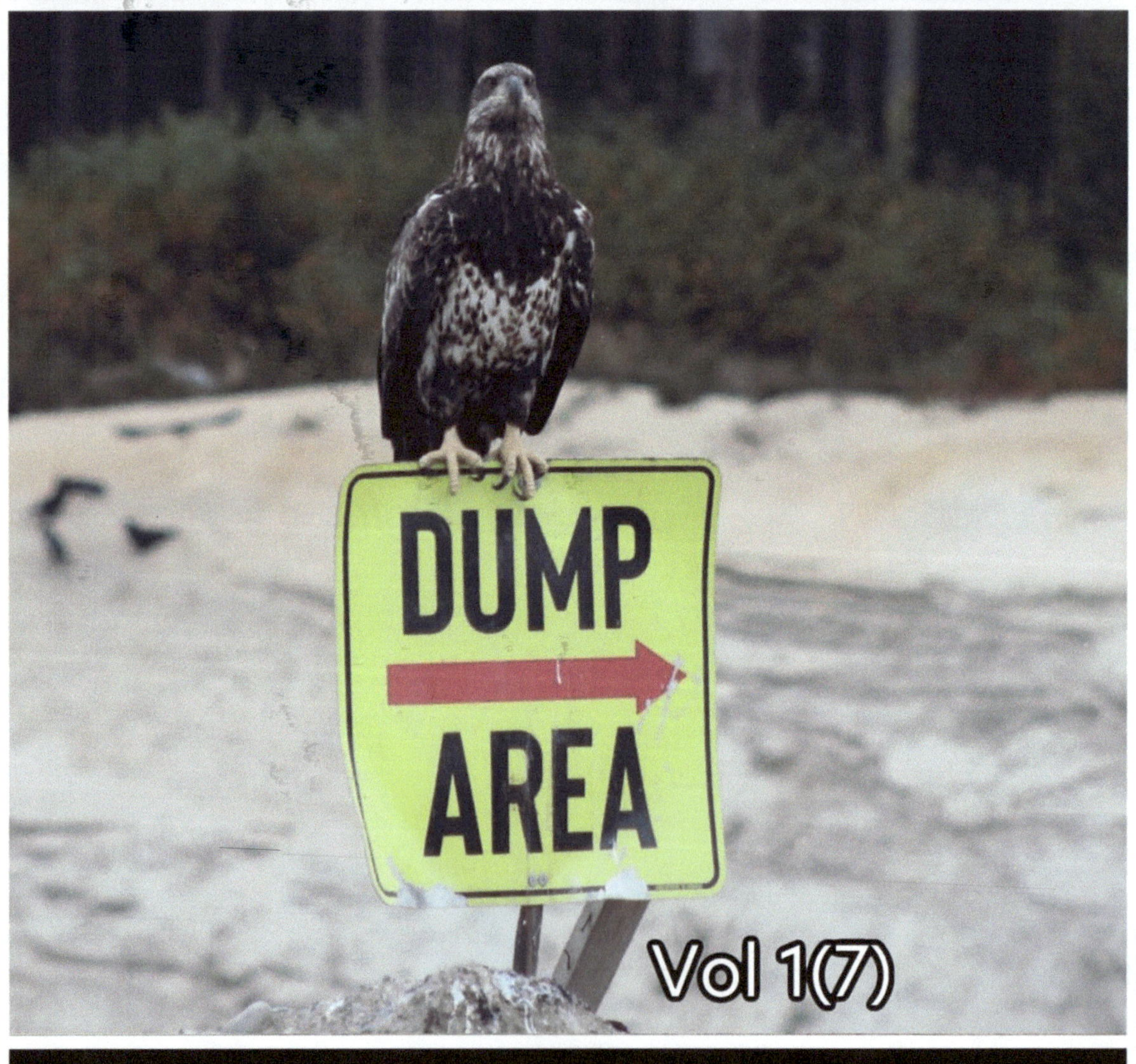
SHATTERED PSYCHE
DUMP
AREA
Vol 1(7)
I Ain't Your Marionette

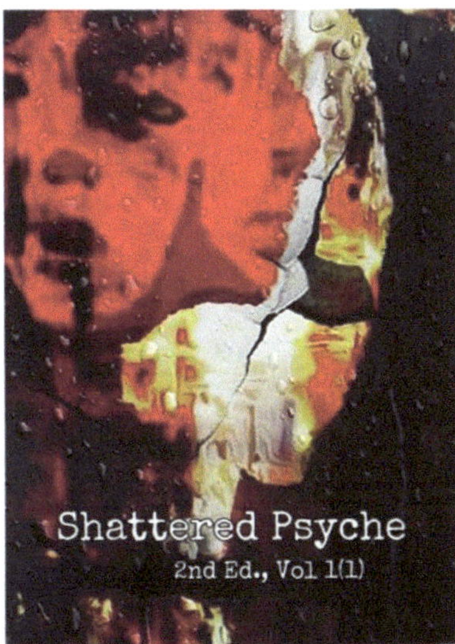

A behind the lens statement about Shattered Psyche 1(7) by artist Joe Mykut:

The span of this book and it's images feel like one is following the journey of a single life force energy as it experiences existence in infinite forms all at once. The false line between man and nature is blurred back to nonexistence as we bare witness to them both entangled as one. From wildlife to human form, each one neglected by the other and by self, it becomes more apparent than ever that we are all connected to the same source as the source. Divinity within dumps and symbolism of the journey through life and death, and a face seen in various values, each express a life being simultaneously and omnipotently lived out frame by frame. Like a still movie brought to life by the scanning of the readers eyes this mental movie reel is captivating and fascinating.

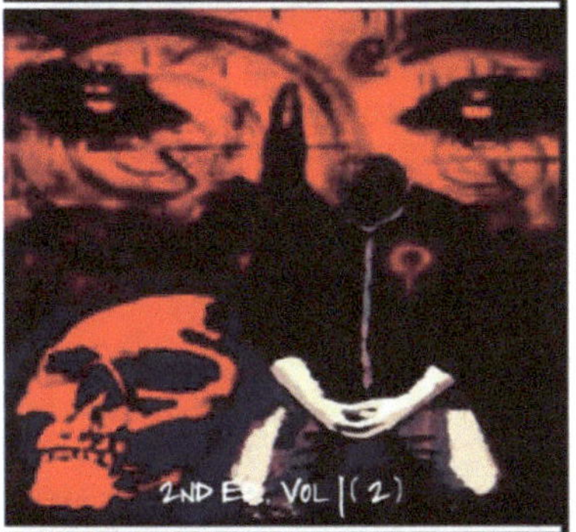

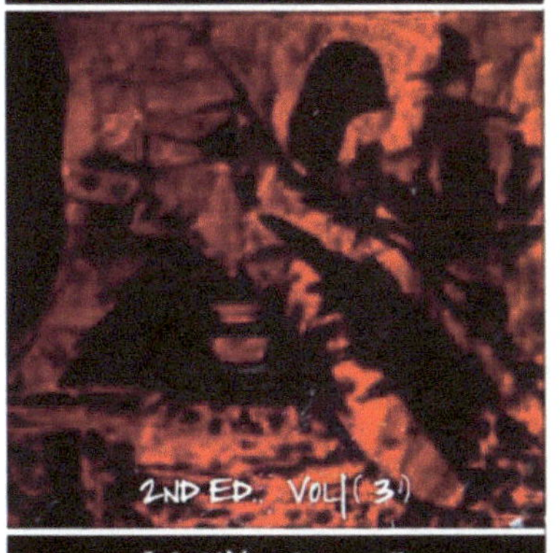

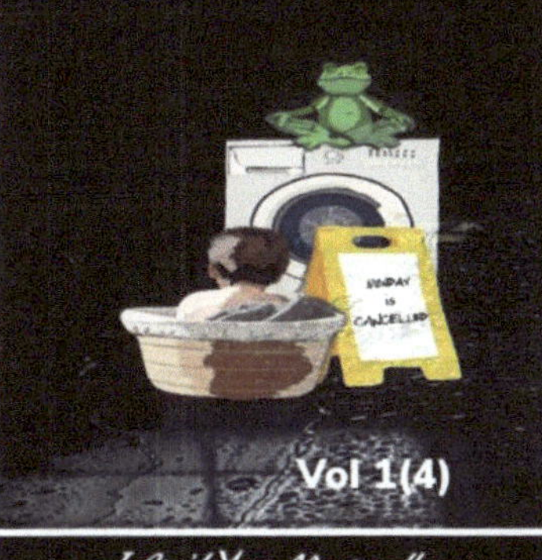

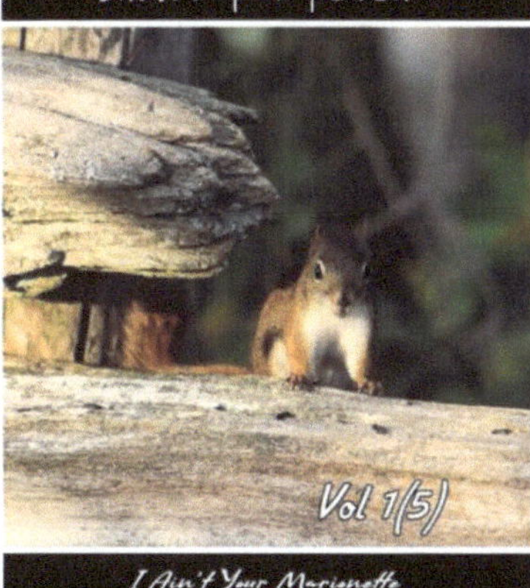

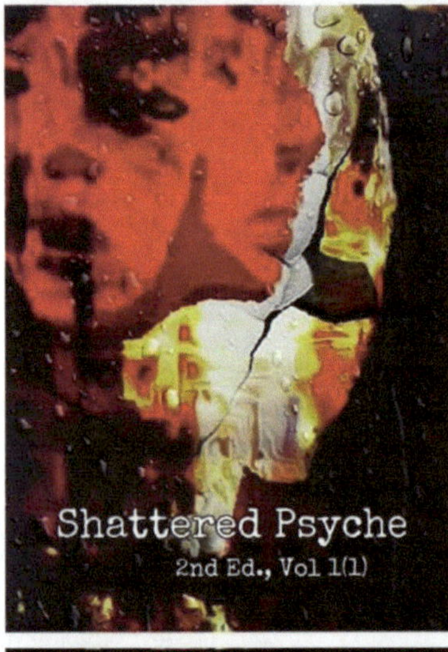

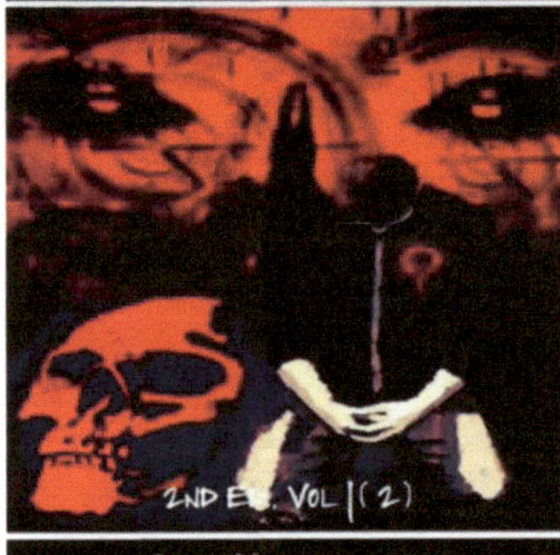

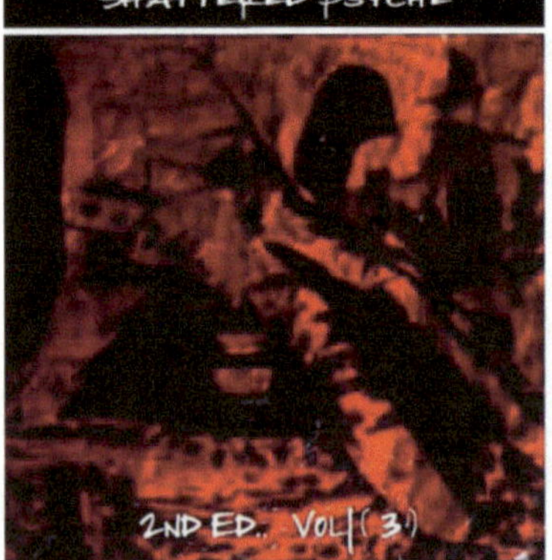

Dedicated to those seeking inner peace

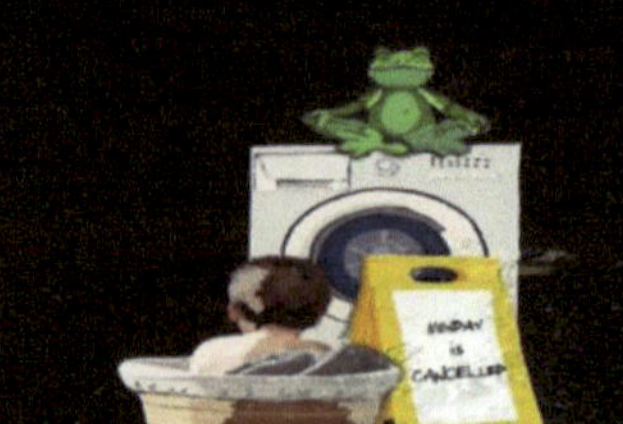

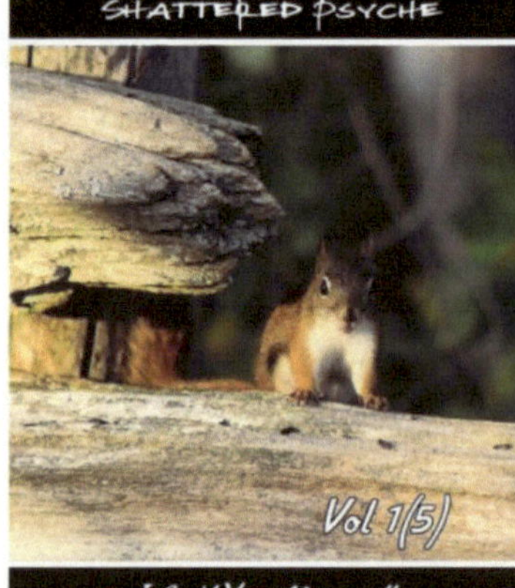

TABLE OF CONTENTS

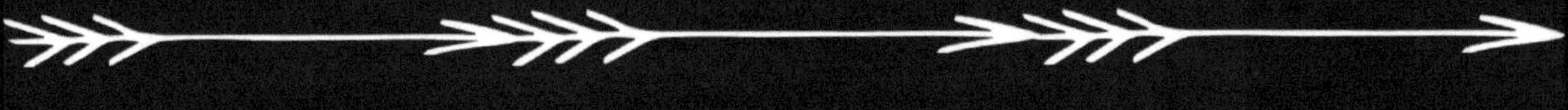

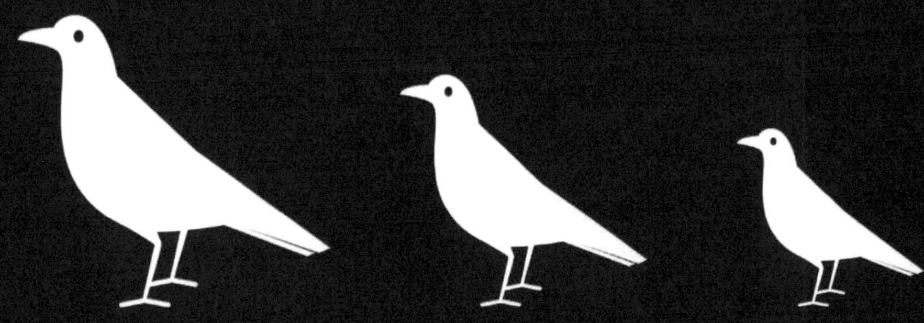

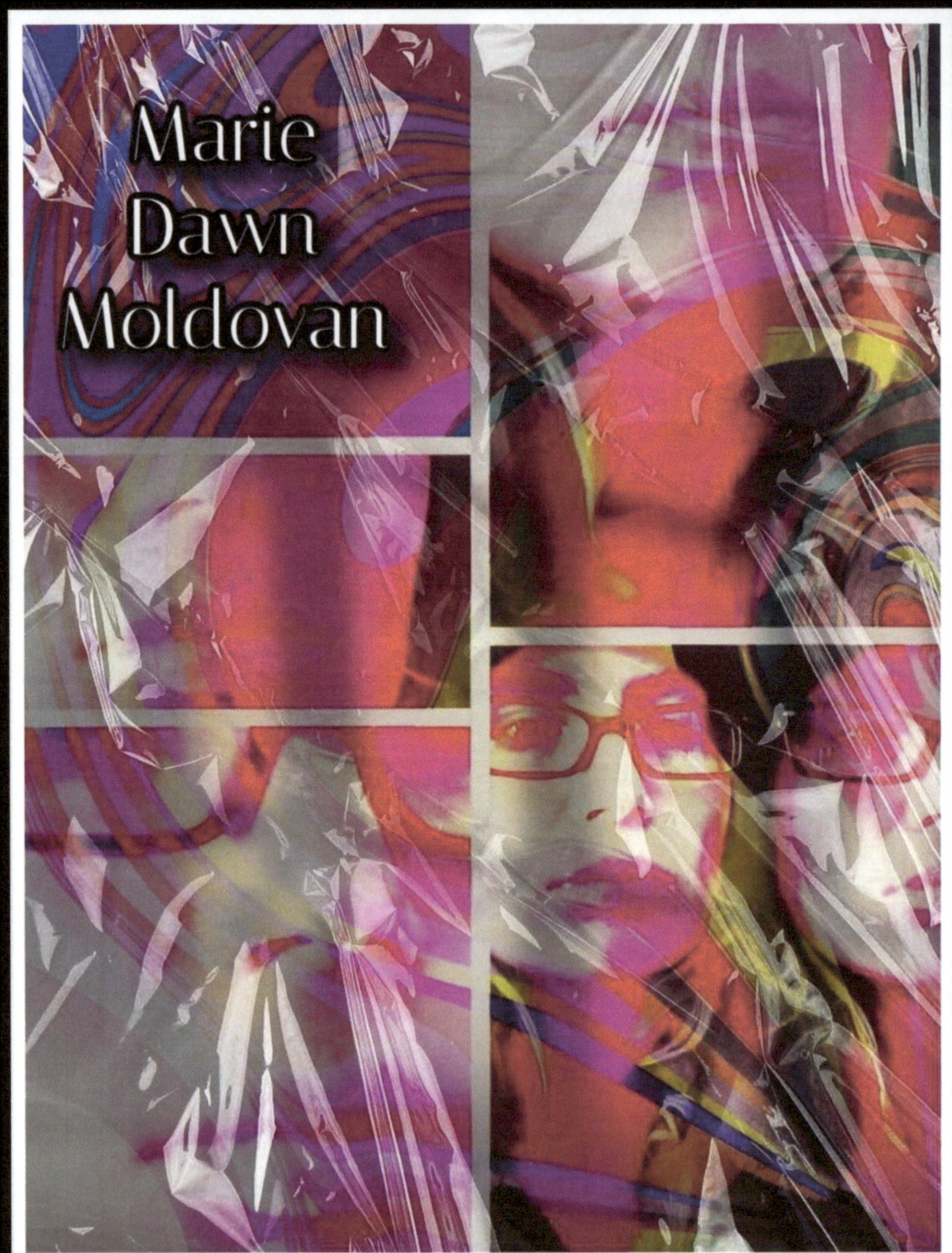
Marie
Dawn
Moldovan

About the Artist

Marie Moldovan is a writer, artist, Canadian Forces veteran, jack-of-all-trades, and independent publisher at I Ain't Your Marionette. Shortly after he/r diagnosis with service-related PTSD and the passing of he/r husband in 2018, s/he began writing poetry to free he/r tormented mind. S/he is the author of 20 Years of Winter.

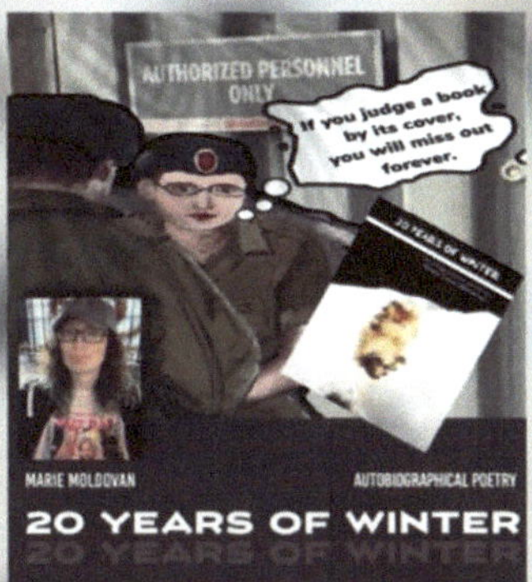

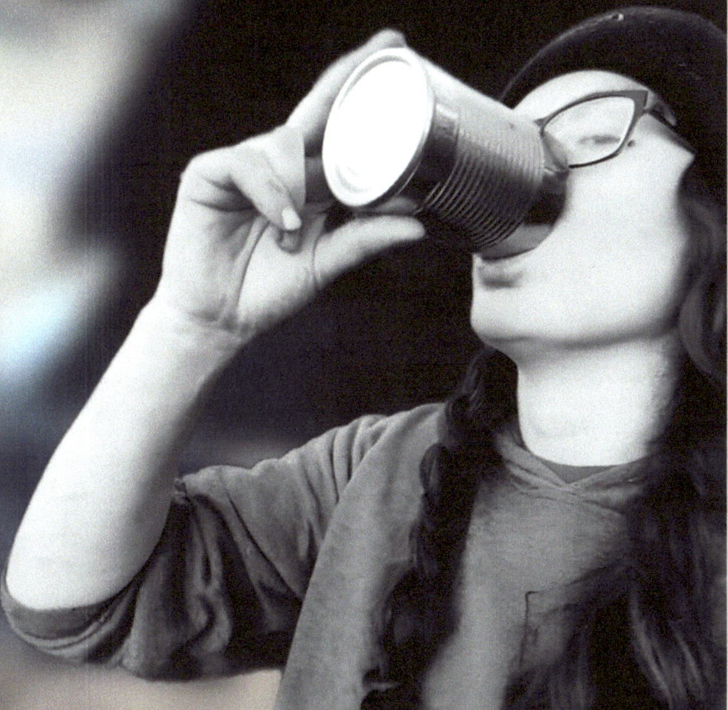

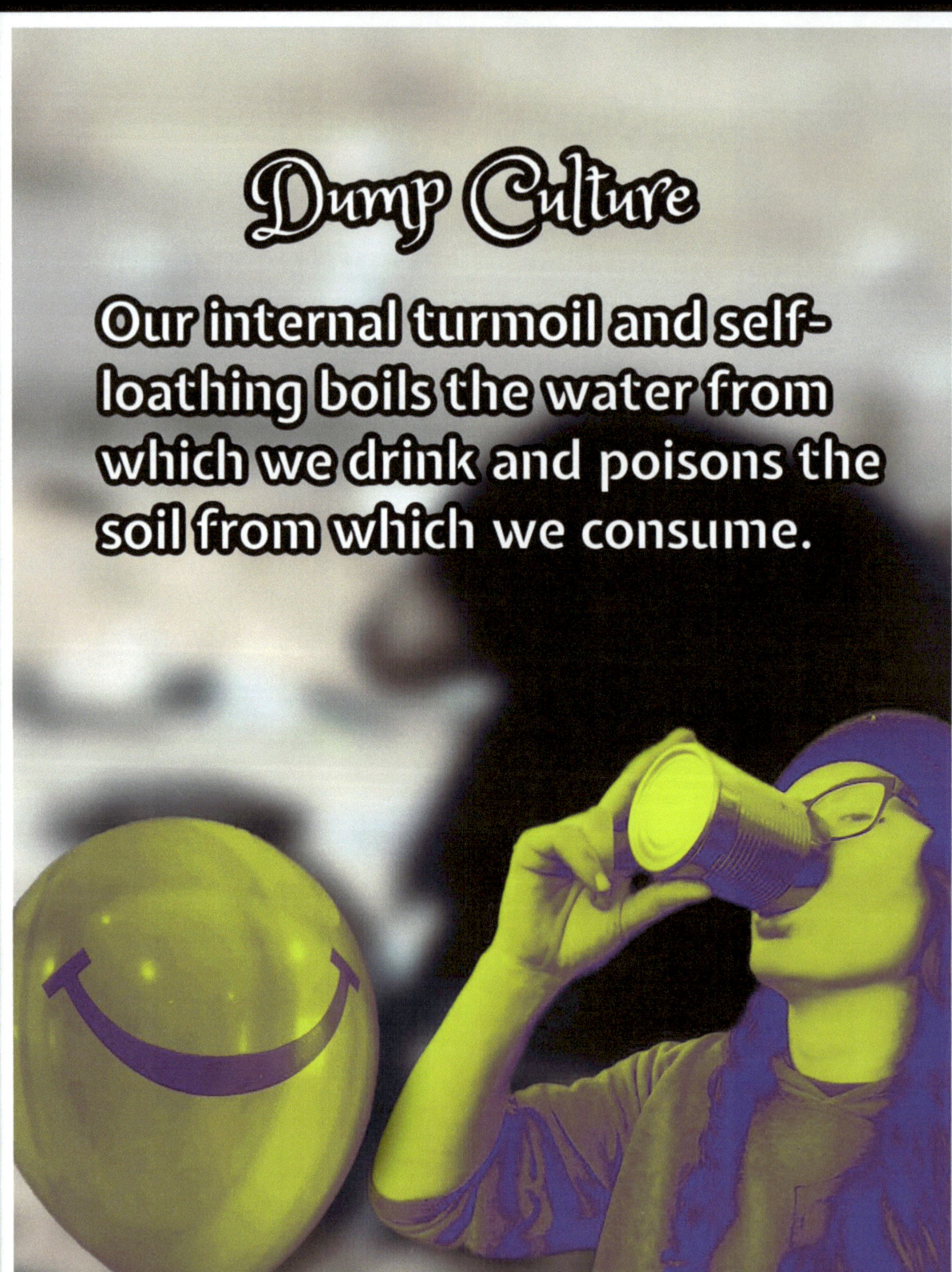
Dump Culture

Our internal turmoil and self-loathing boils the water from which we drink and poisons the soil from which we consume.

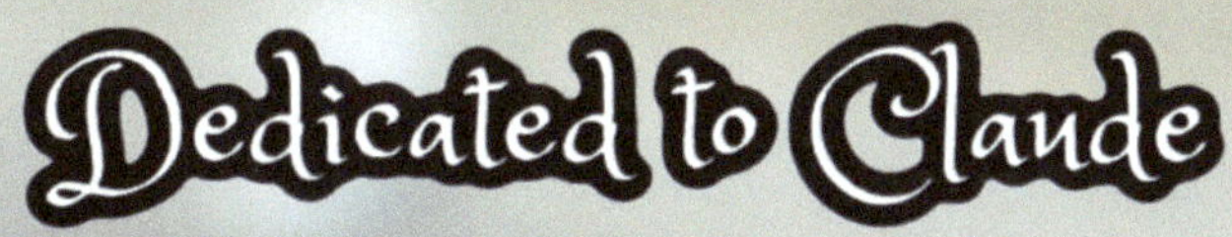

You were "woman" enough for me. I will love you always and forever.

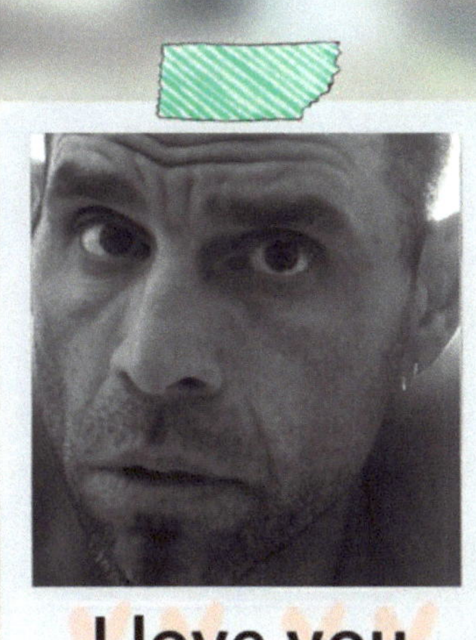

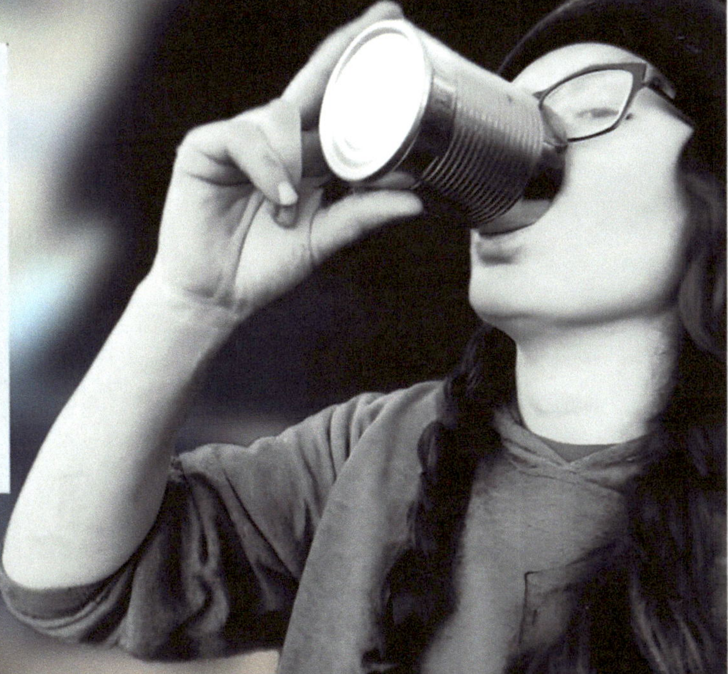

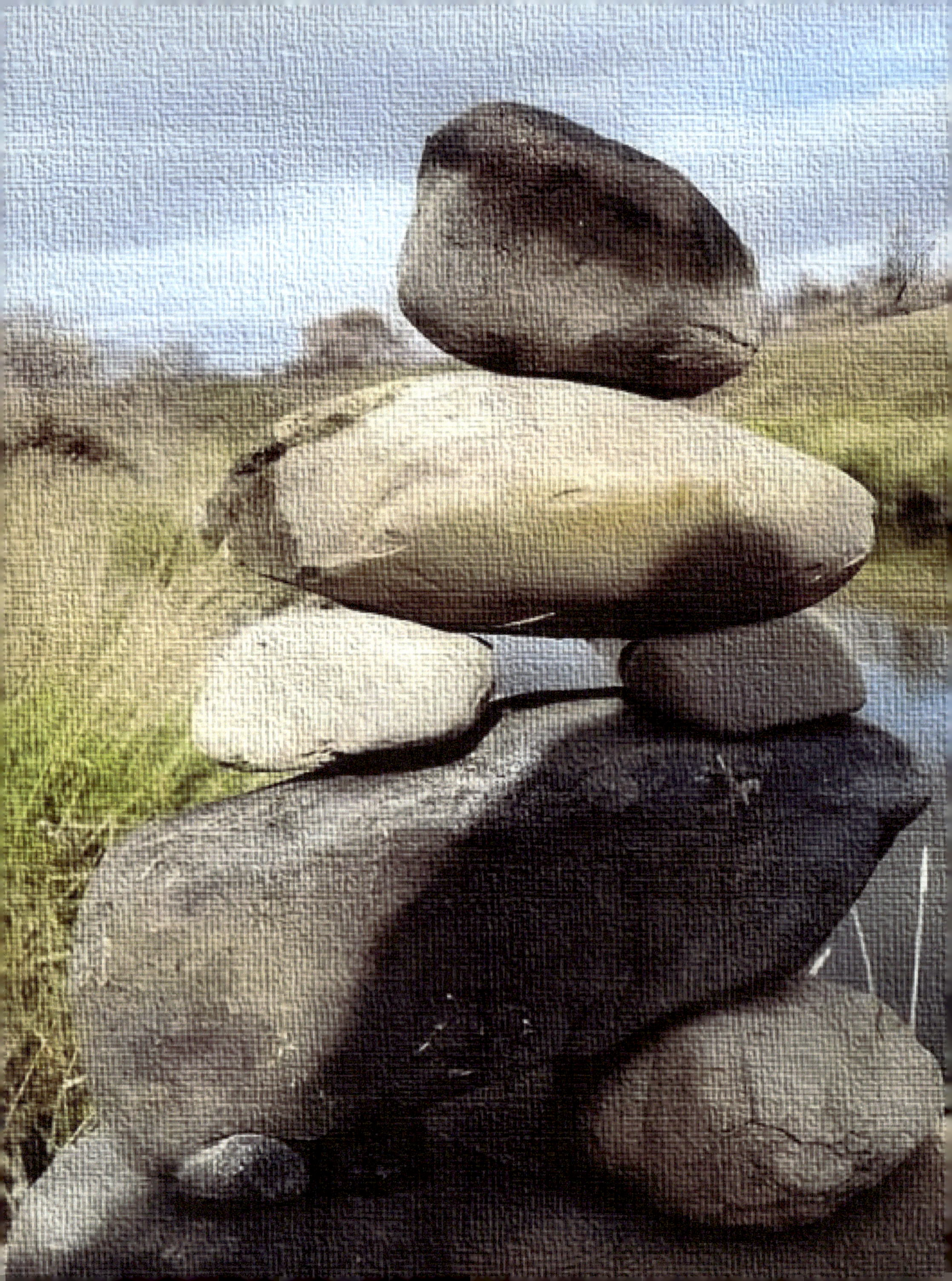

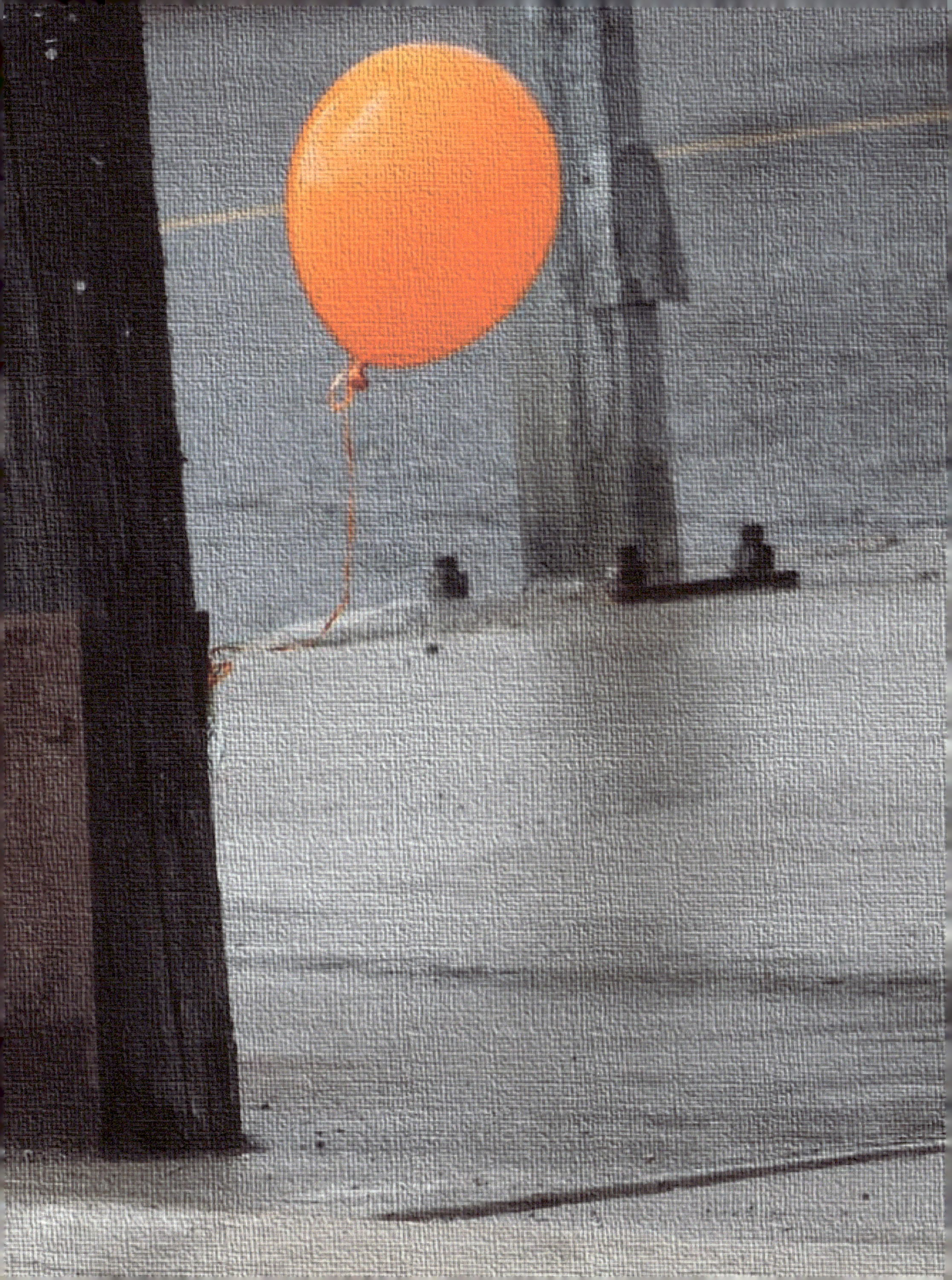

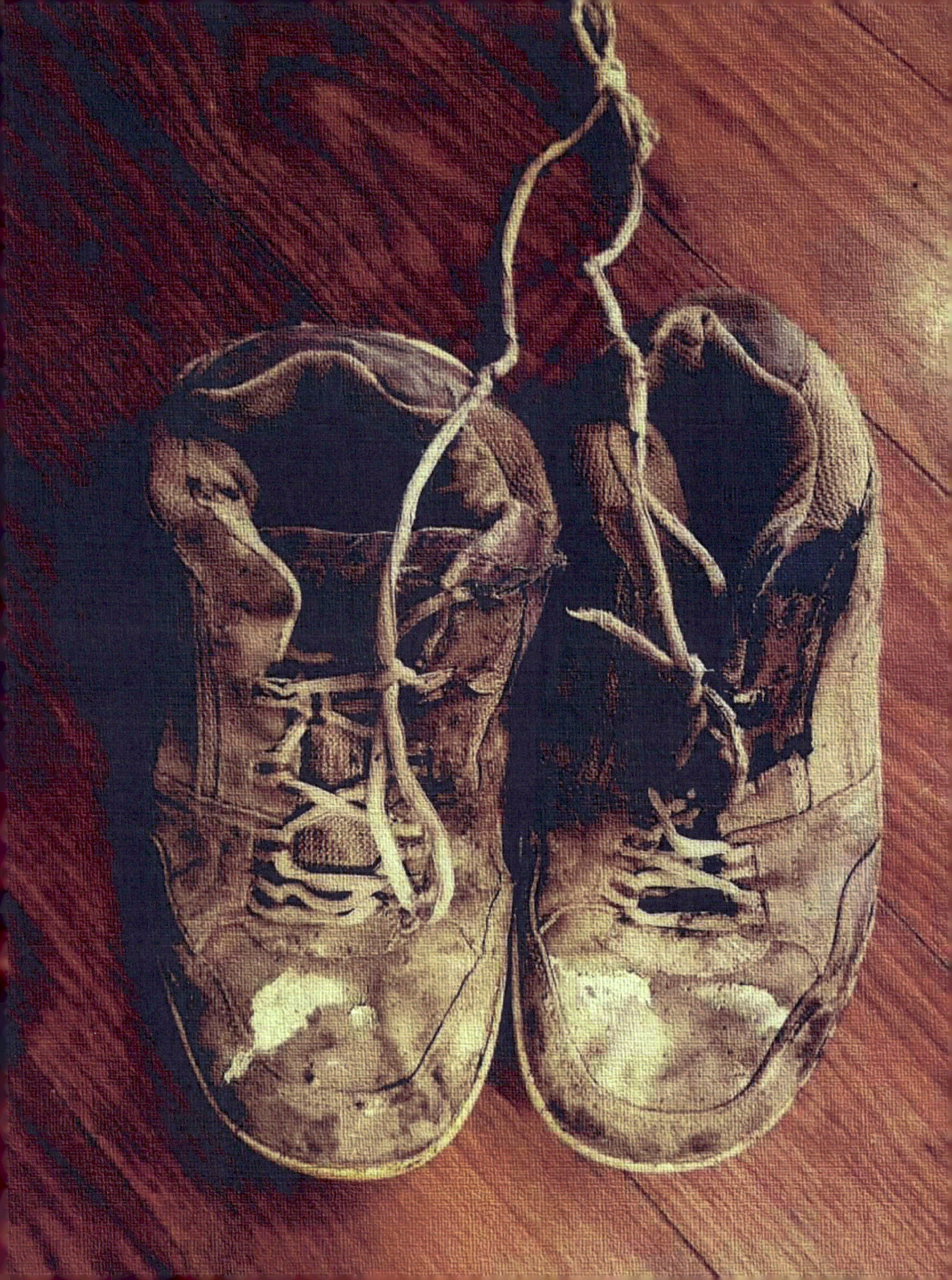

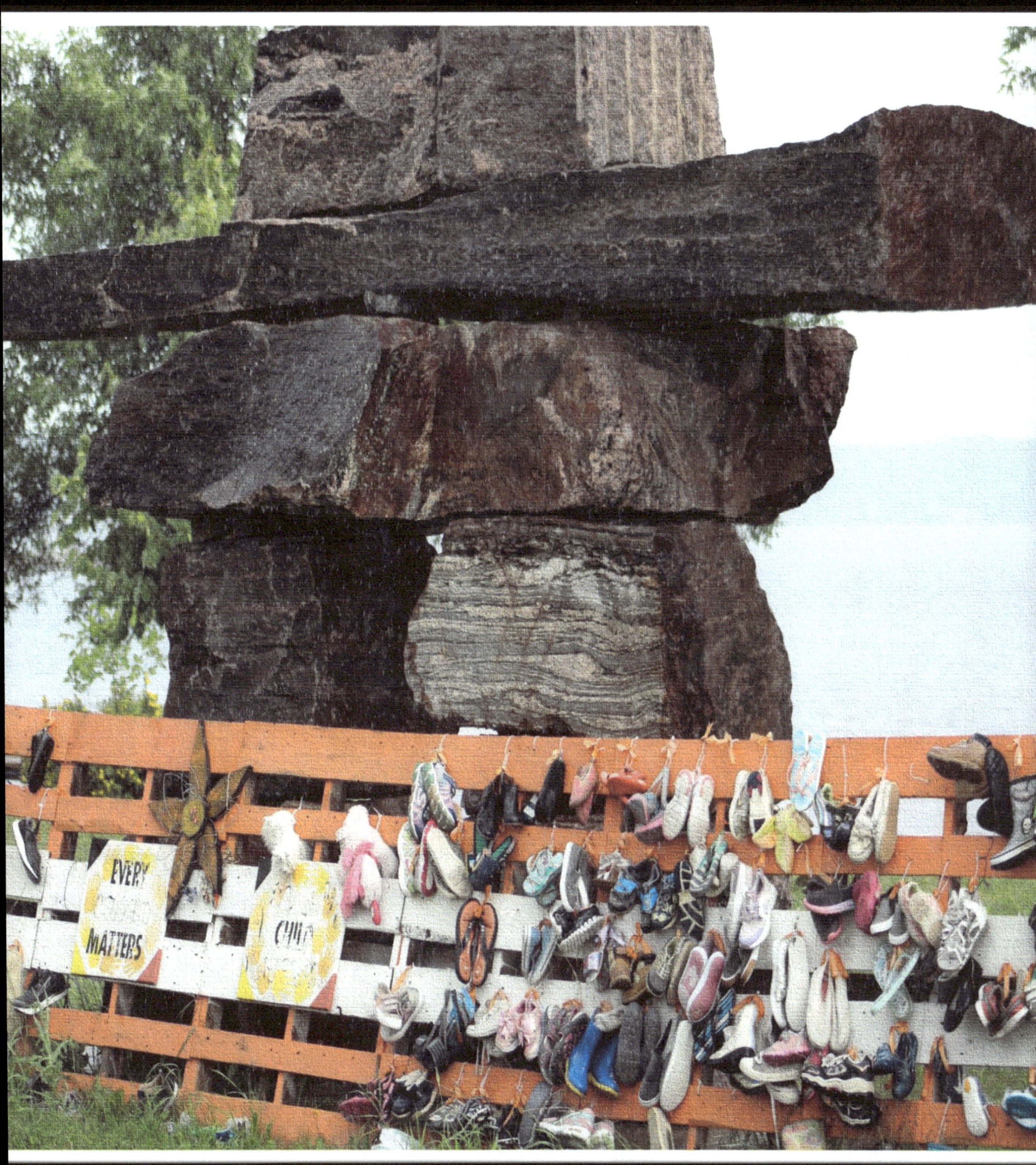
EVERY
MATTERS
CHILD

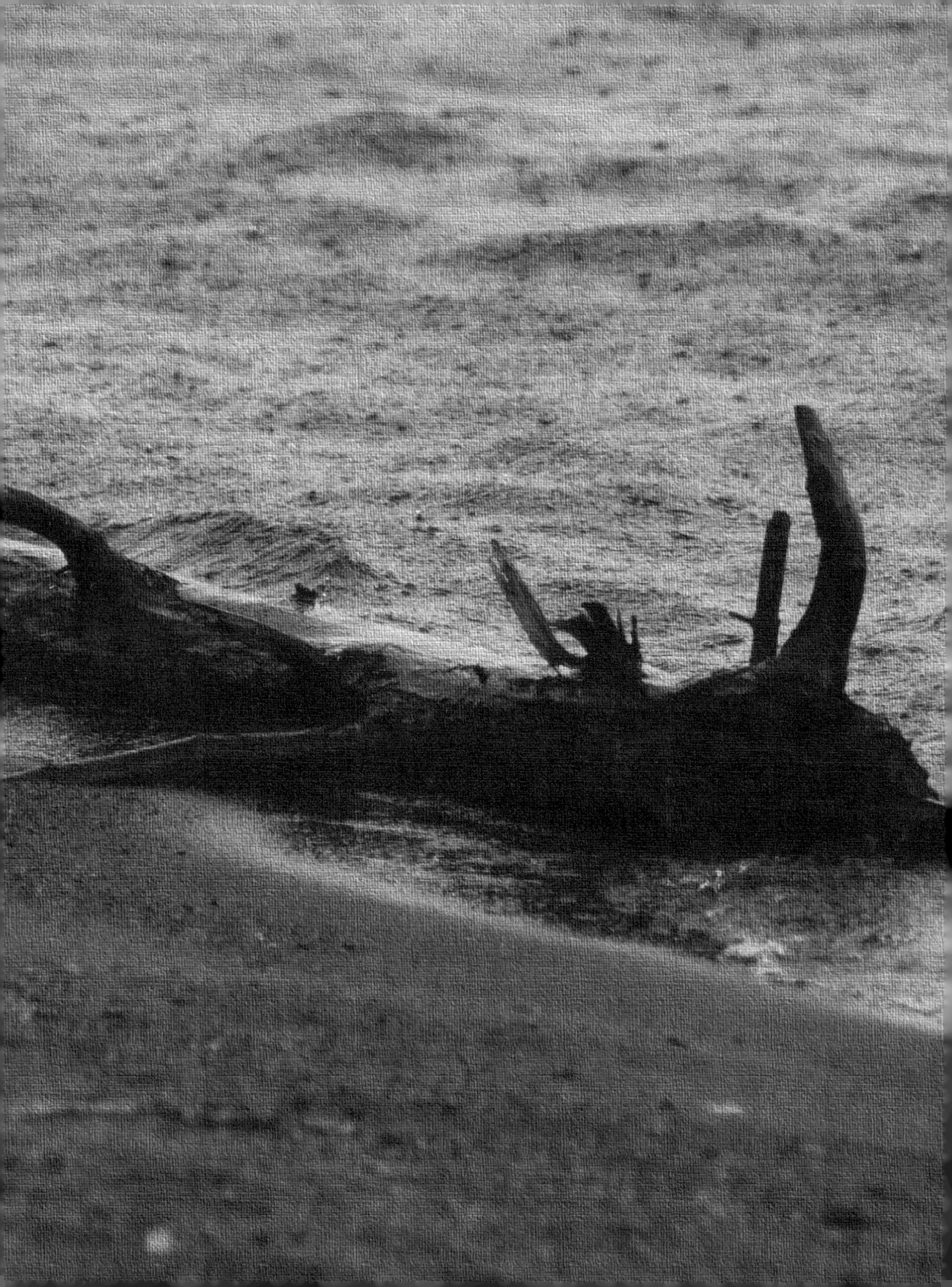

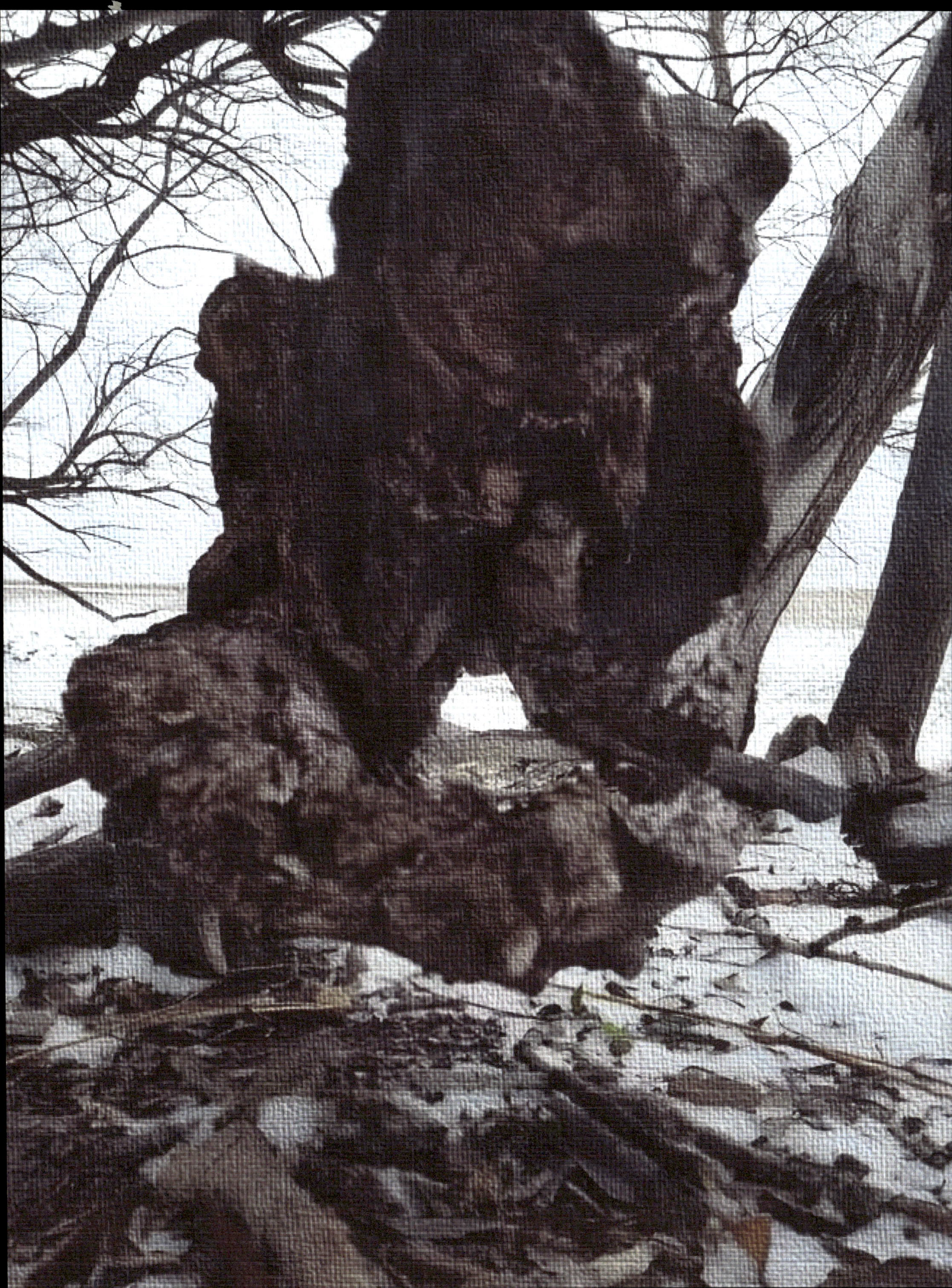

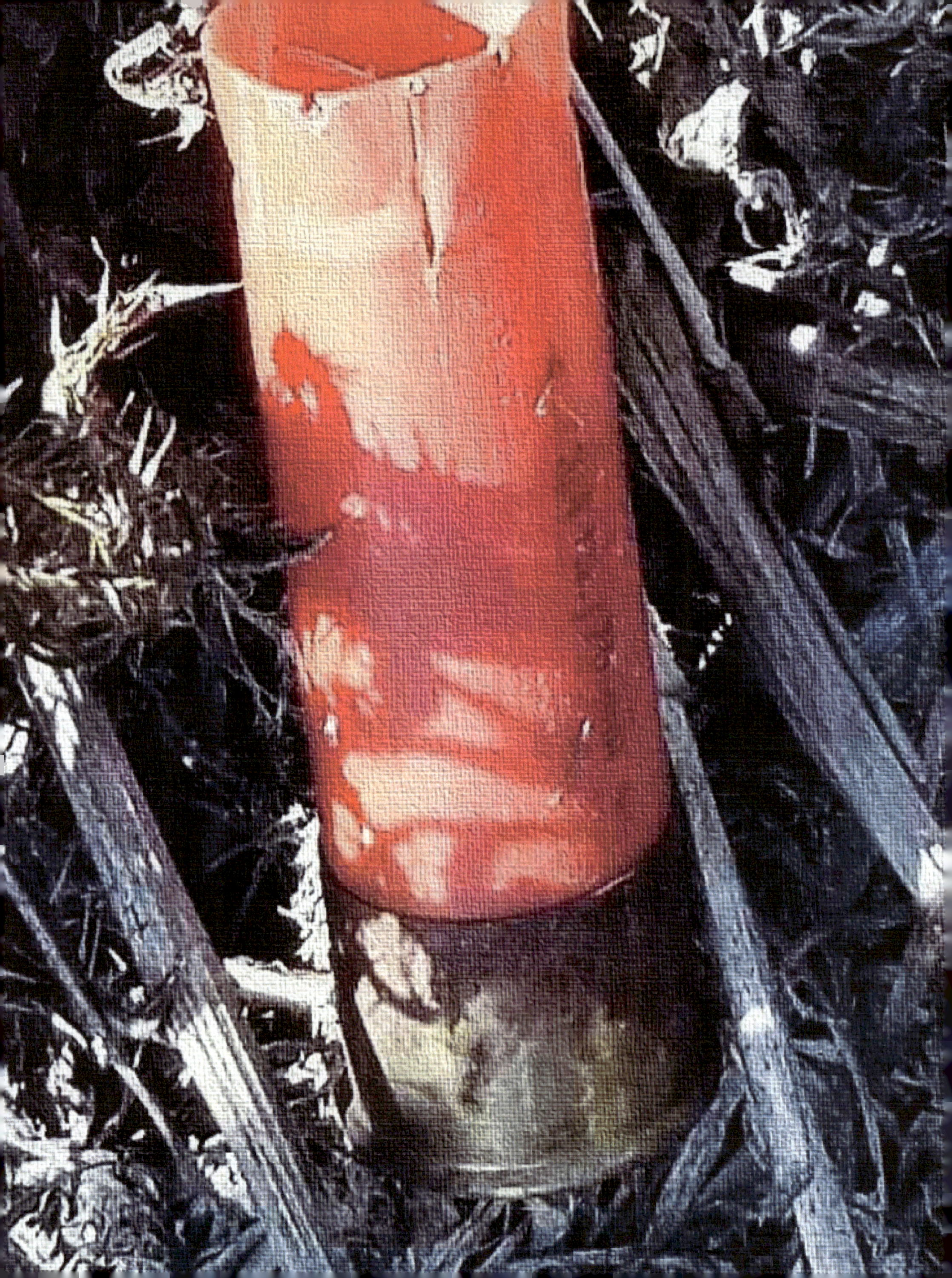

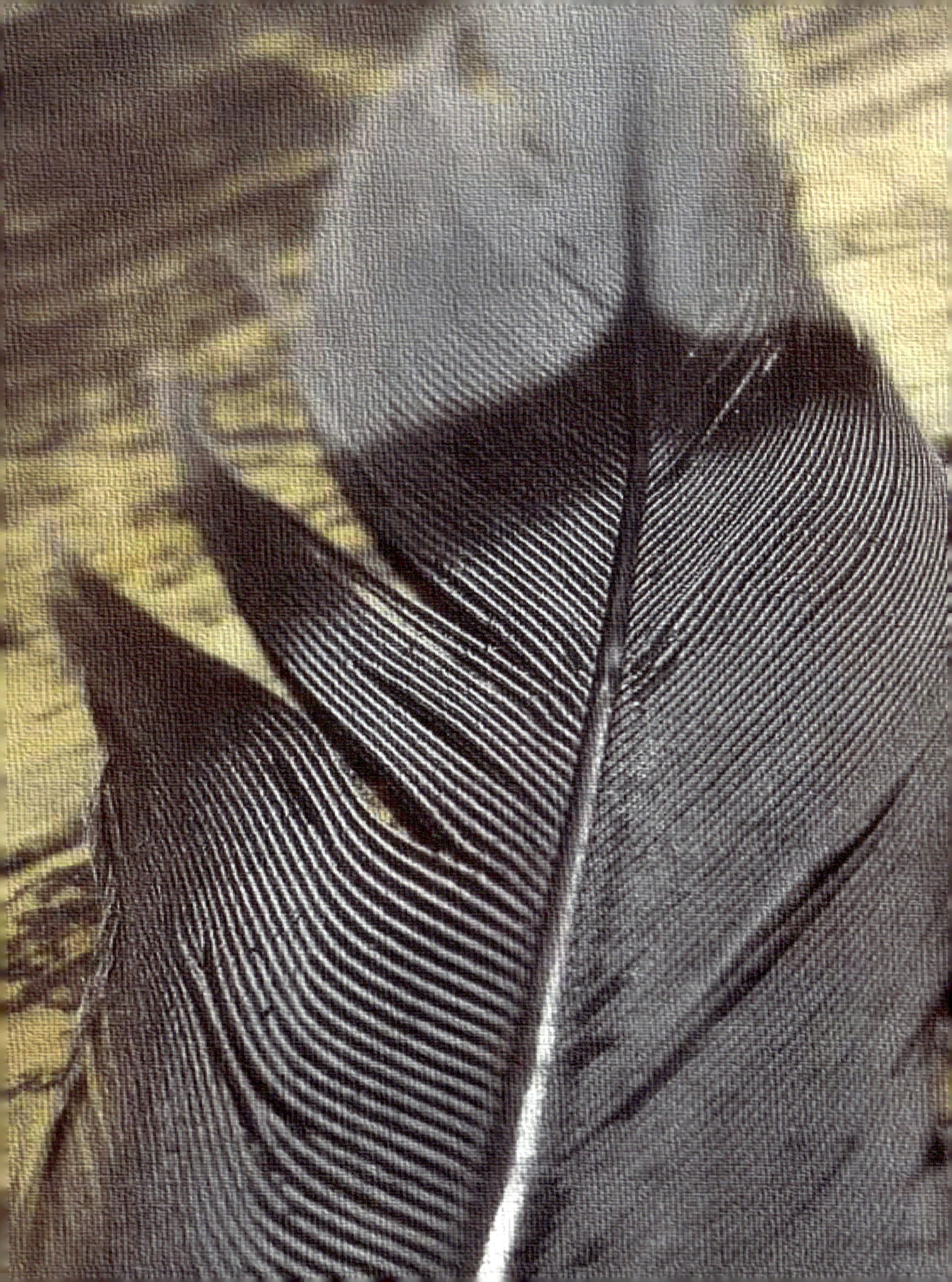

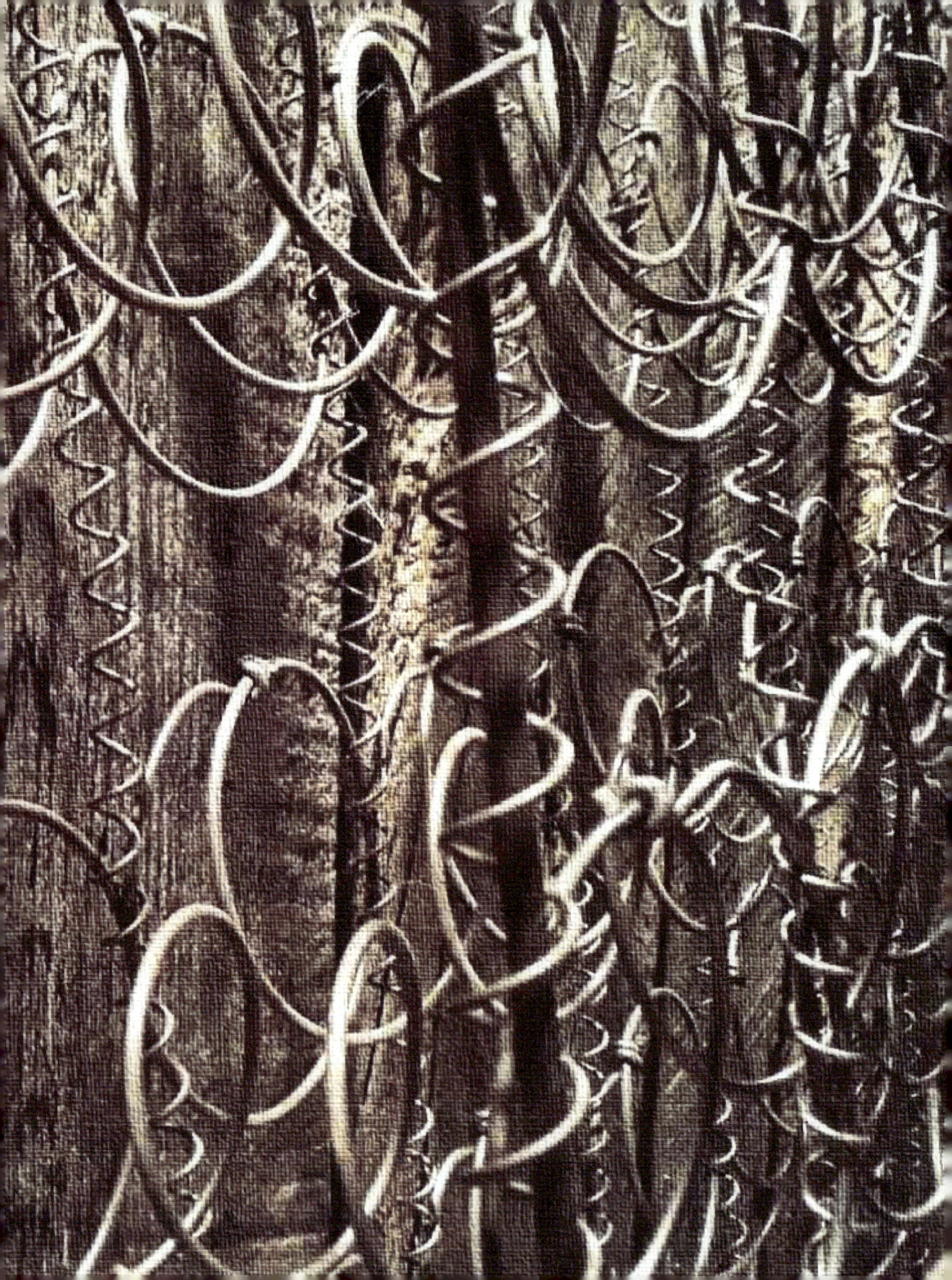

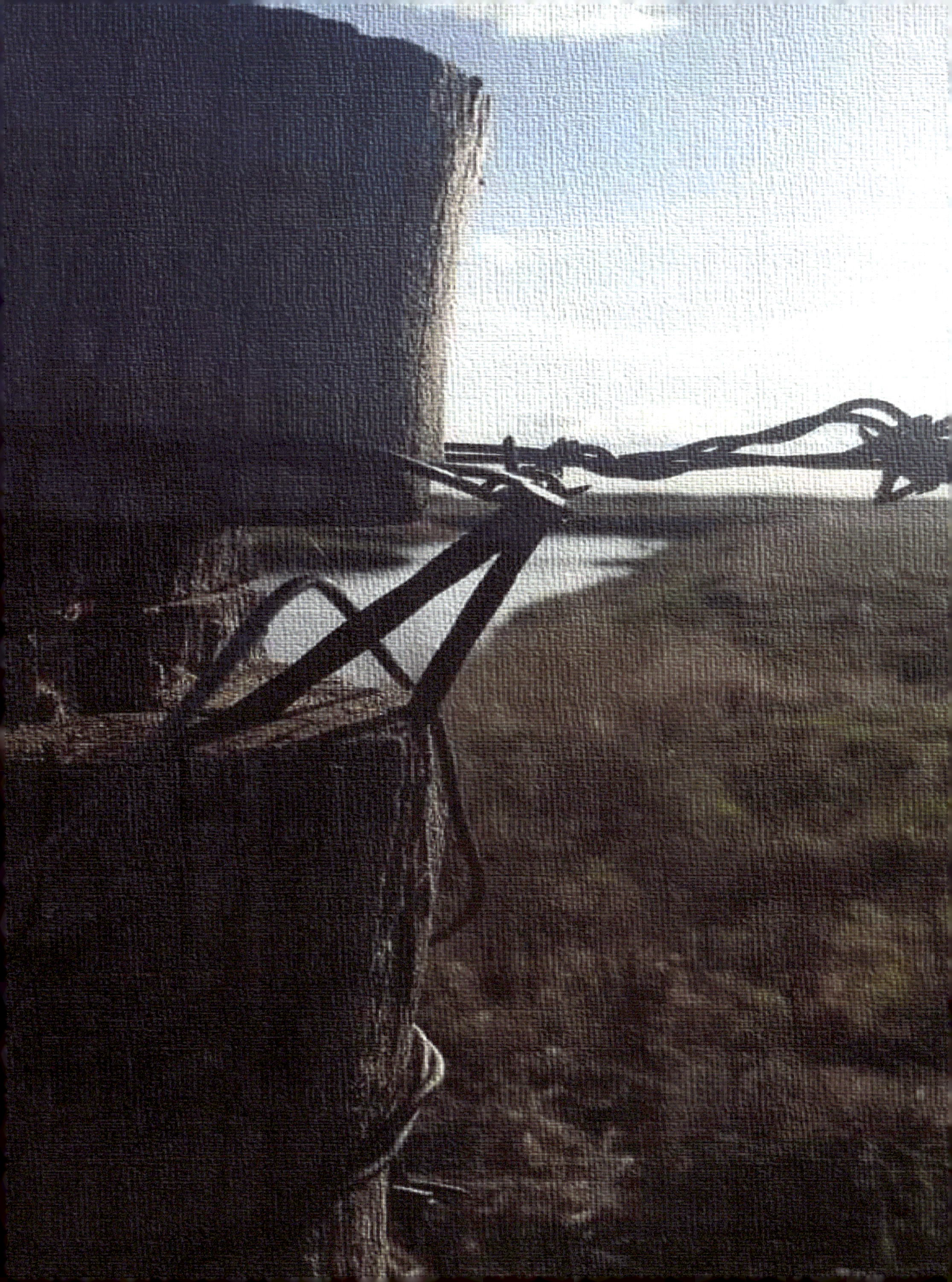

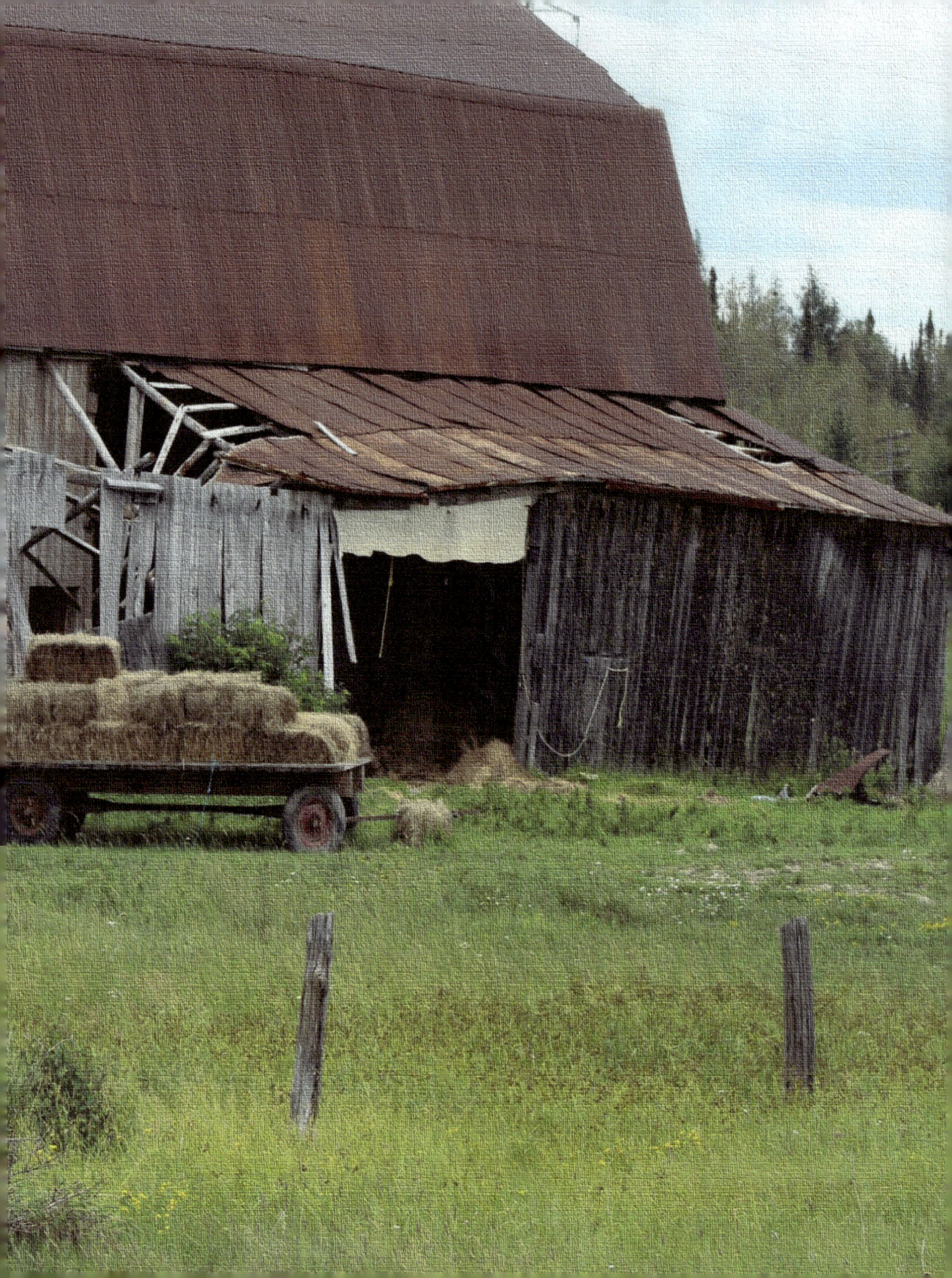

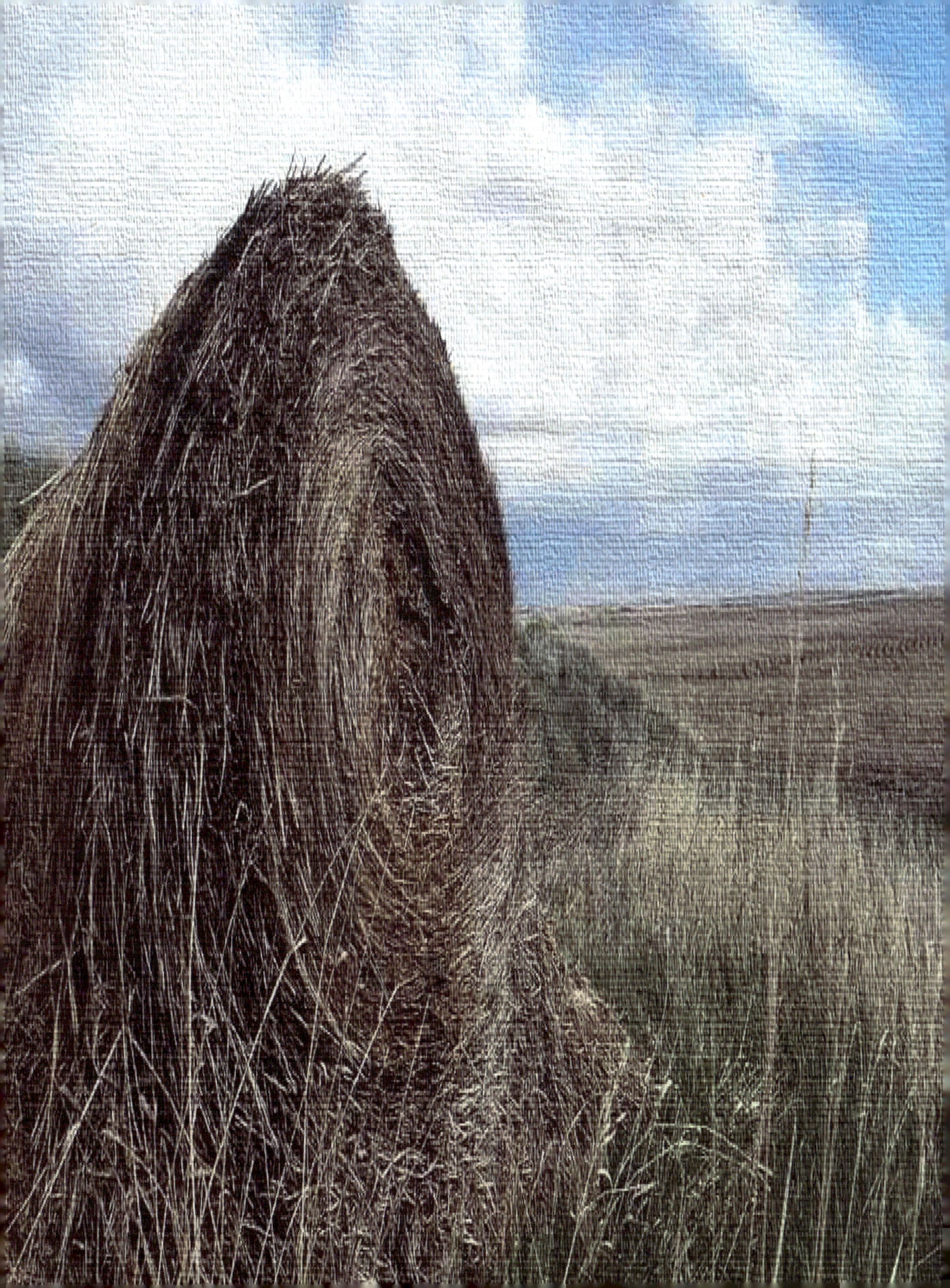

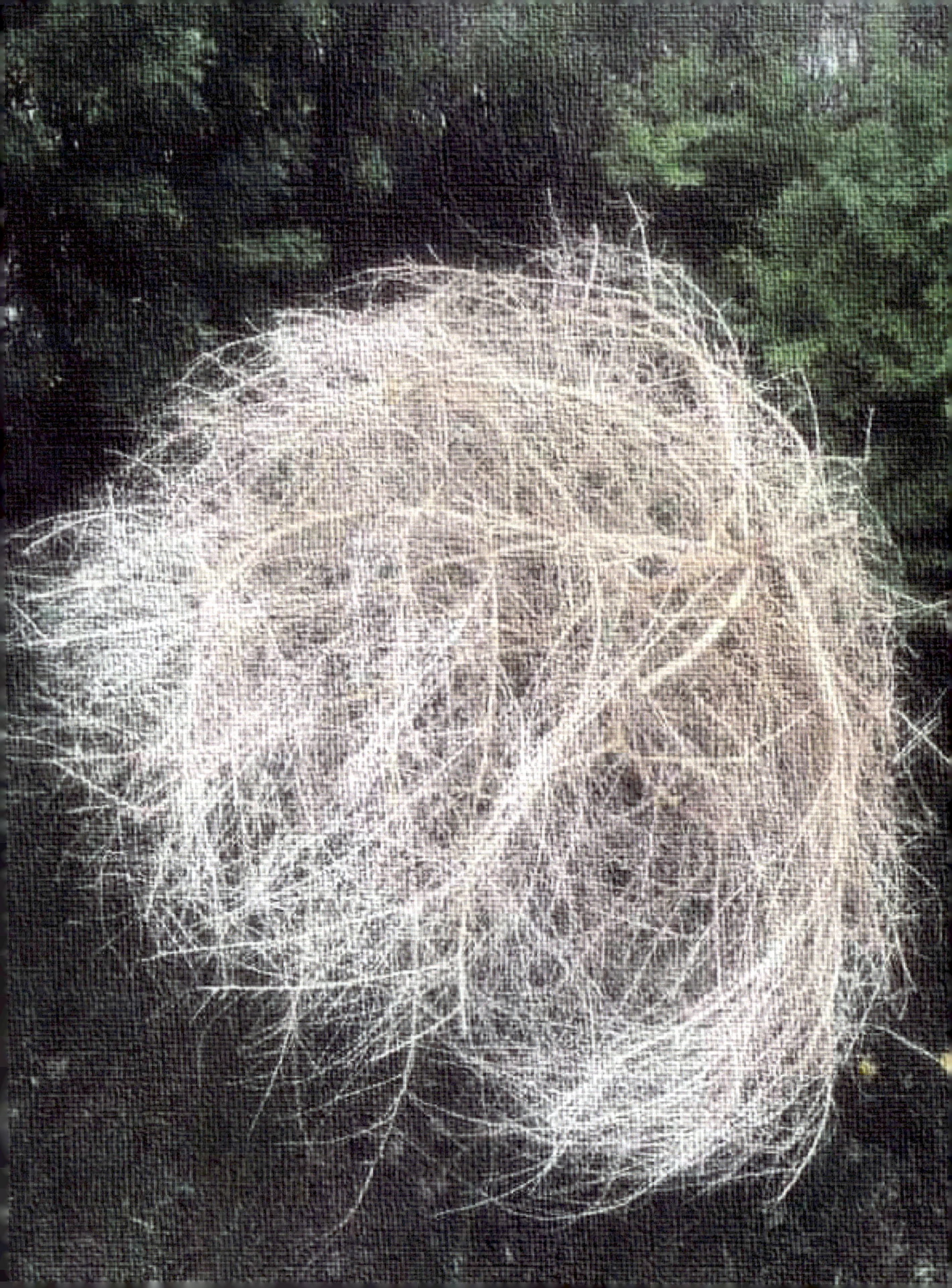

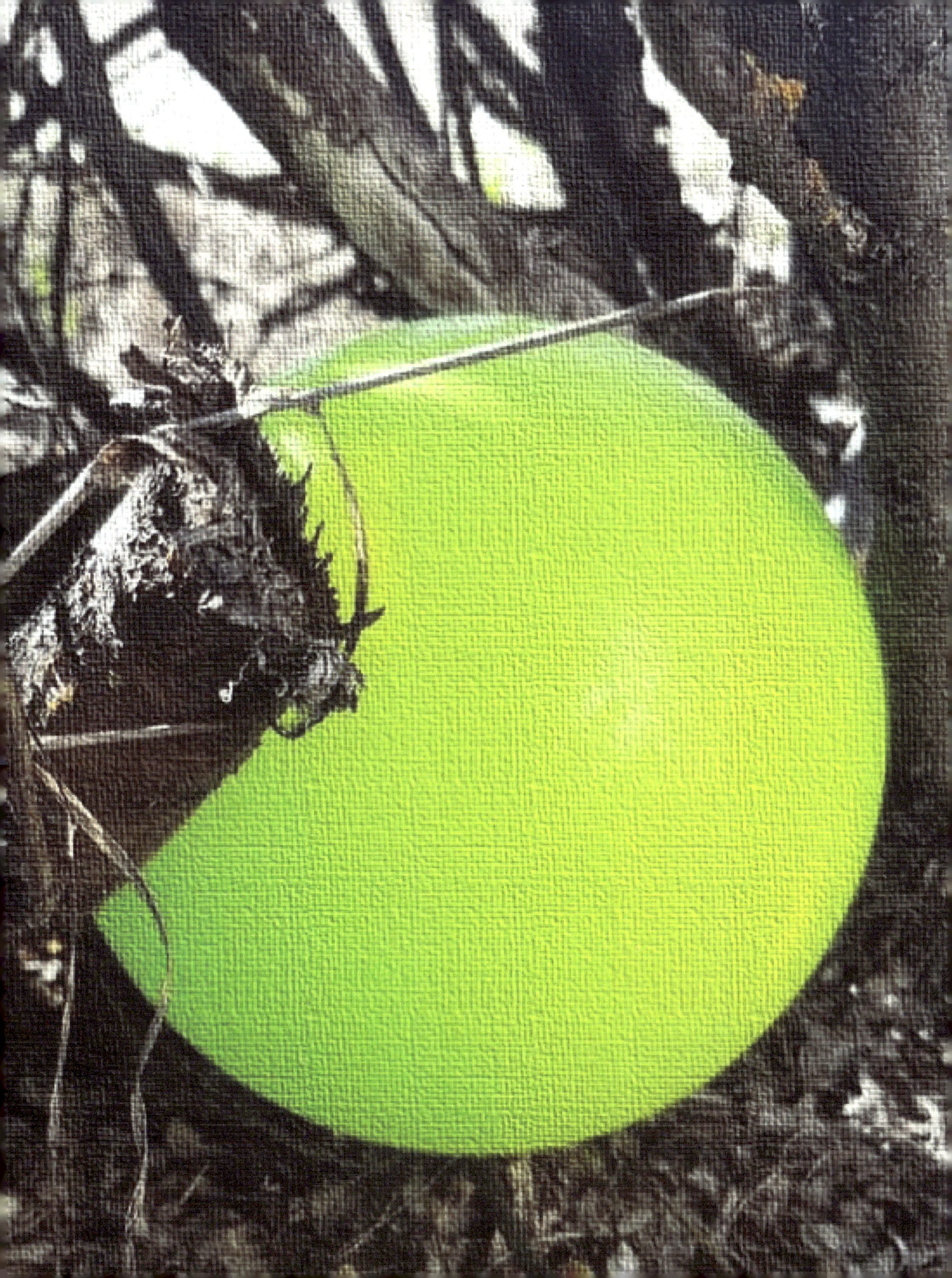

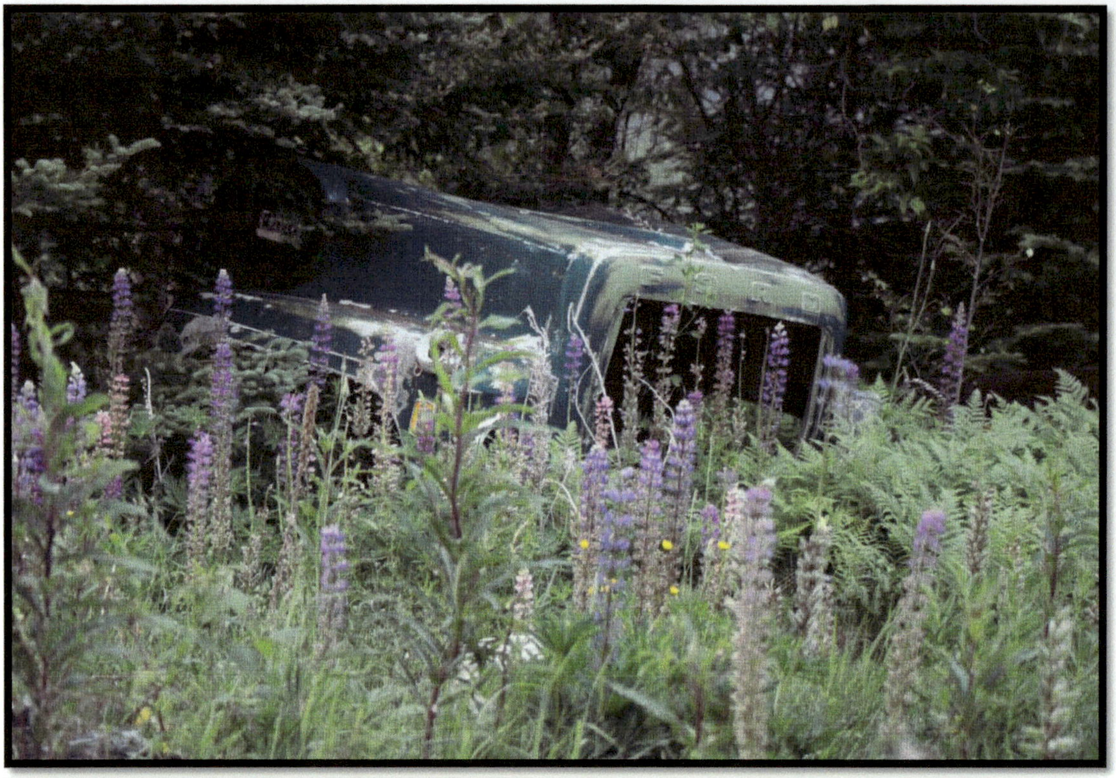

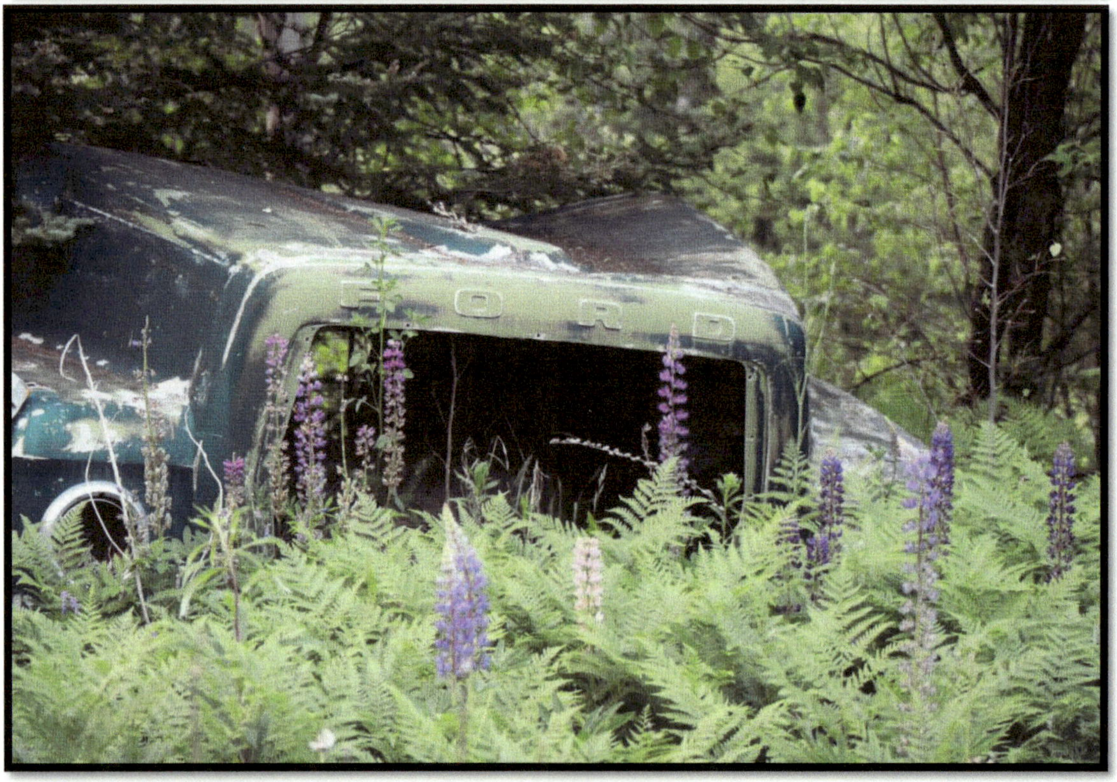

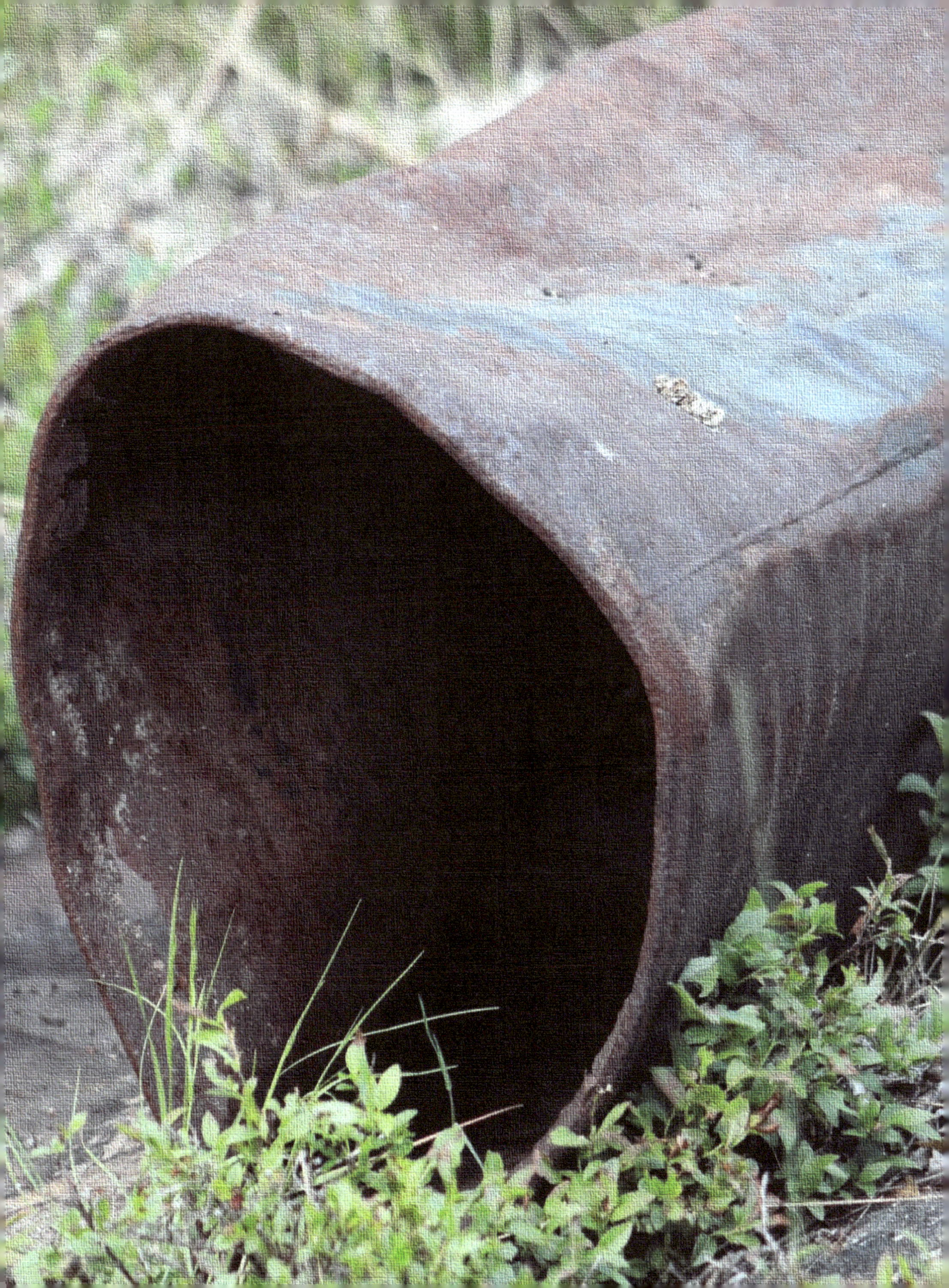

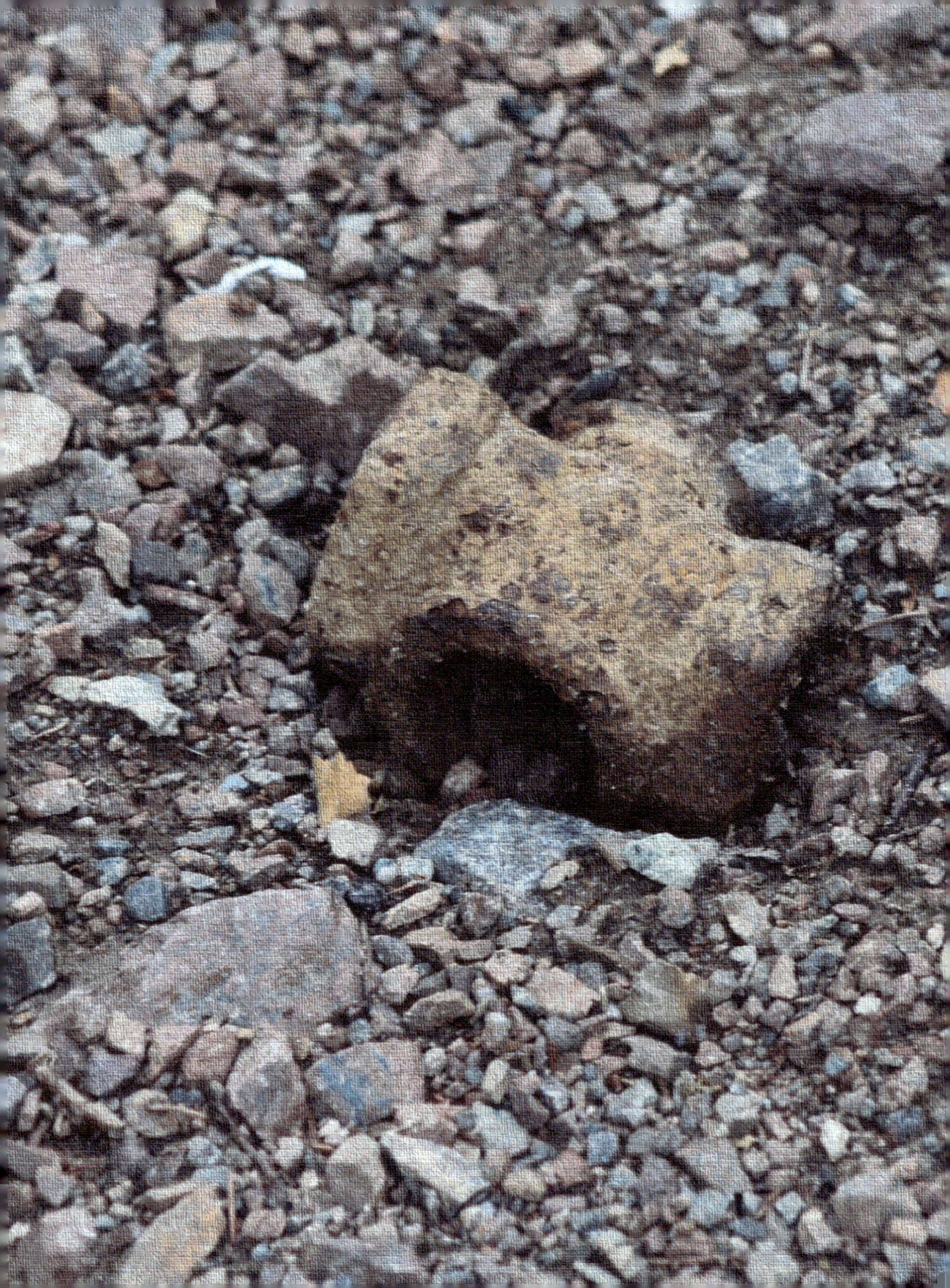

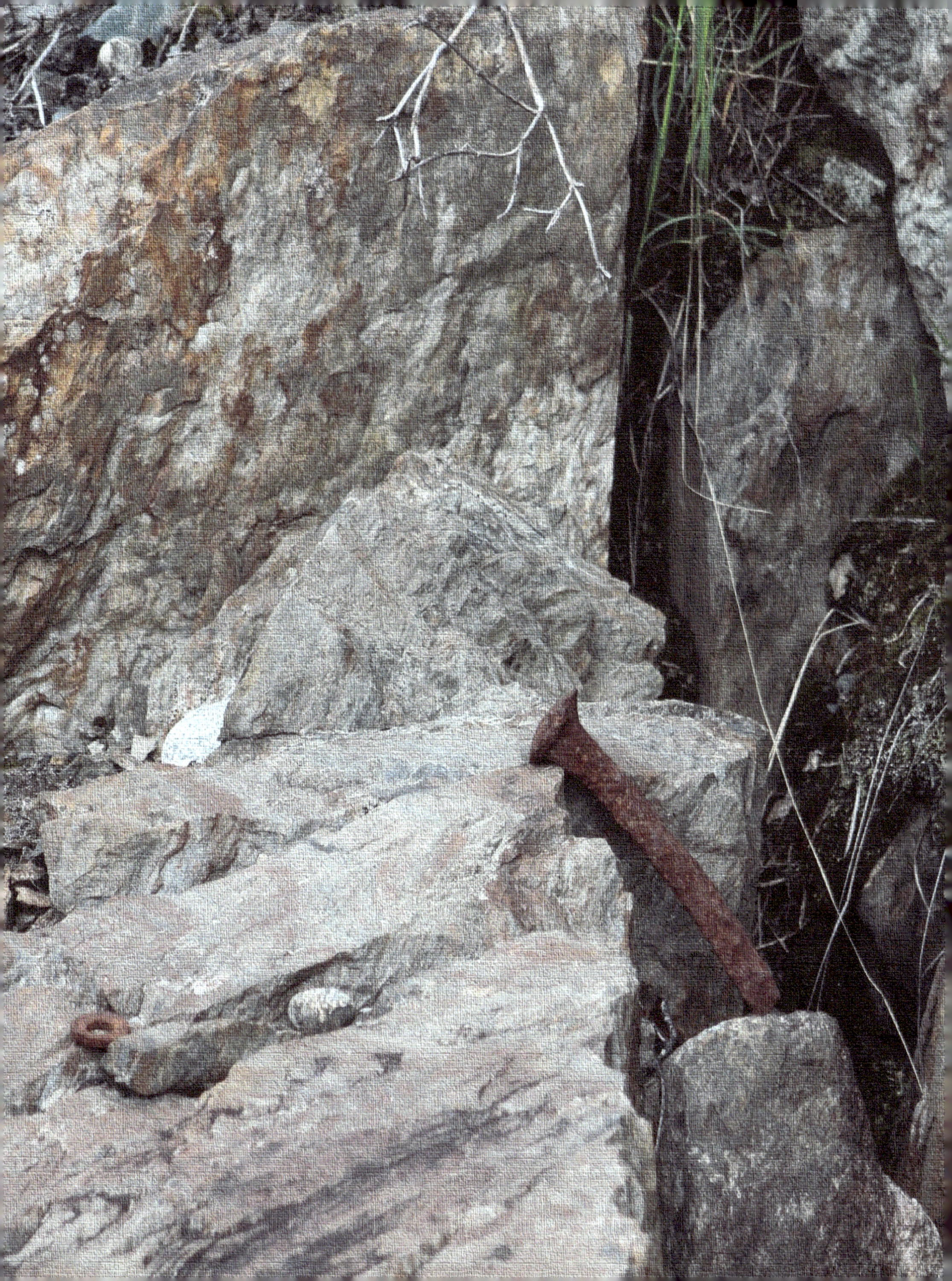

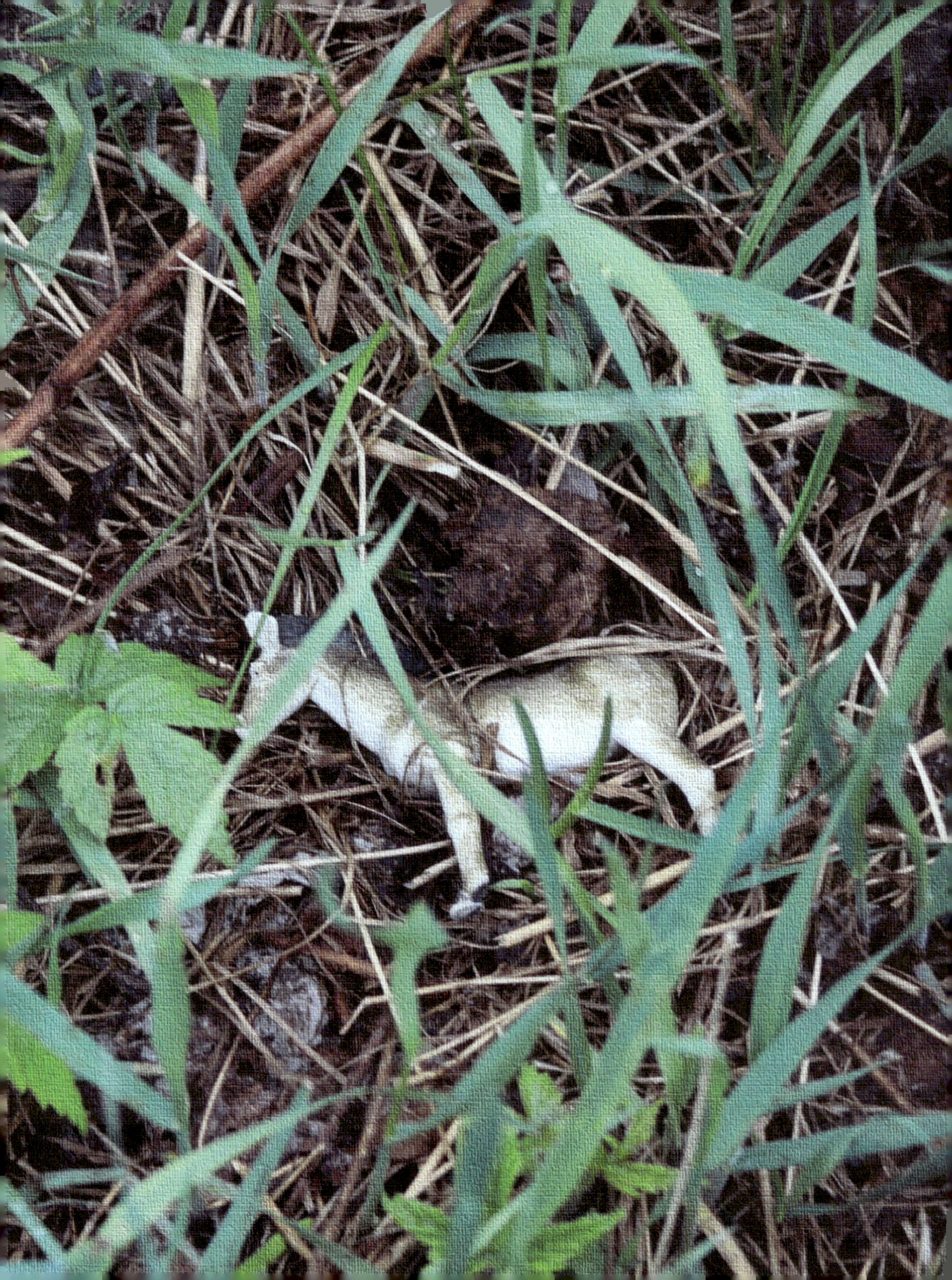

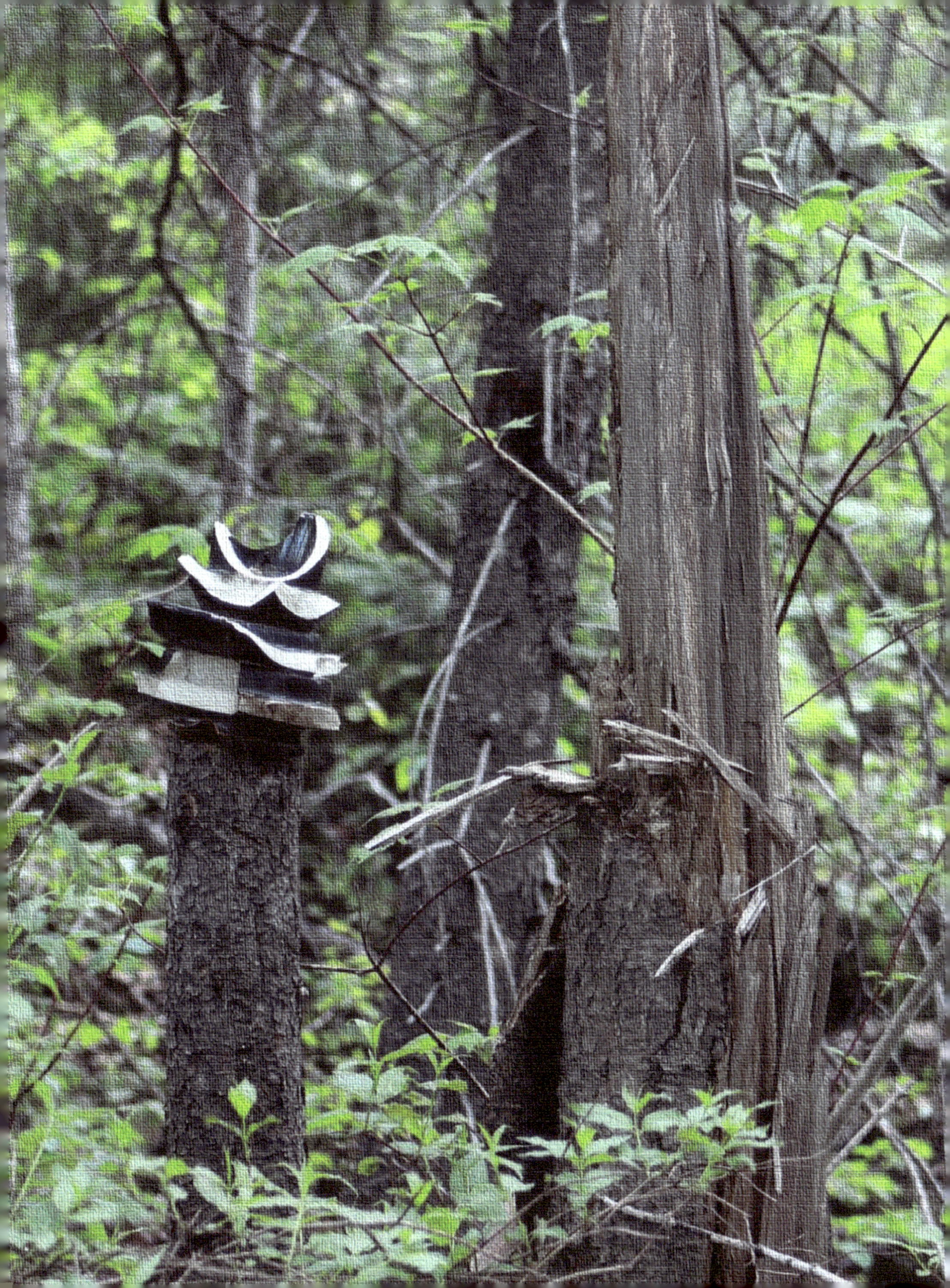

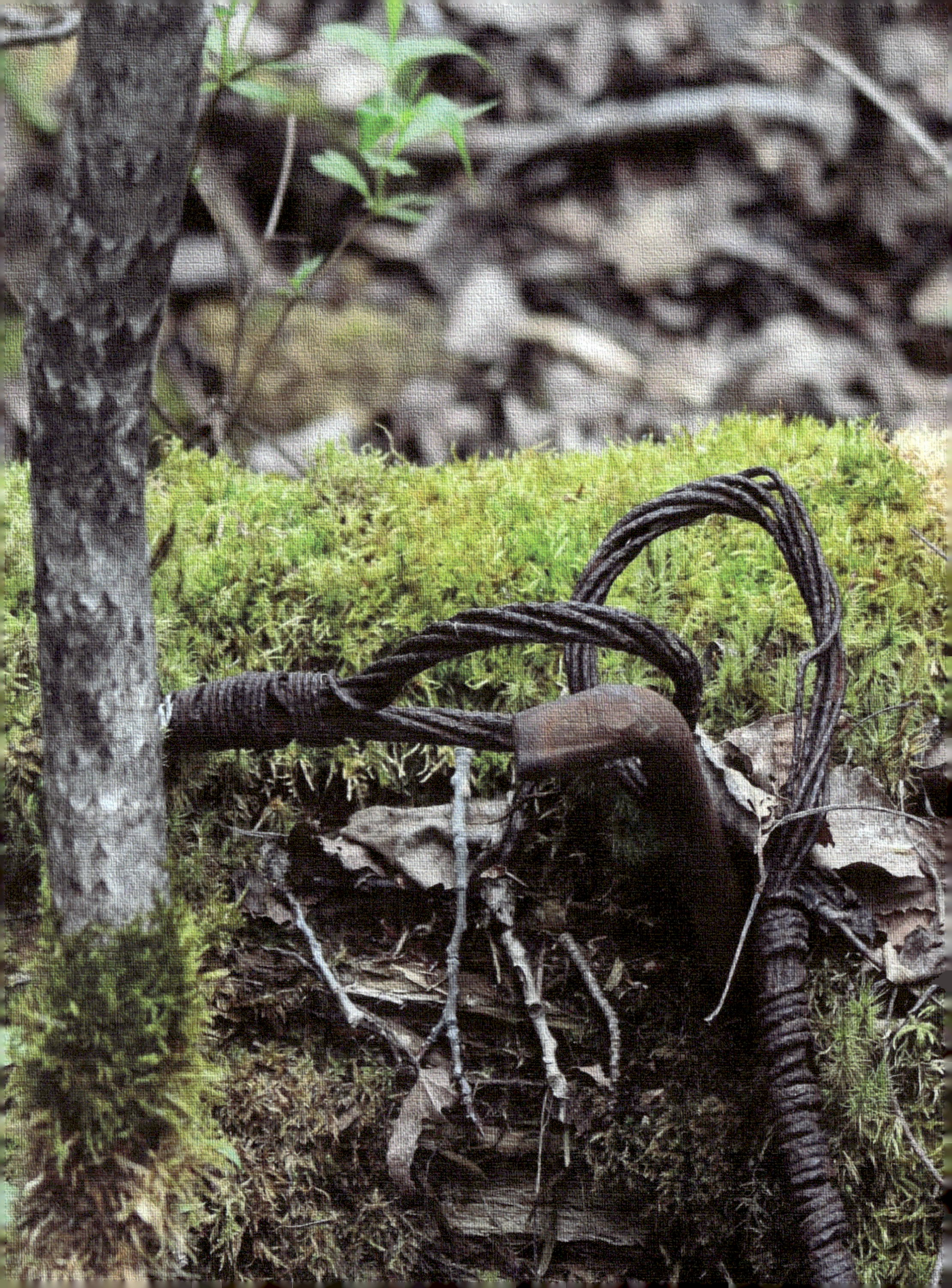

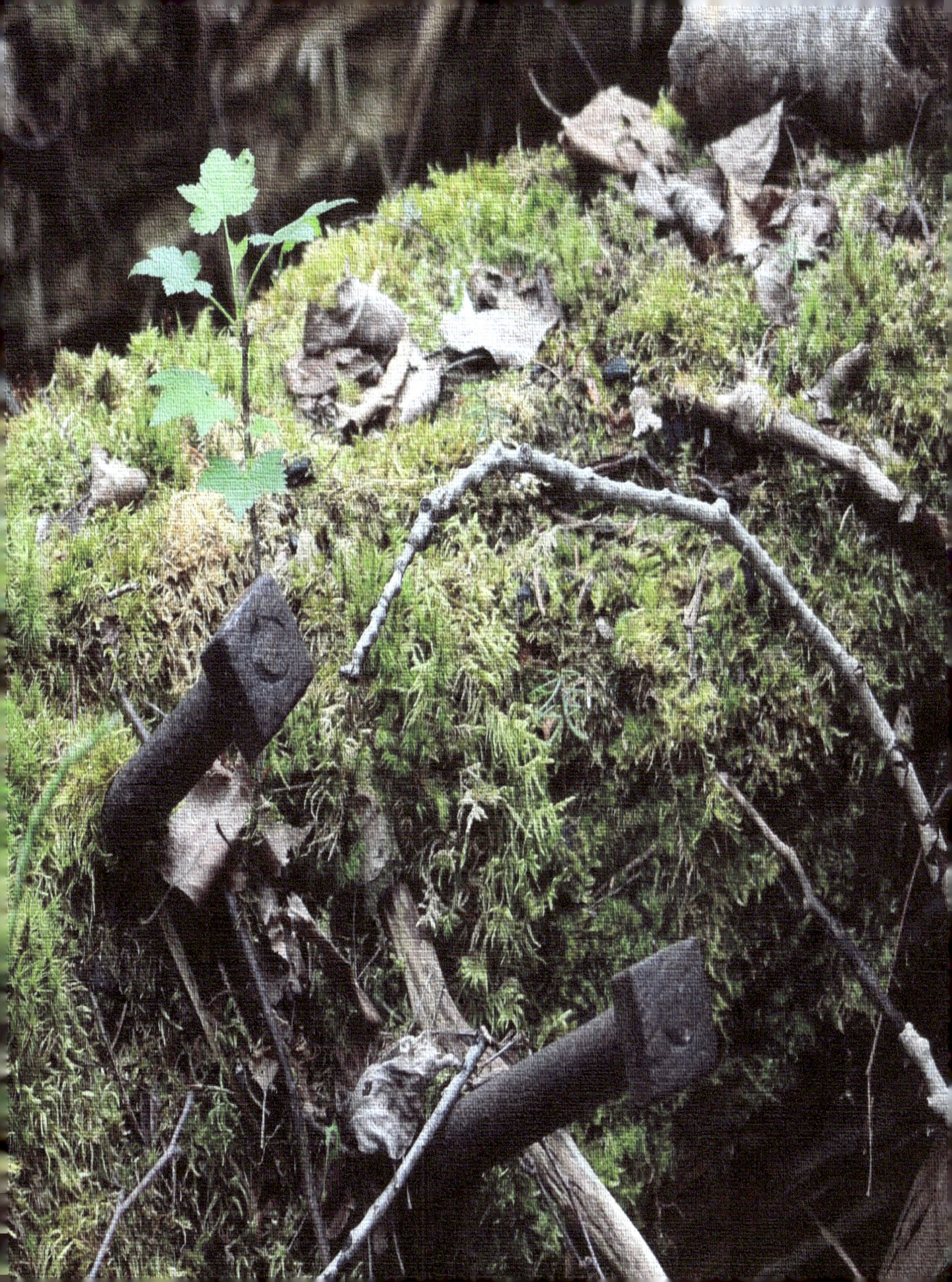

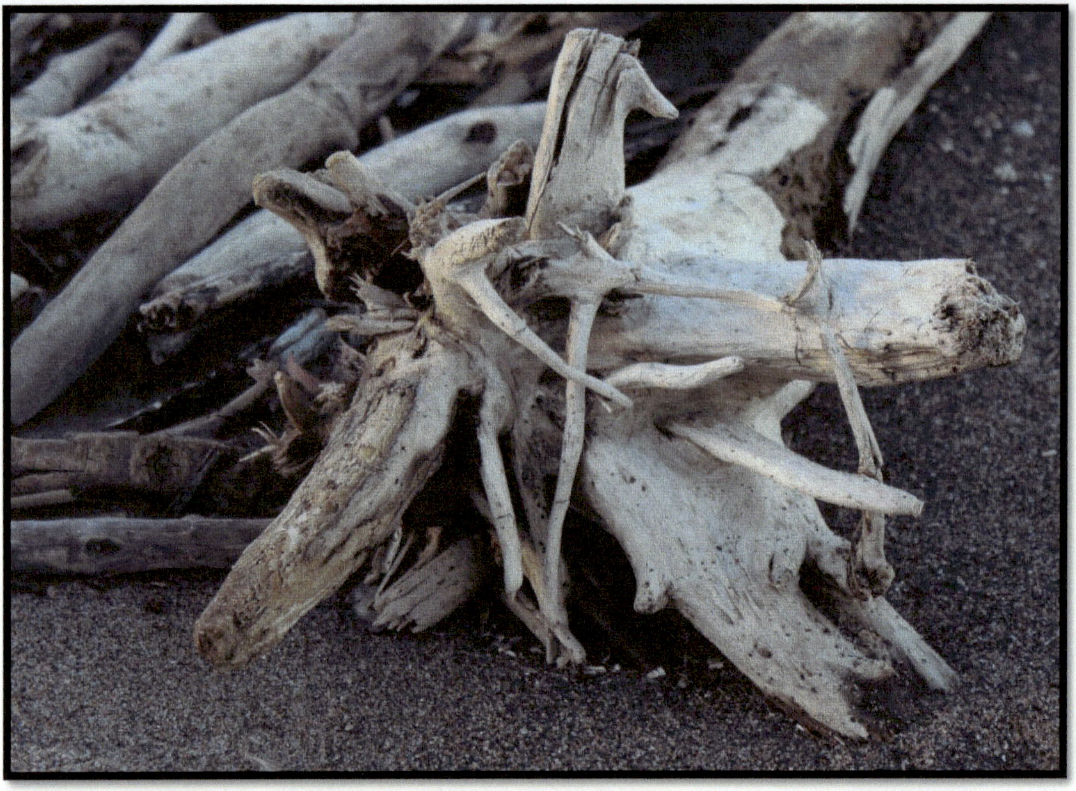

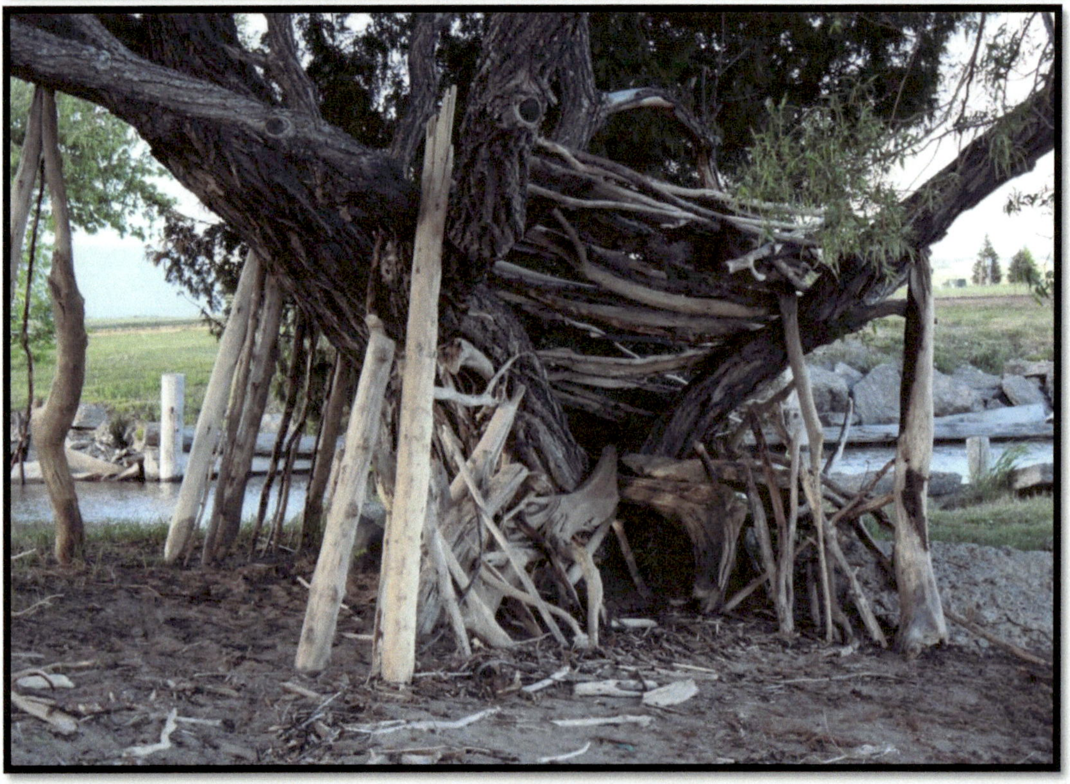

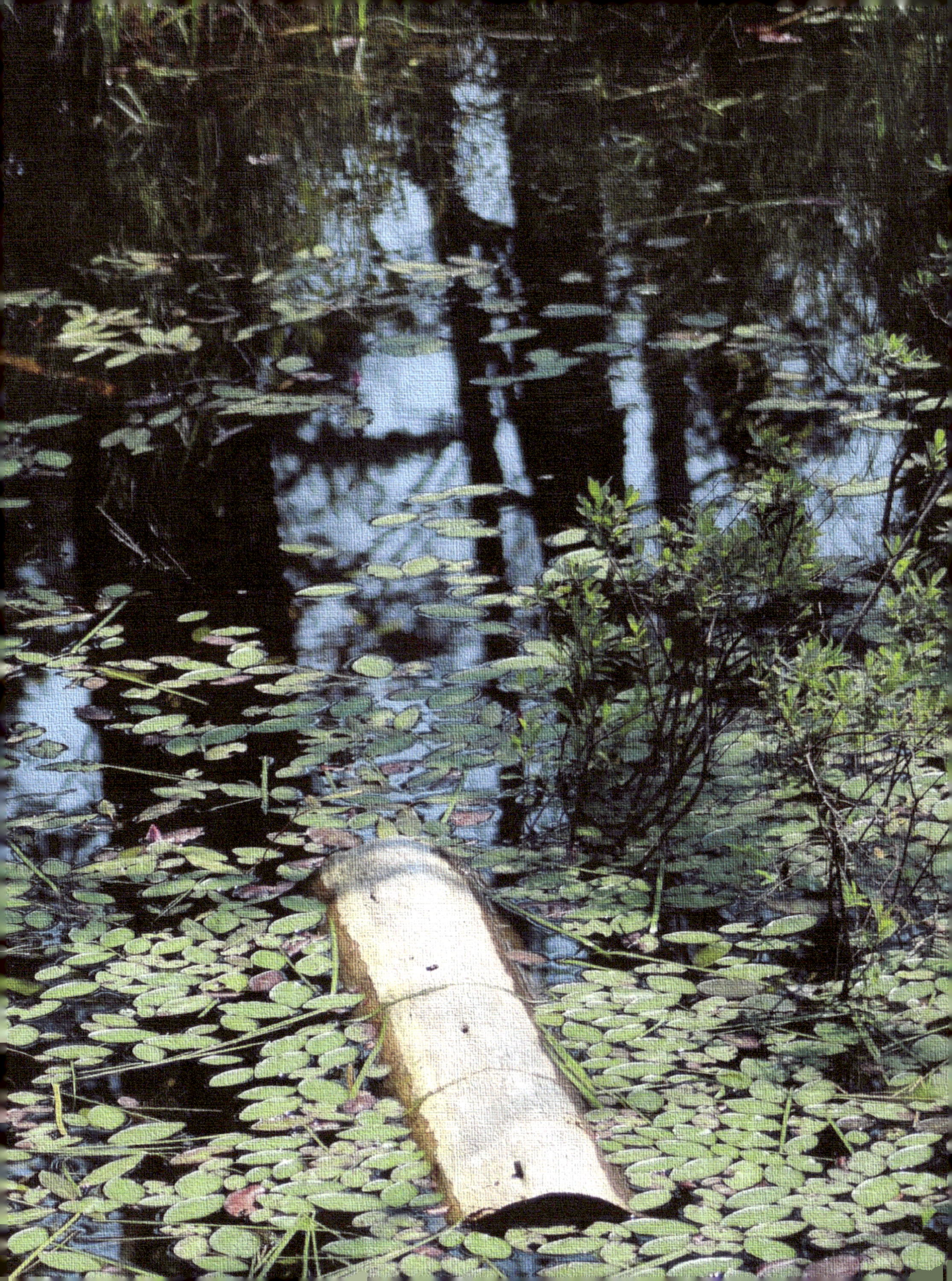

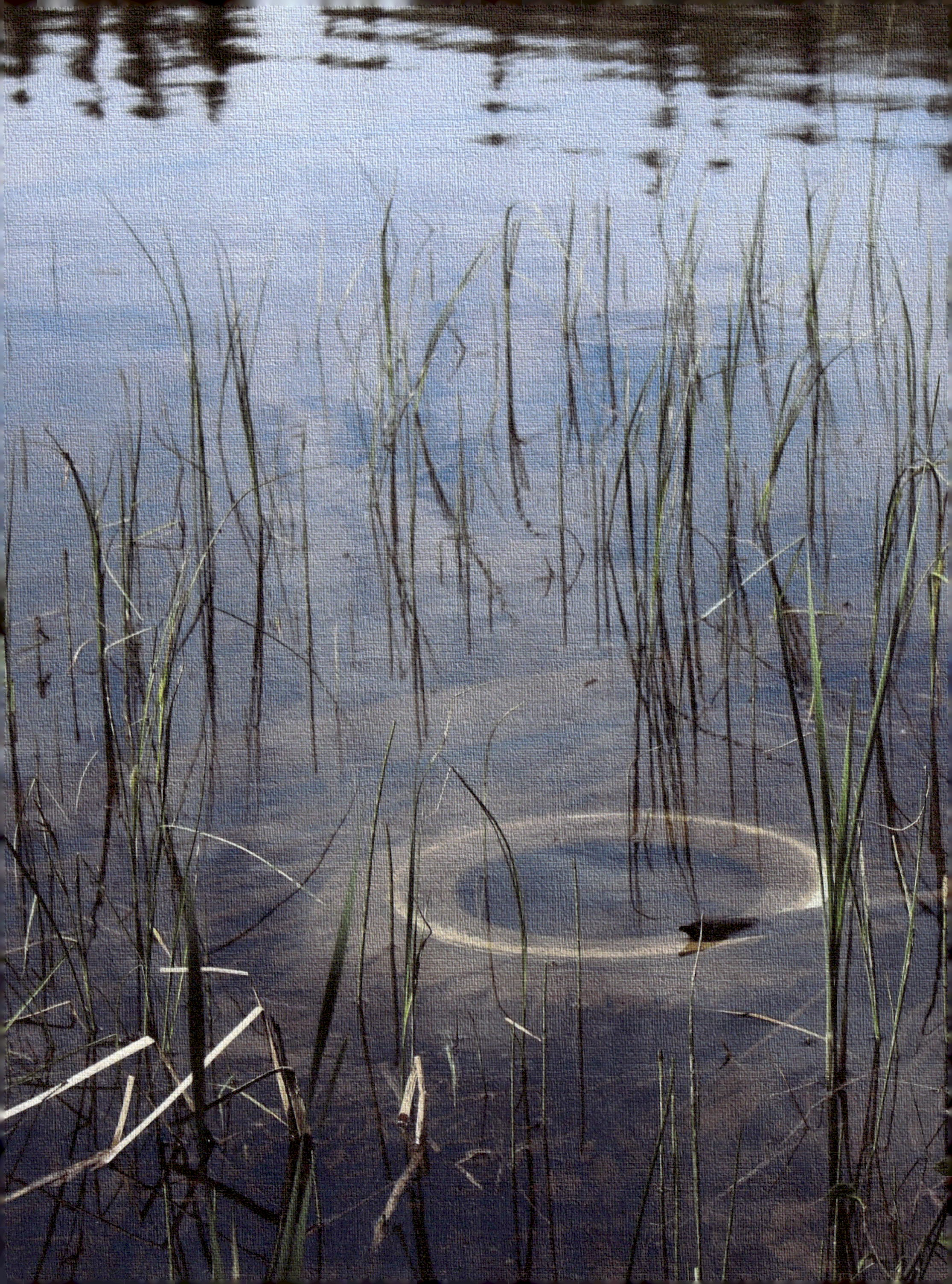

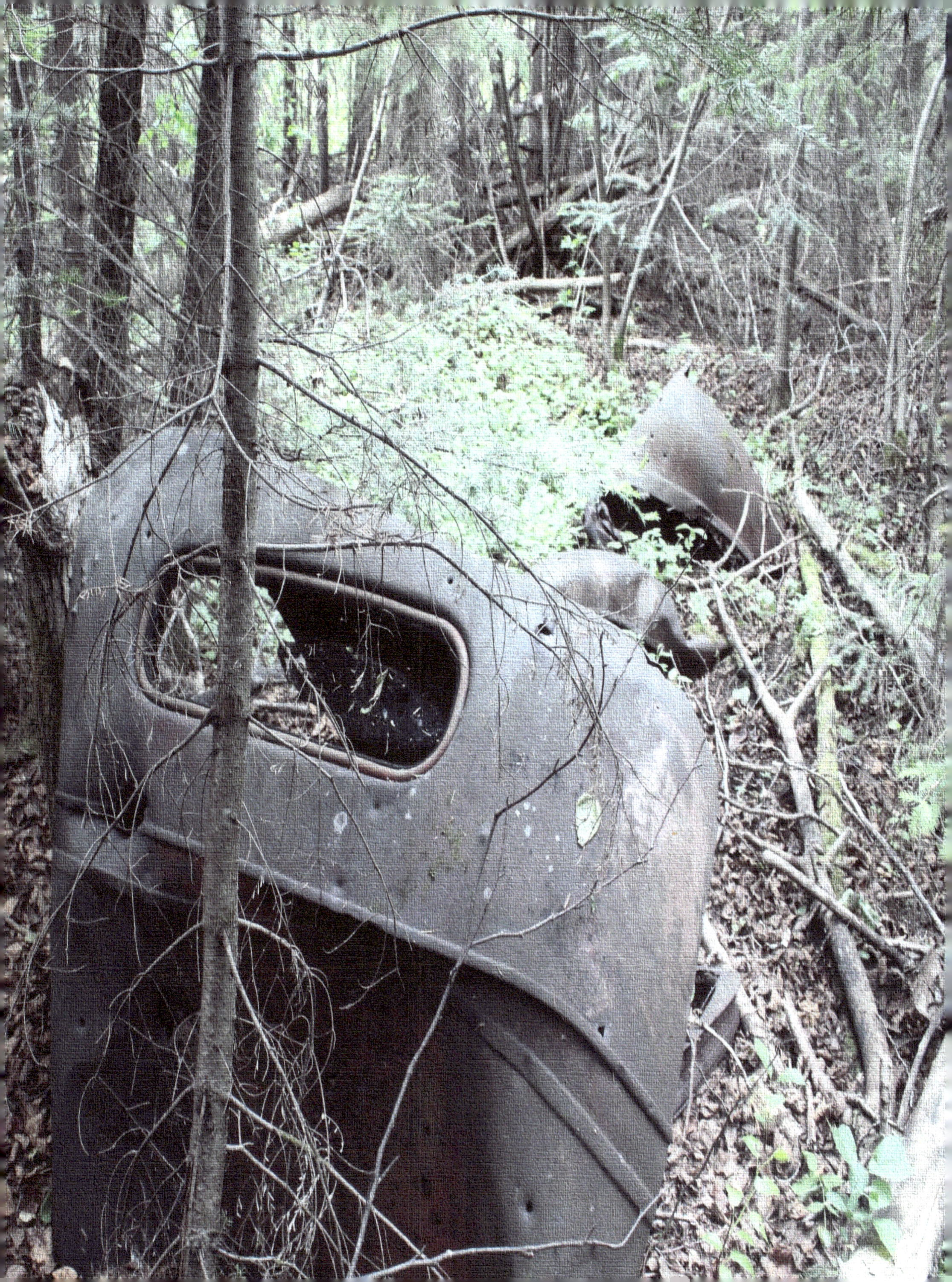

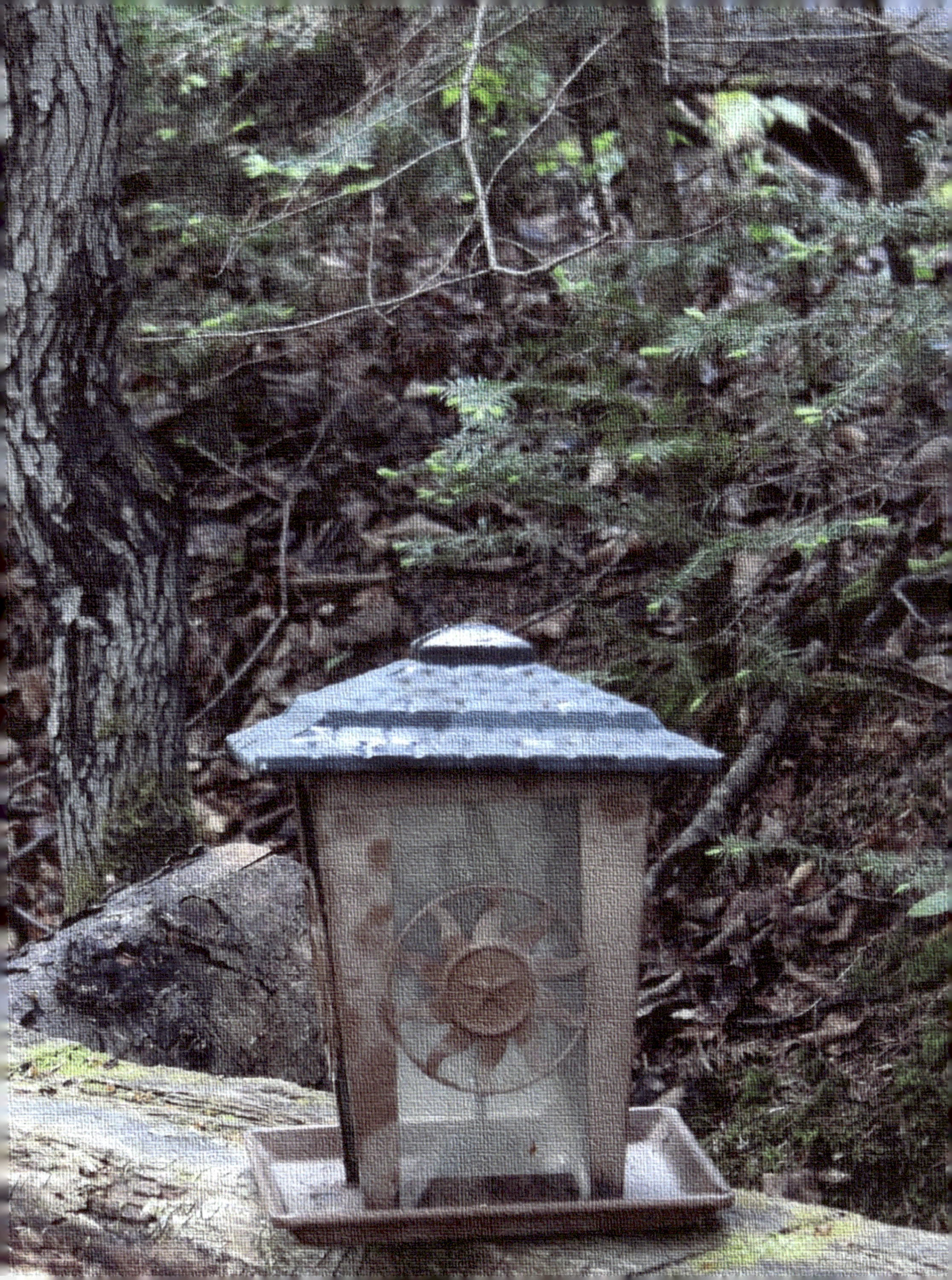

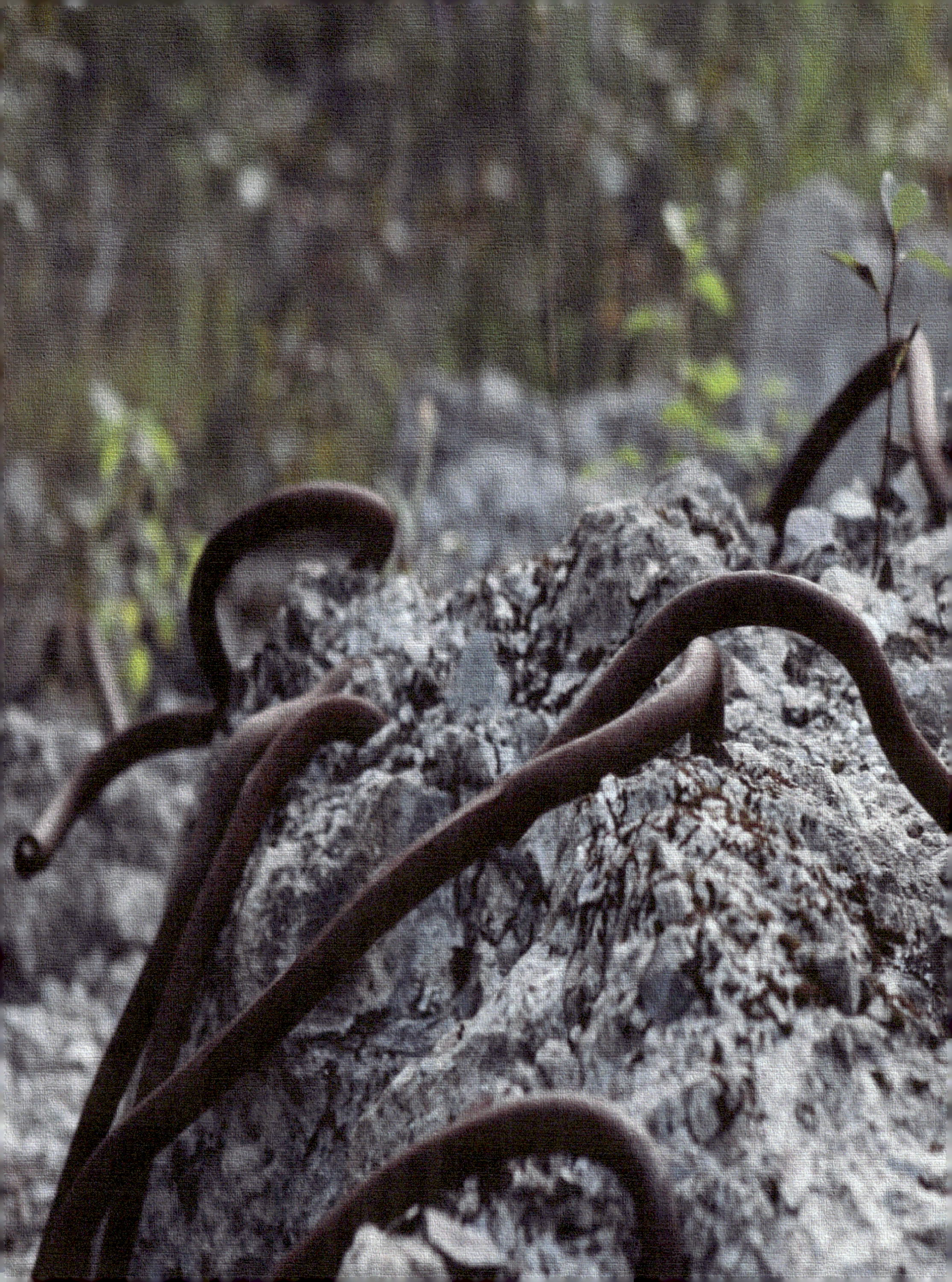

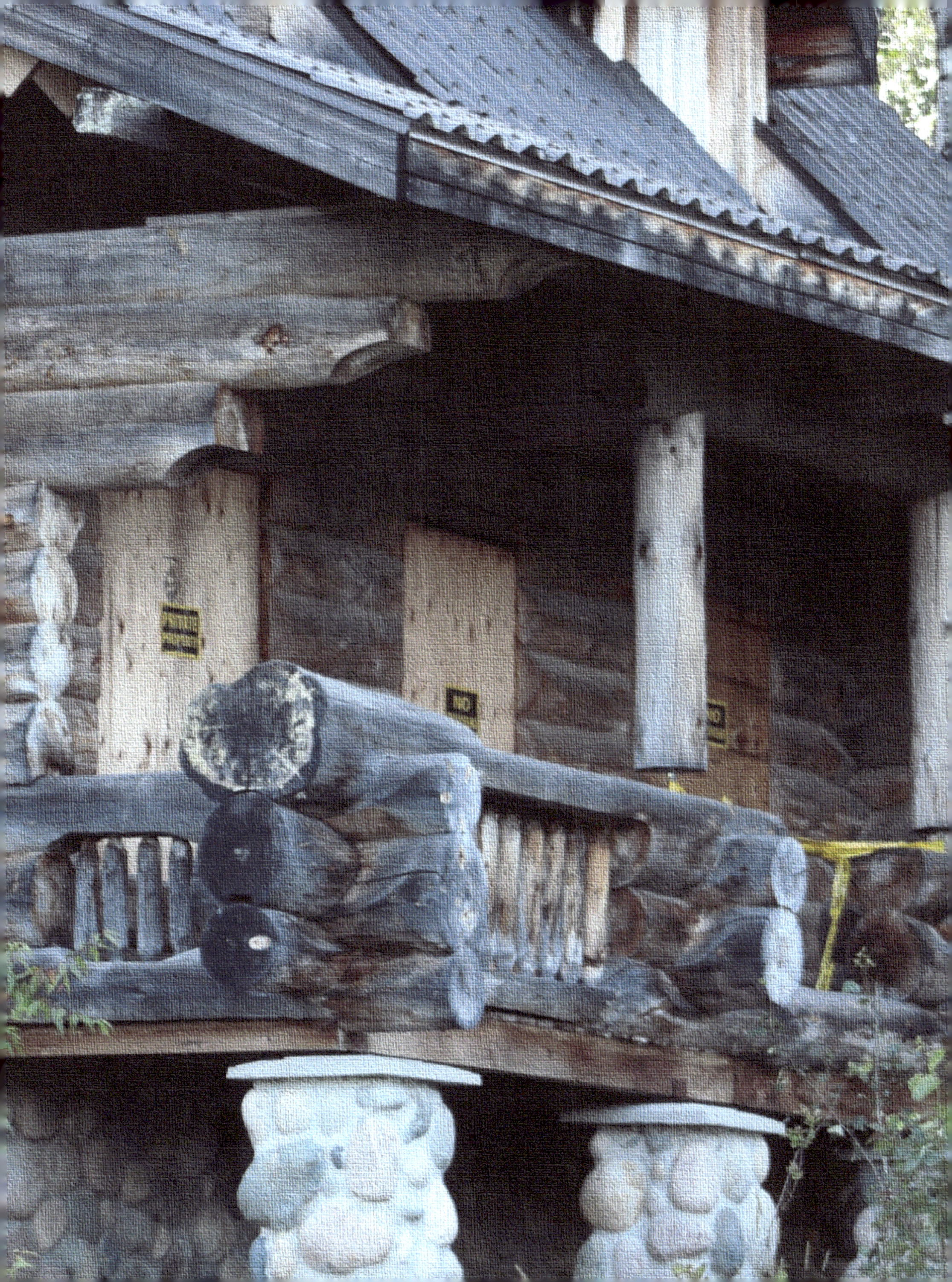

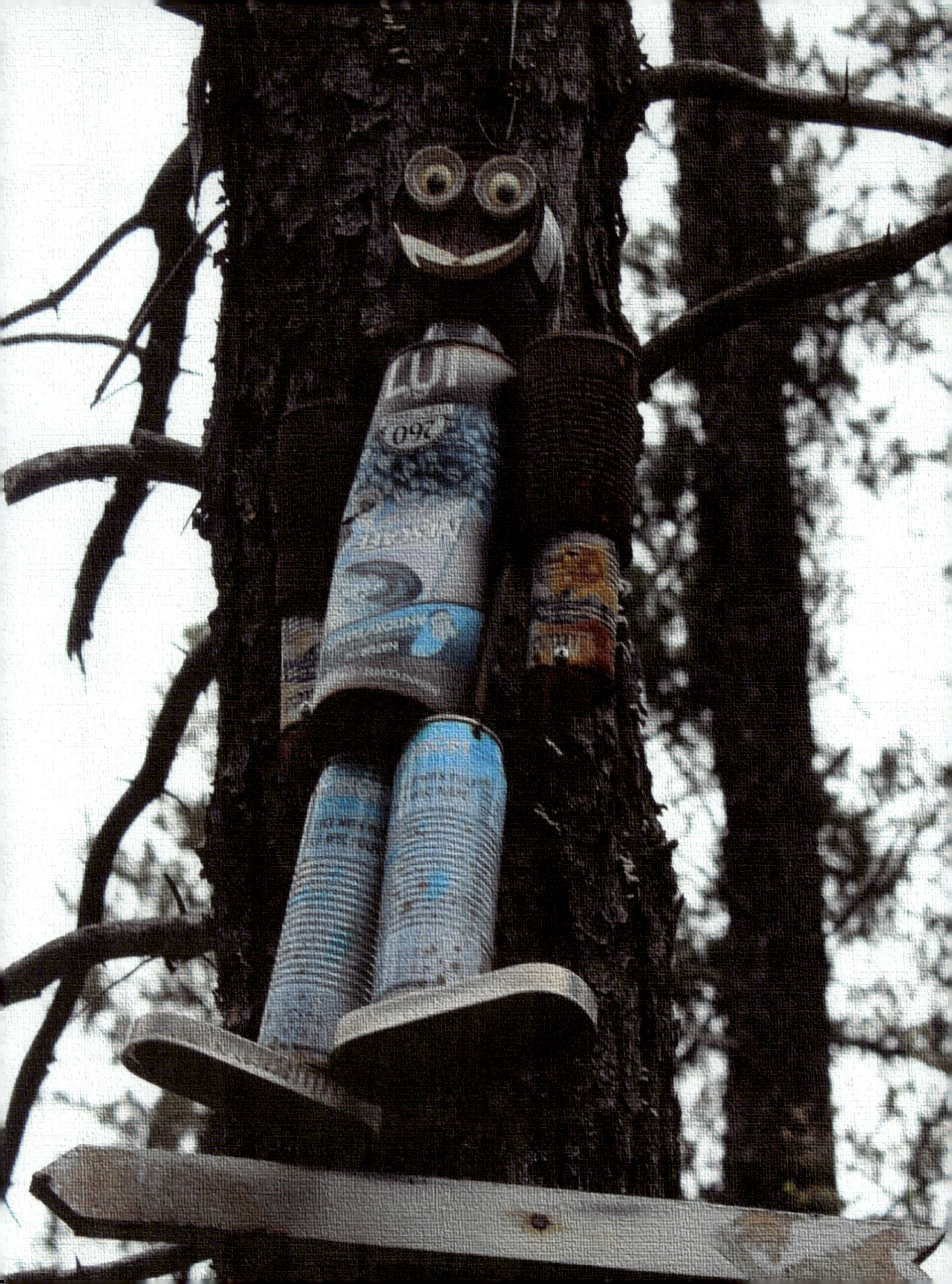

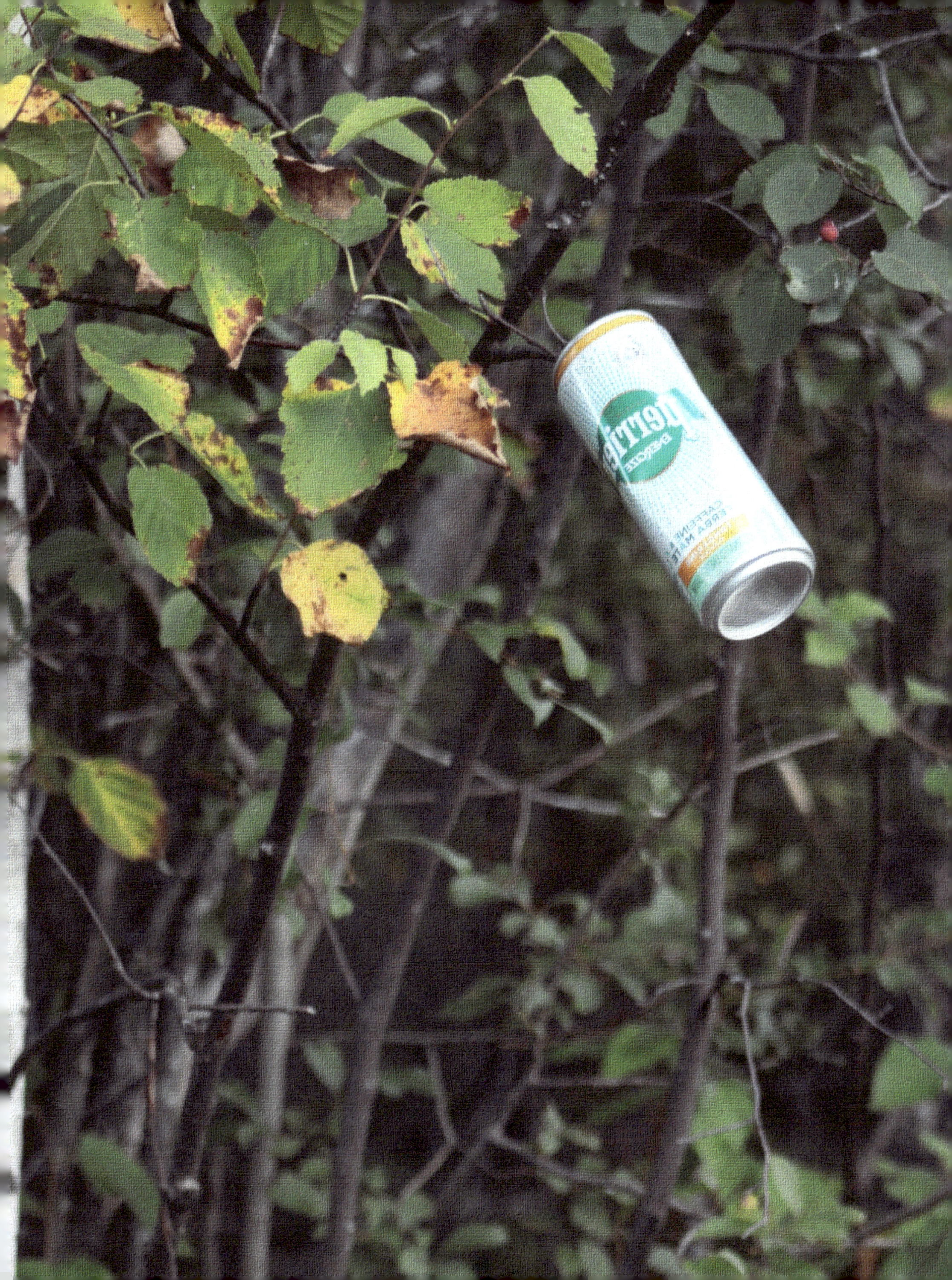
Perrier
ENERGIZE
CAFFEINE &
YERBA MATE

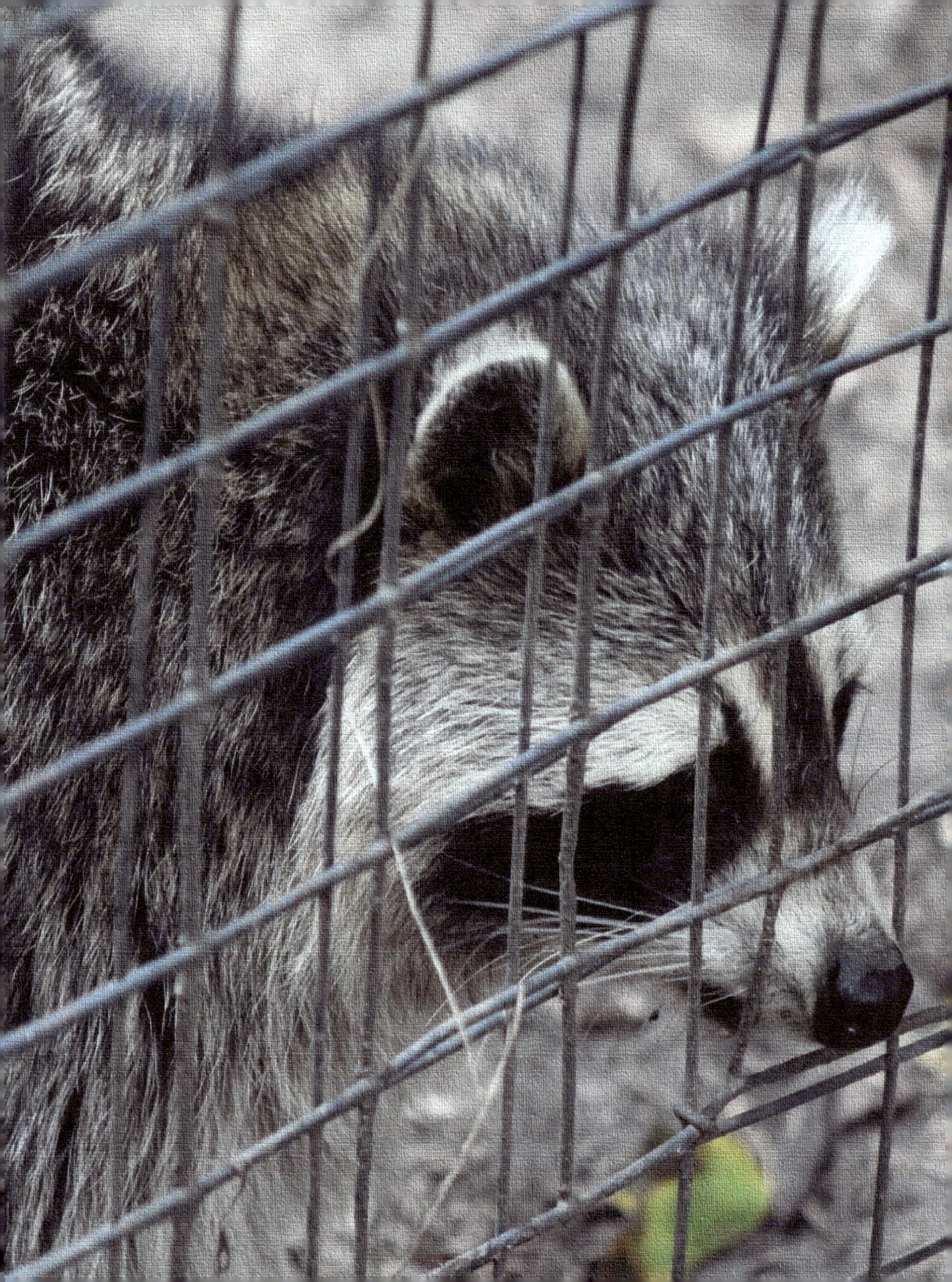

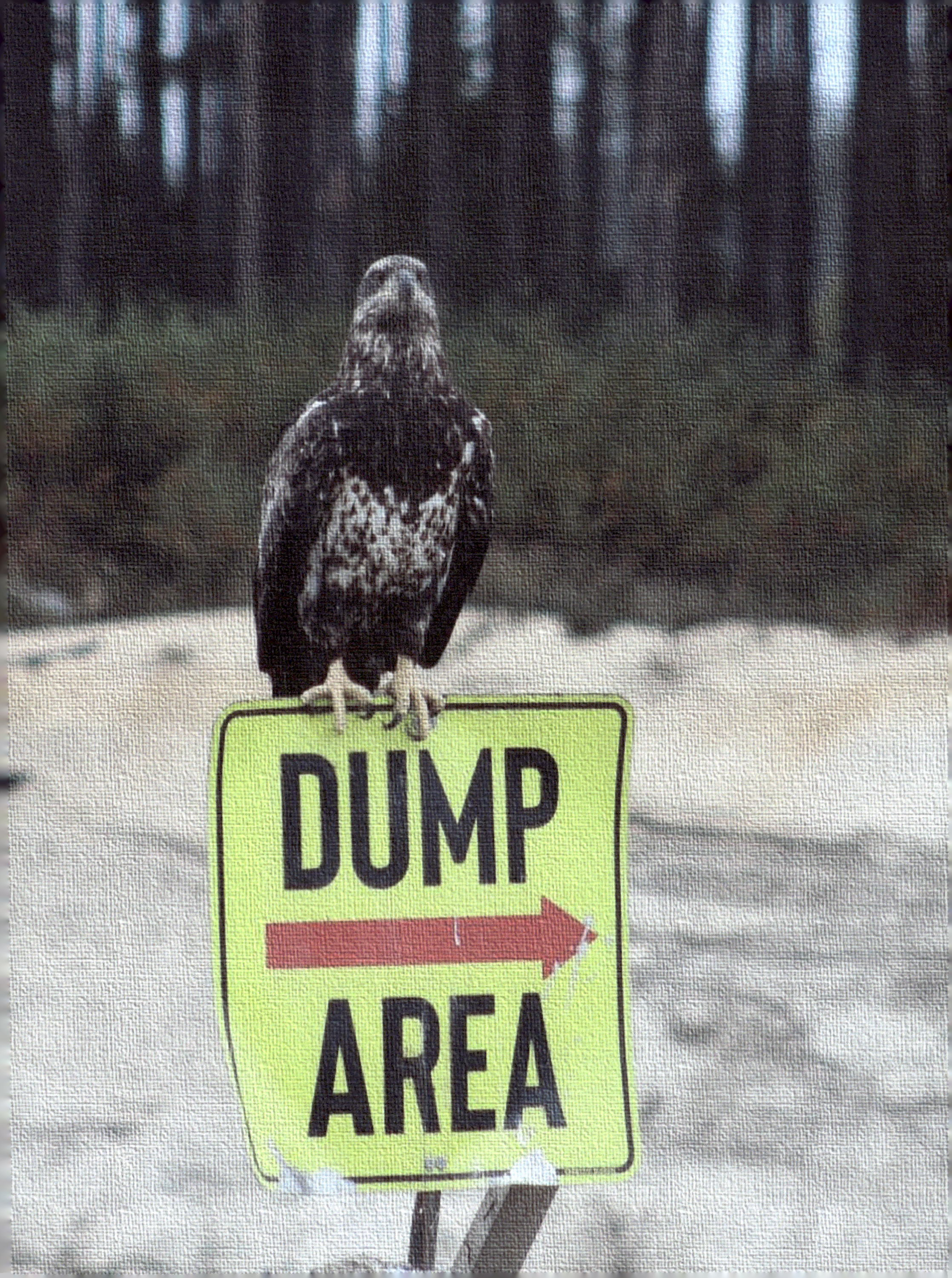

DUMP
AREA

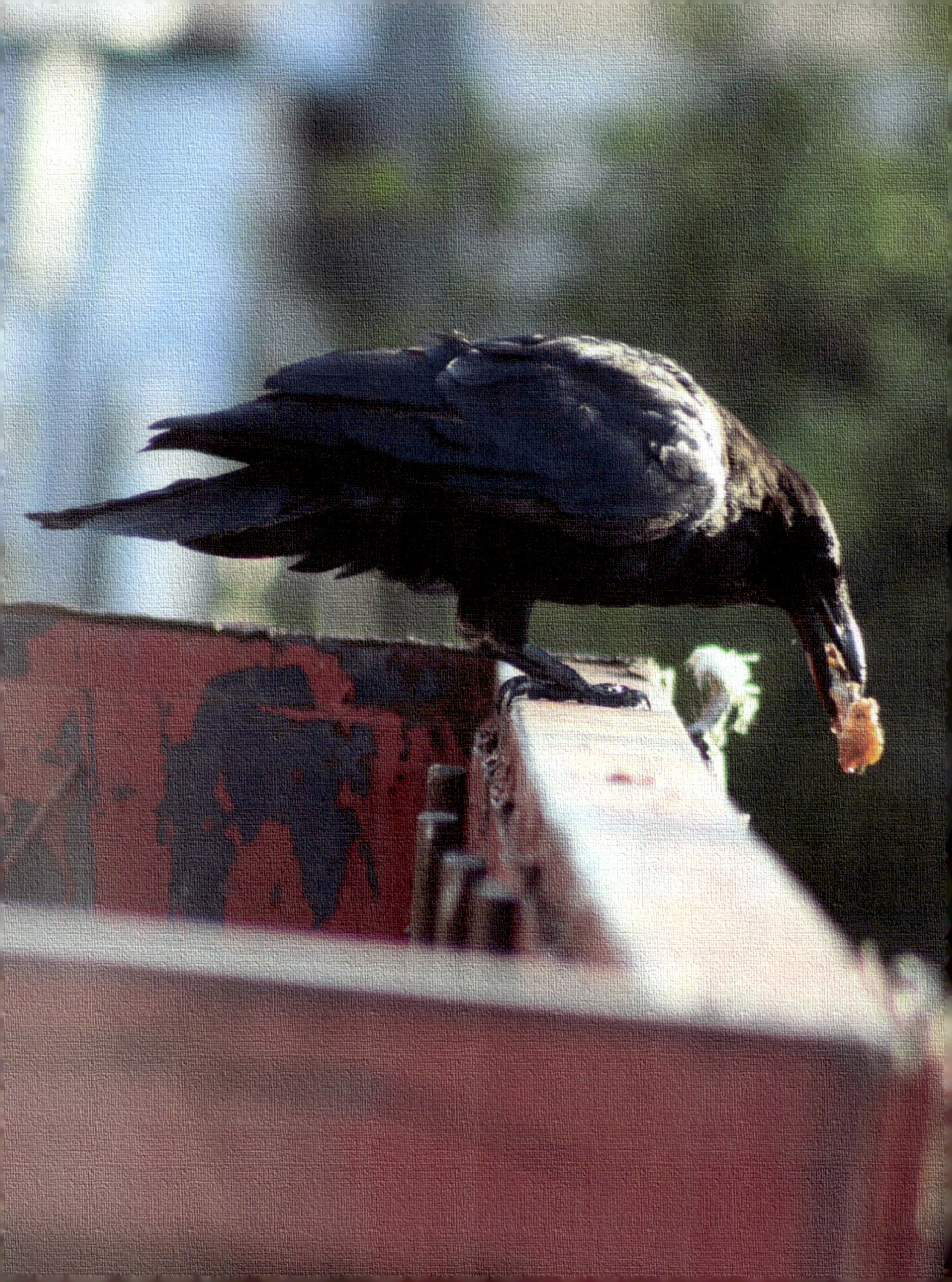

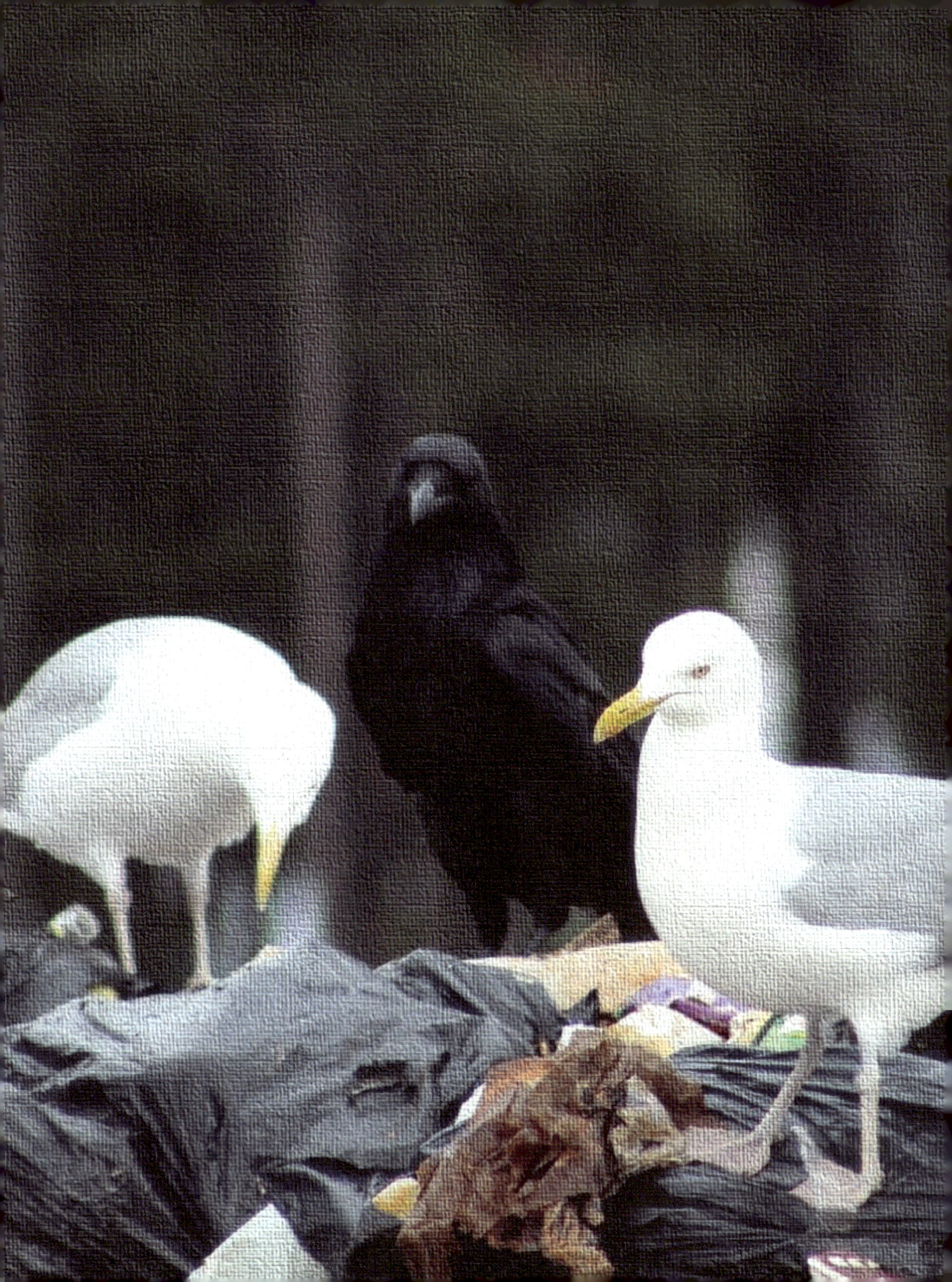

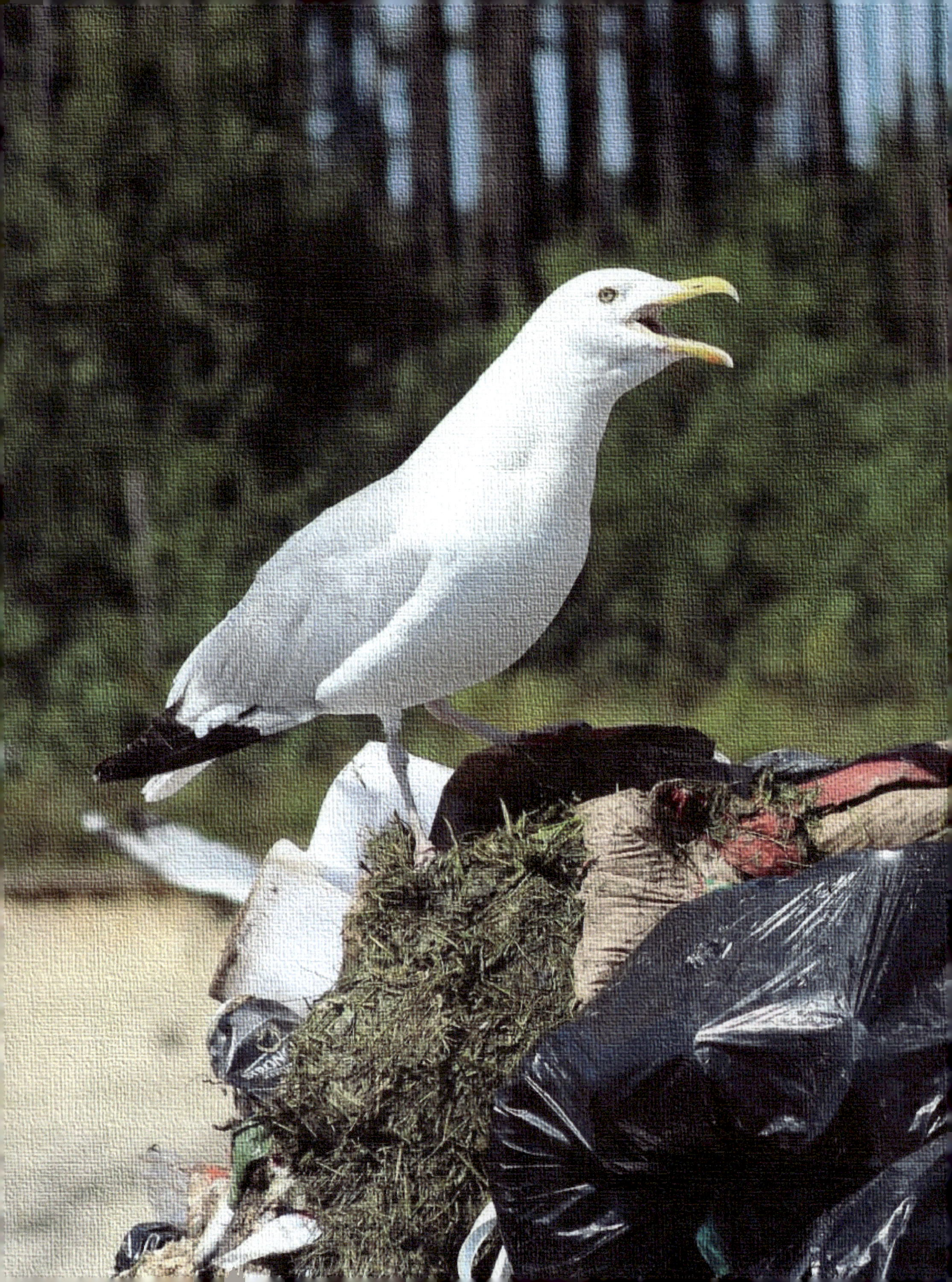

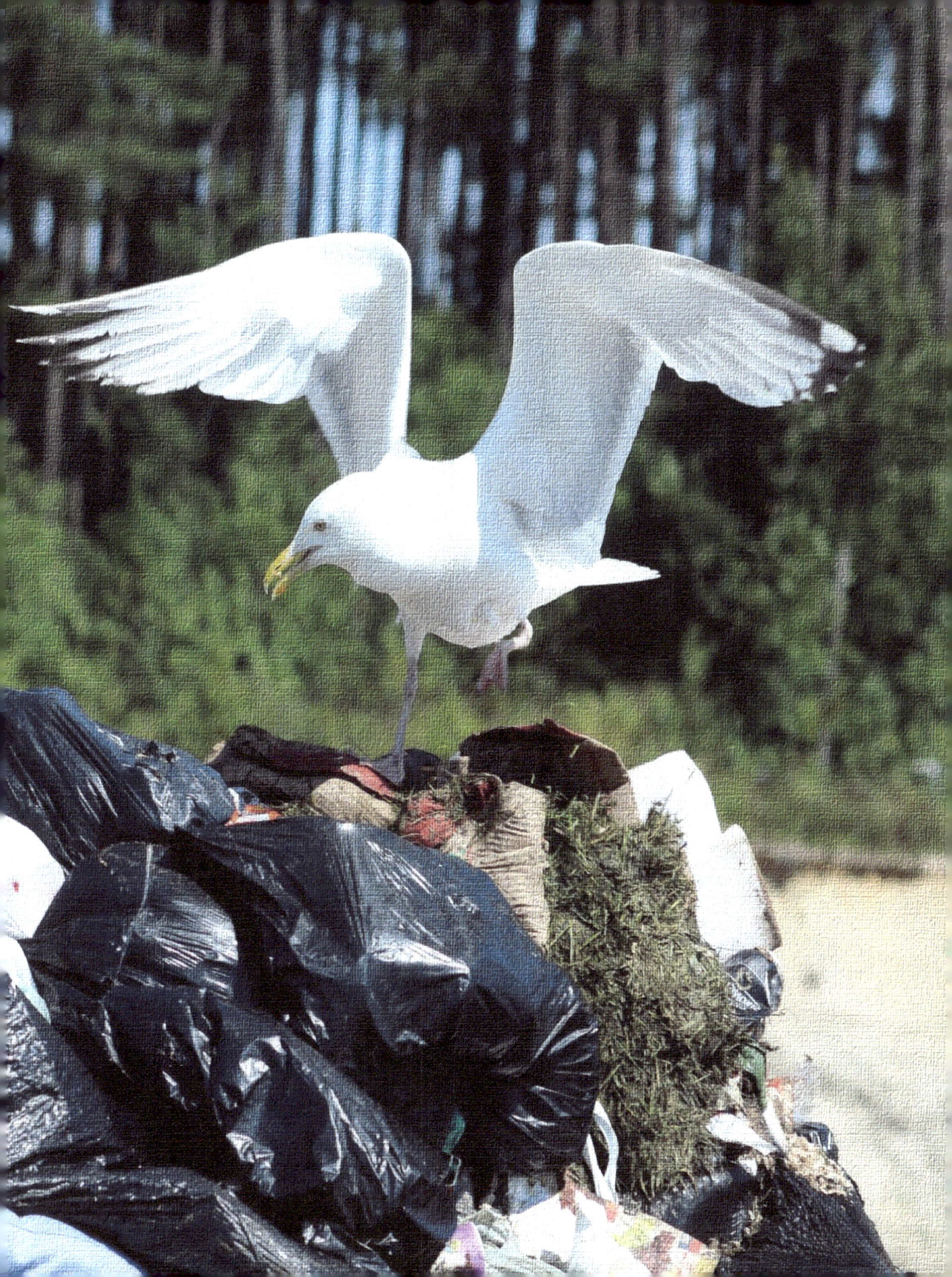

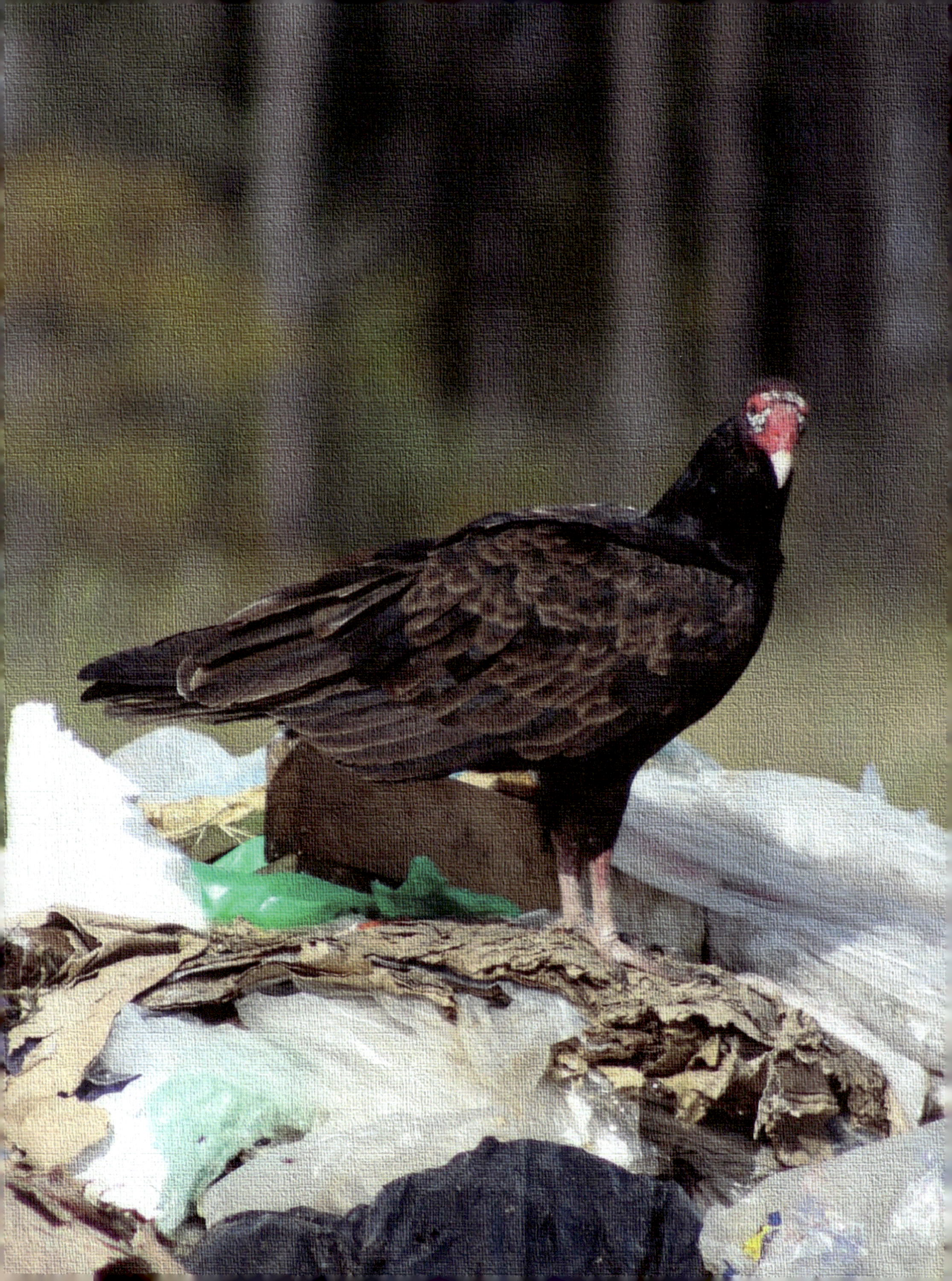

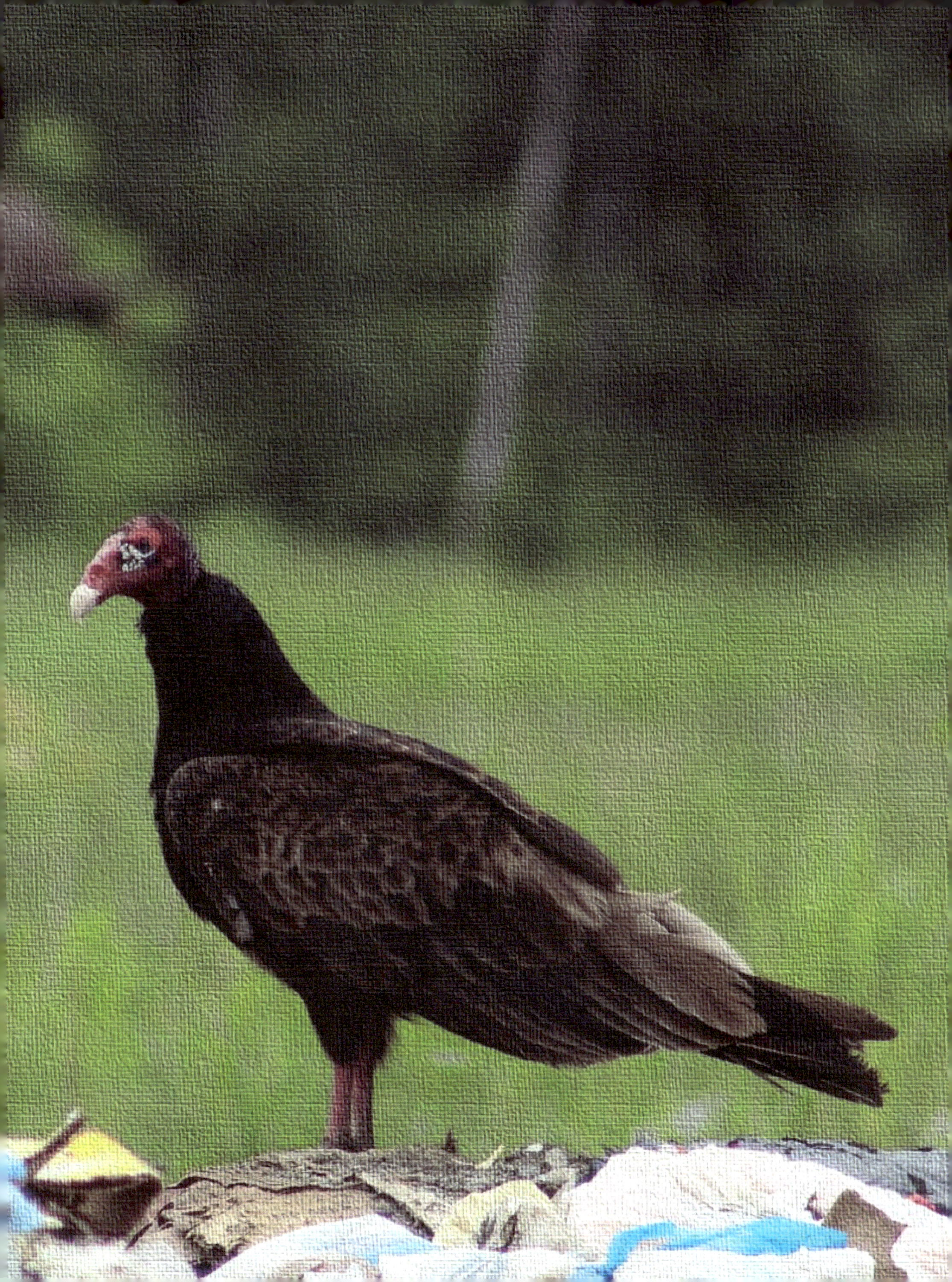

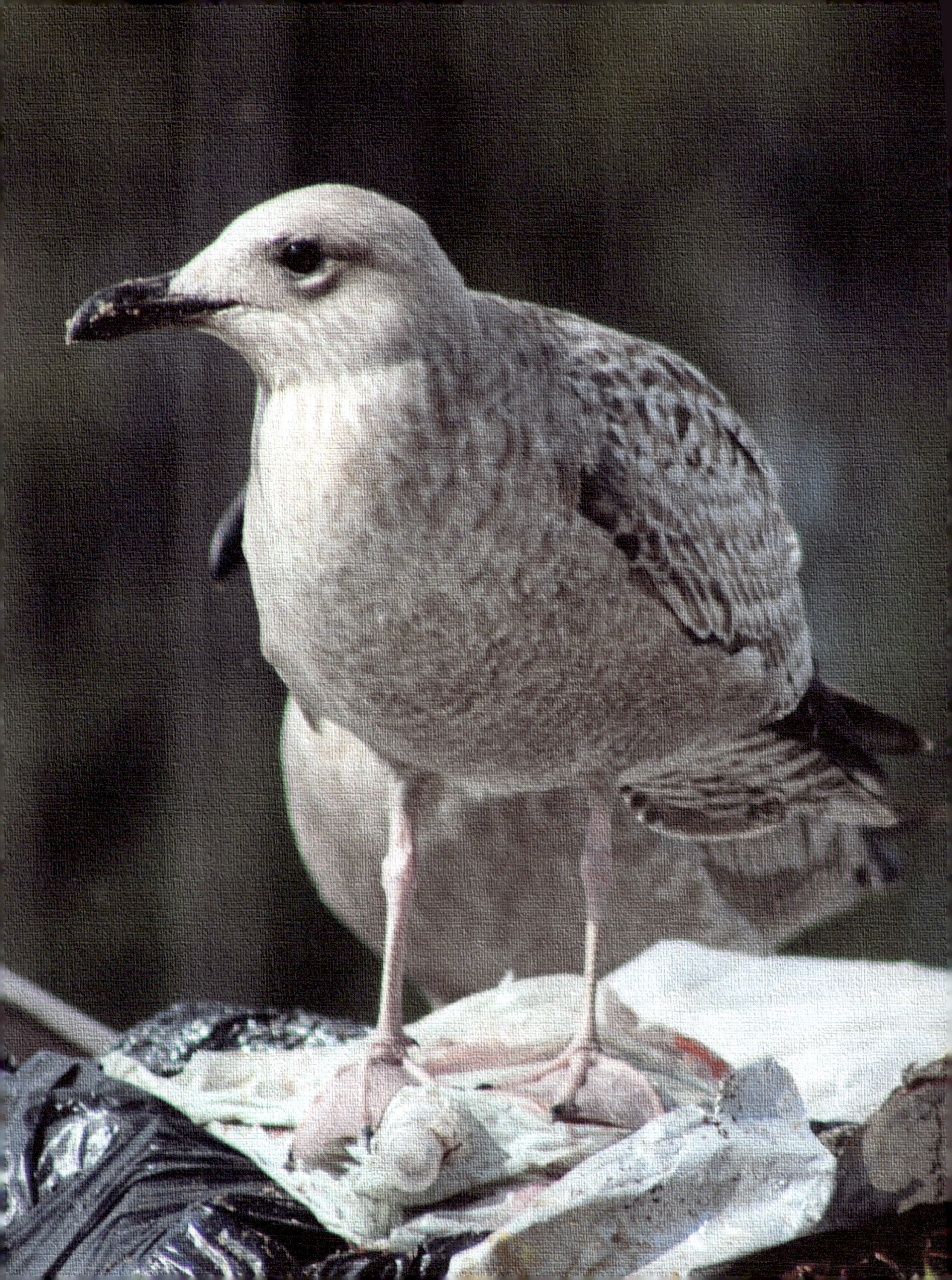

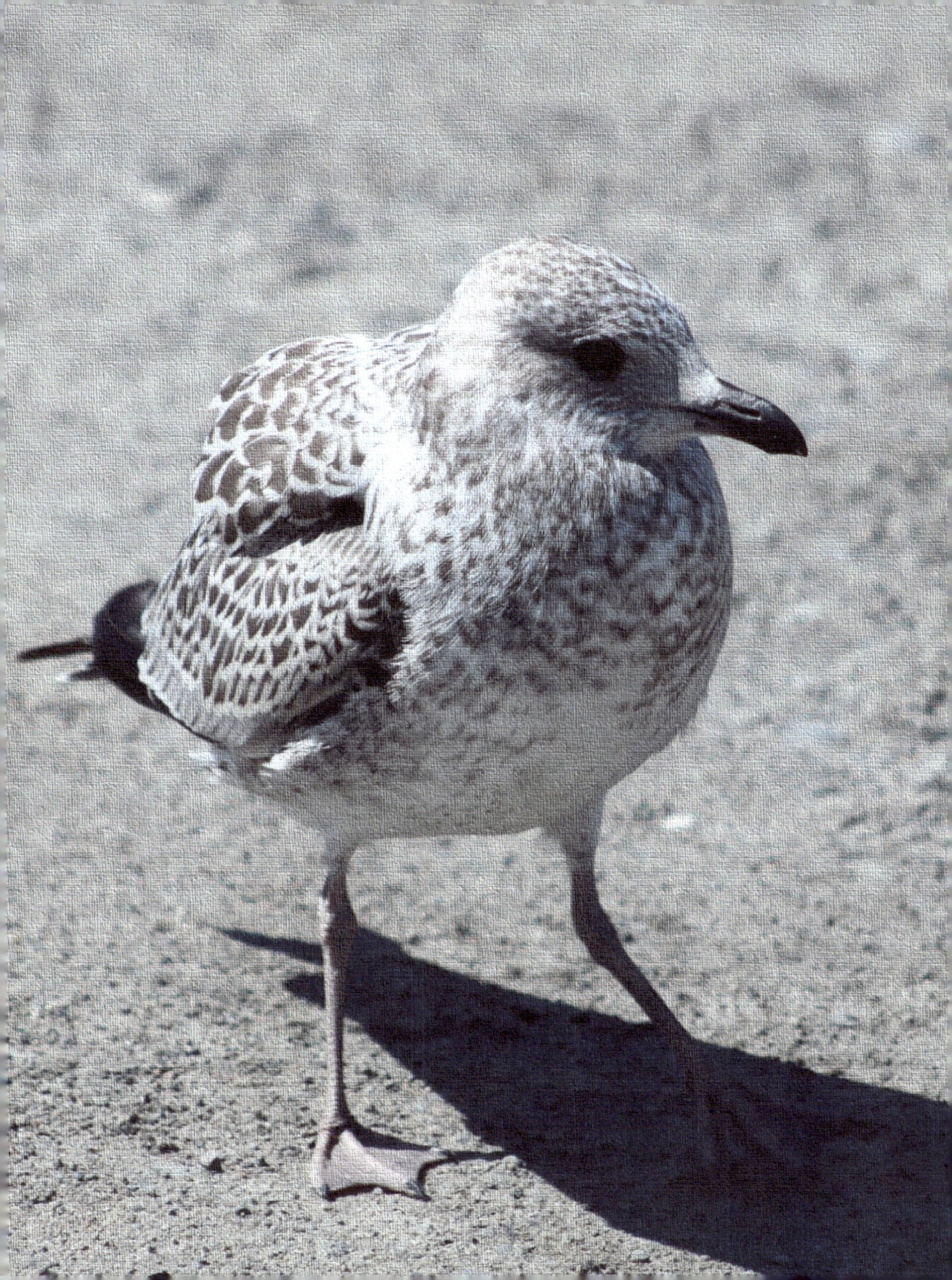

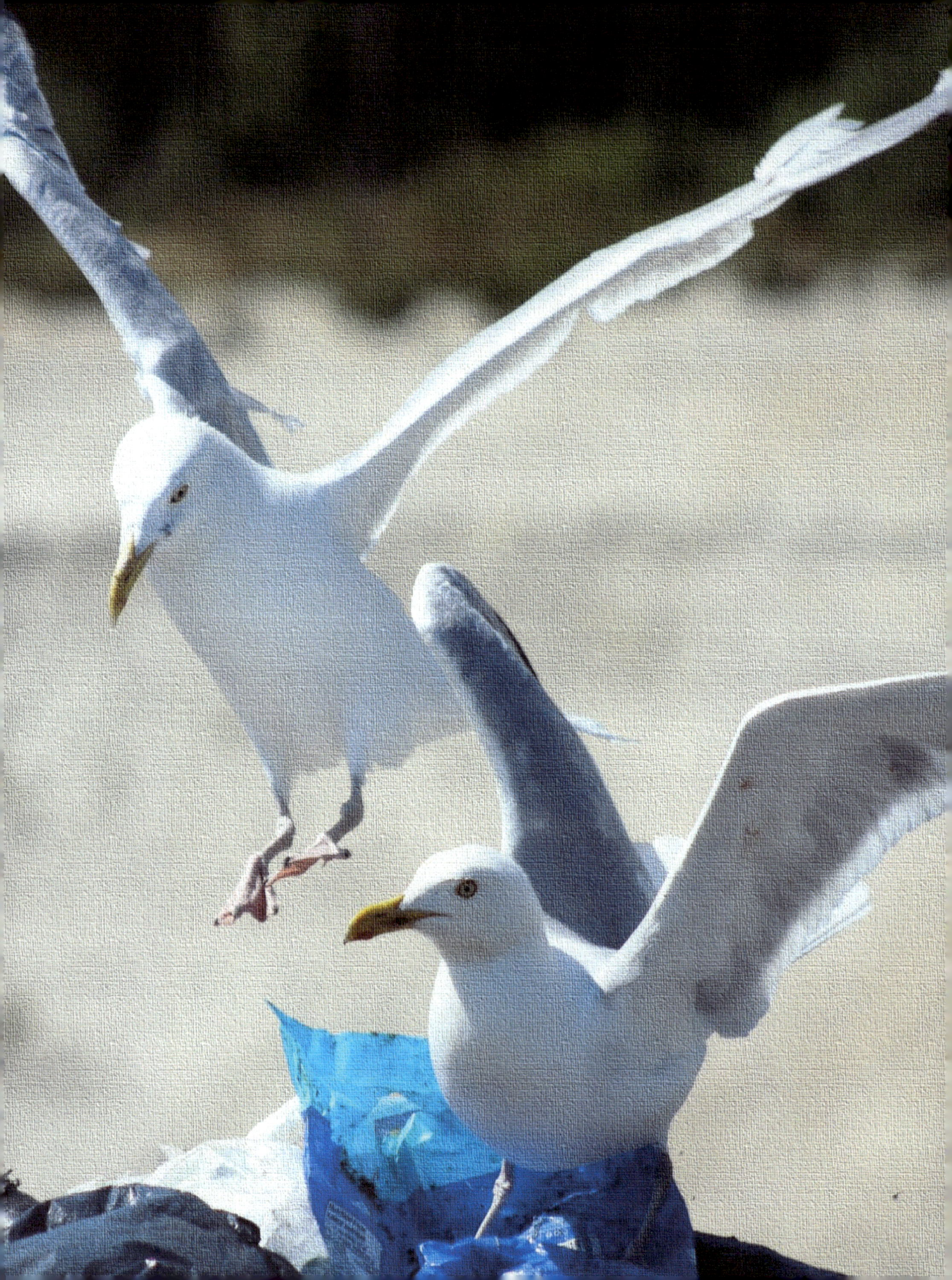

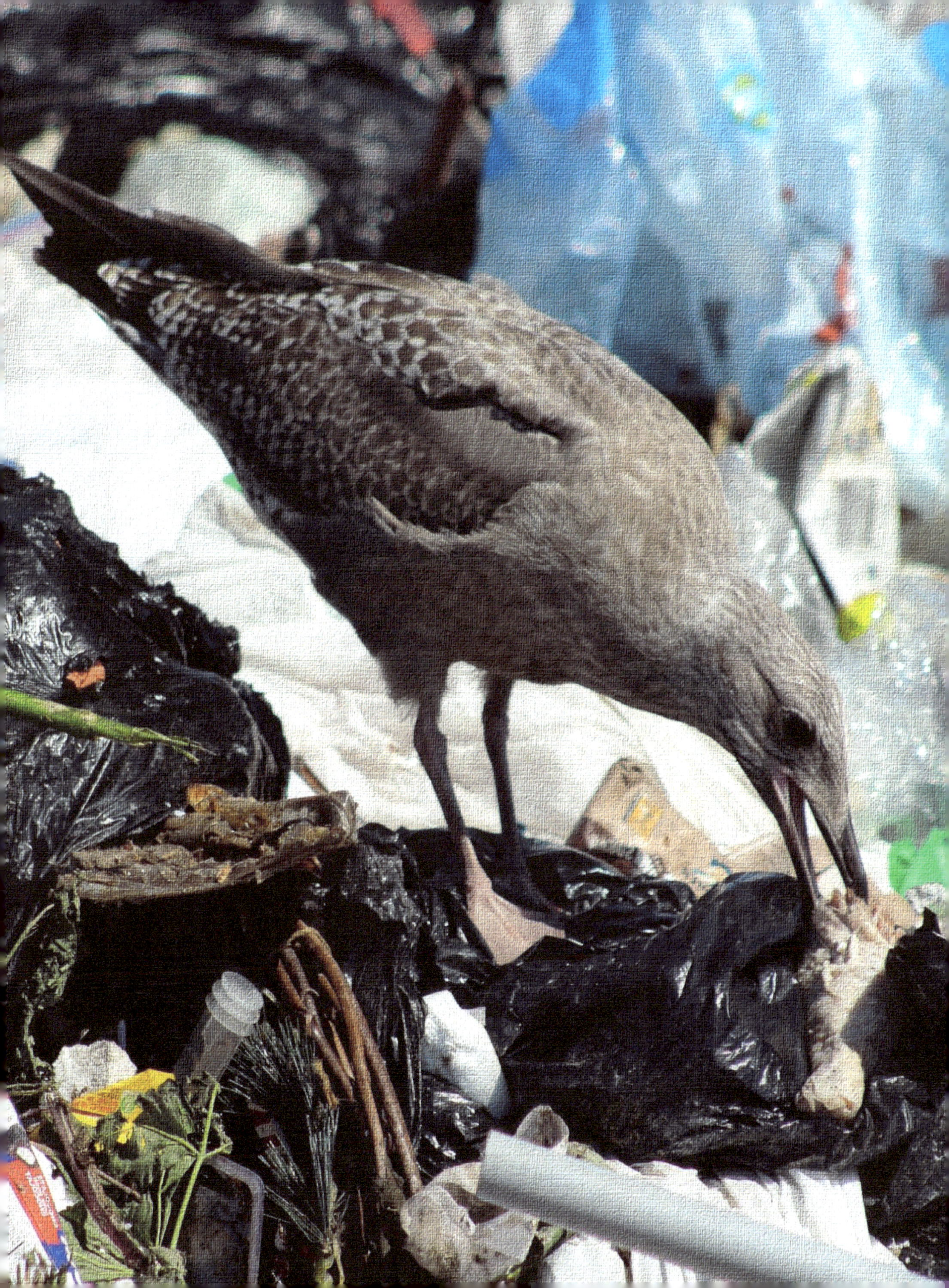

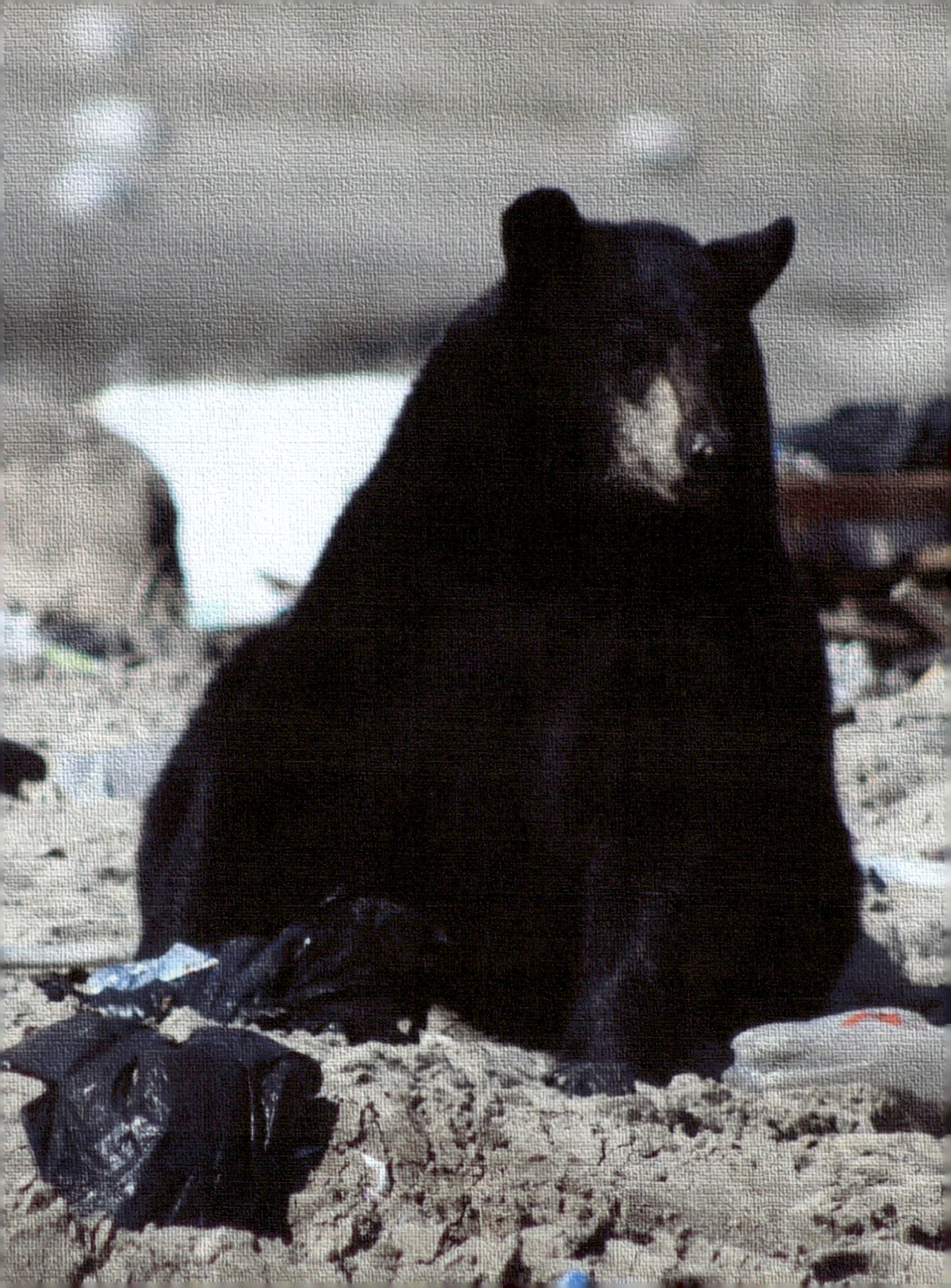

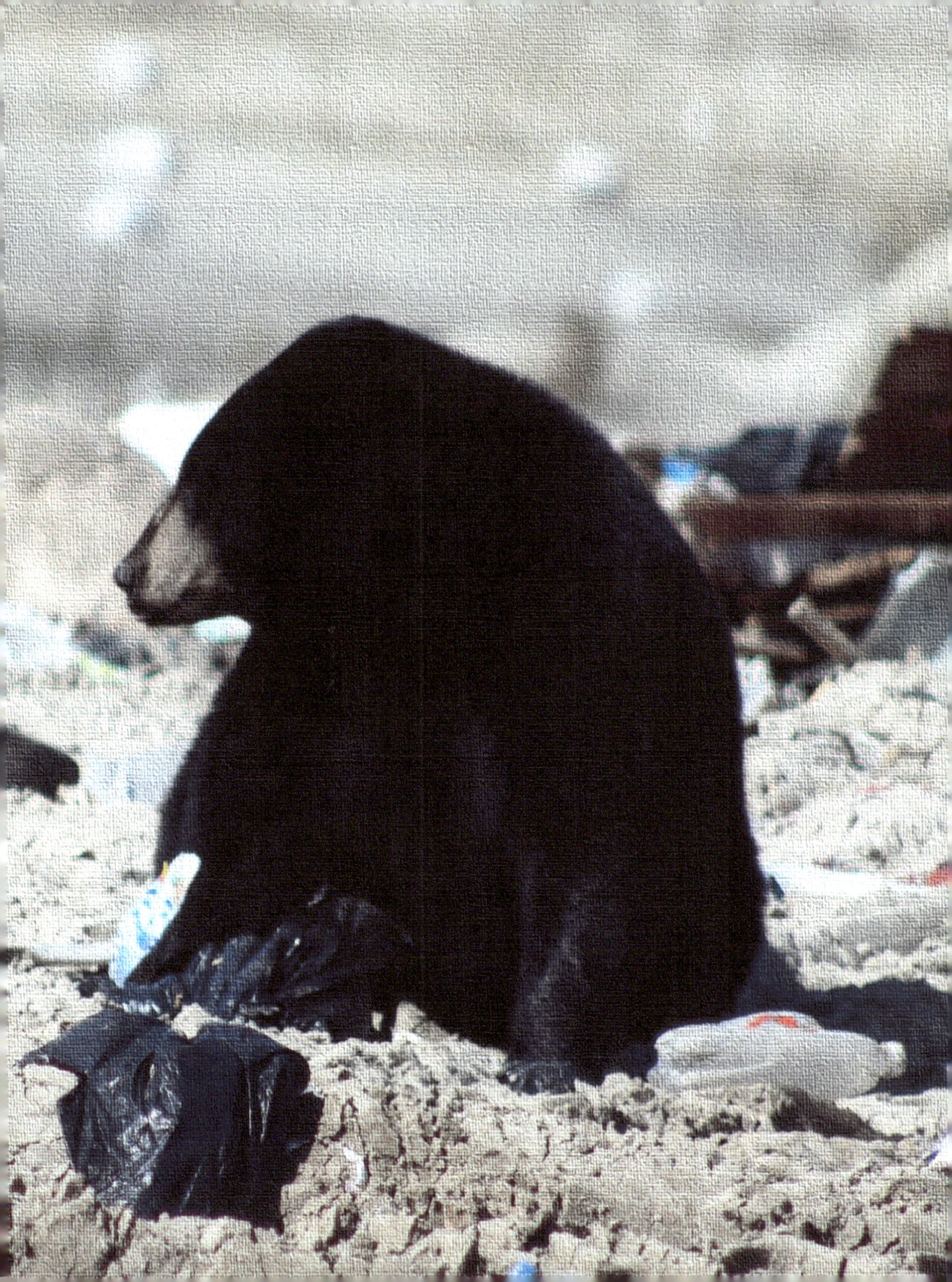

Alycia Hodge

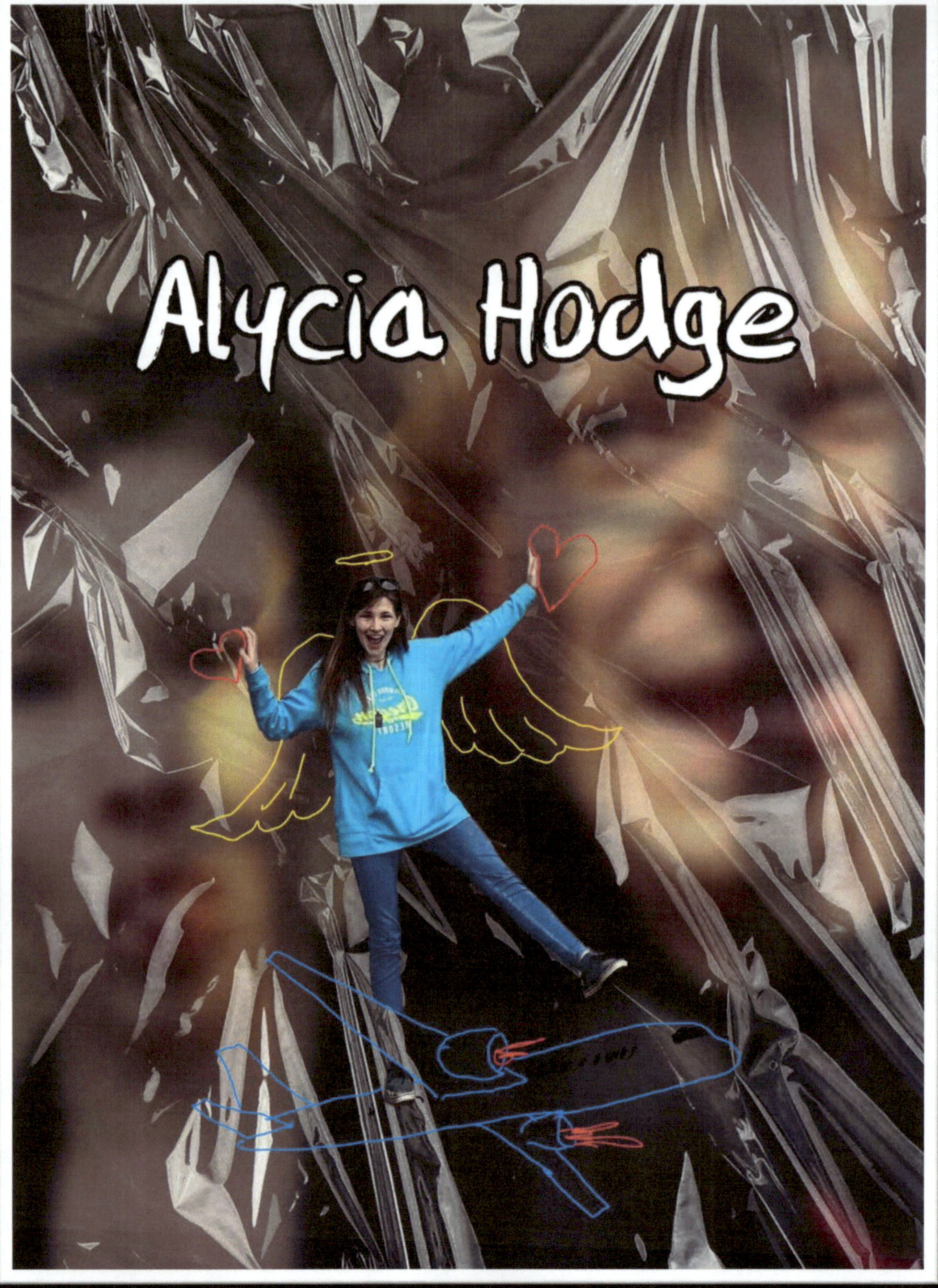

About the Artist

Alycia Hodge is a neurodivergent author, artist and editor living in the state of Oregon, U.S.A with her husband, daughter and 3 cats. She is also a minister with the Universal Life Church and an apprentice Shaman. She believes that art of all forms helps us to heal and connect with others. She is the author of "I May Be a Romantic, But I'm Not Hopeless."

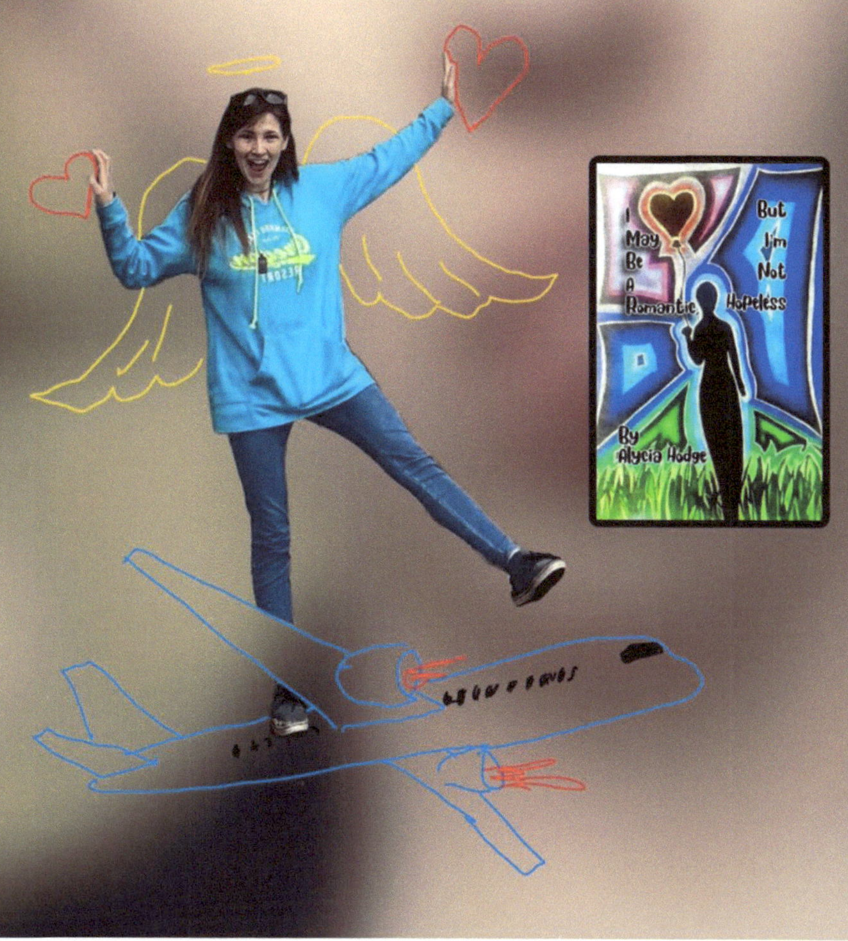

About the Collection

Over the past few years, I have taken a path that has led me through many spiritual, mental and physical trials. While on this journey I discovered many different faces within myself, along with a growing interest in digital art and photo editing. This has been the result thus far of portraying some of the inner faces I have discovered on my journey, with a few edits I did of friends mixed in. Thank you.

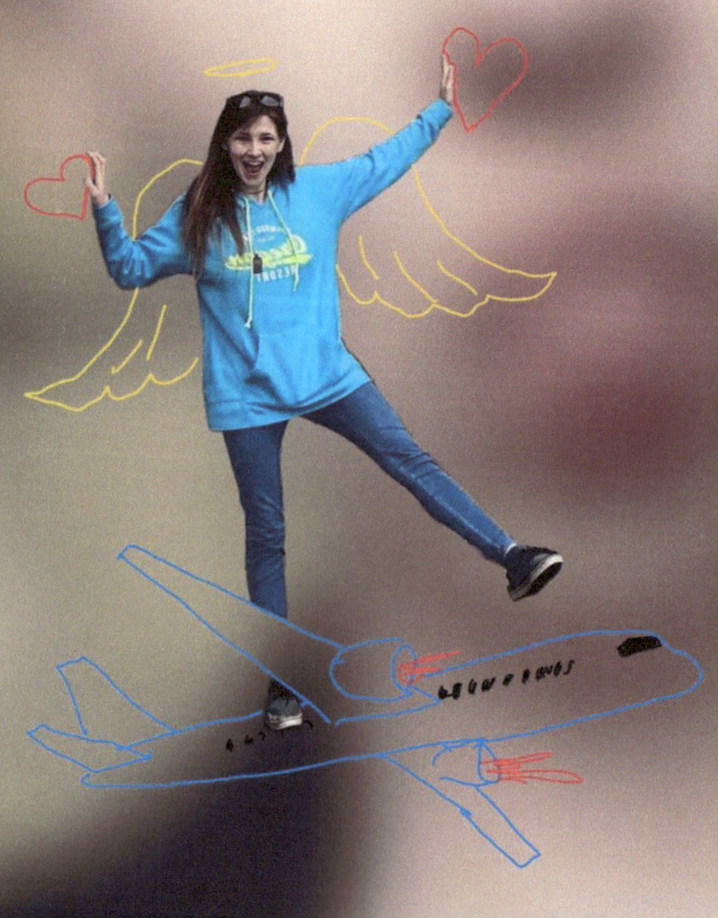

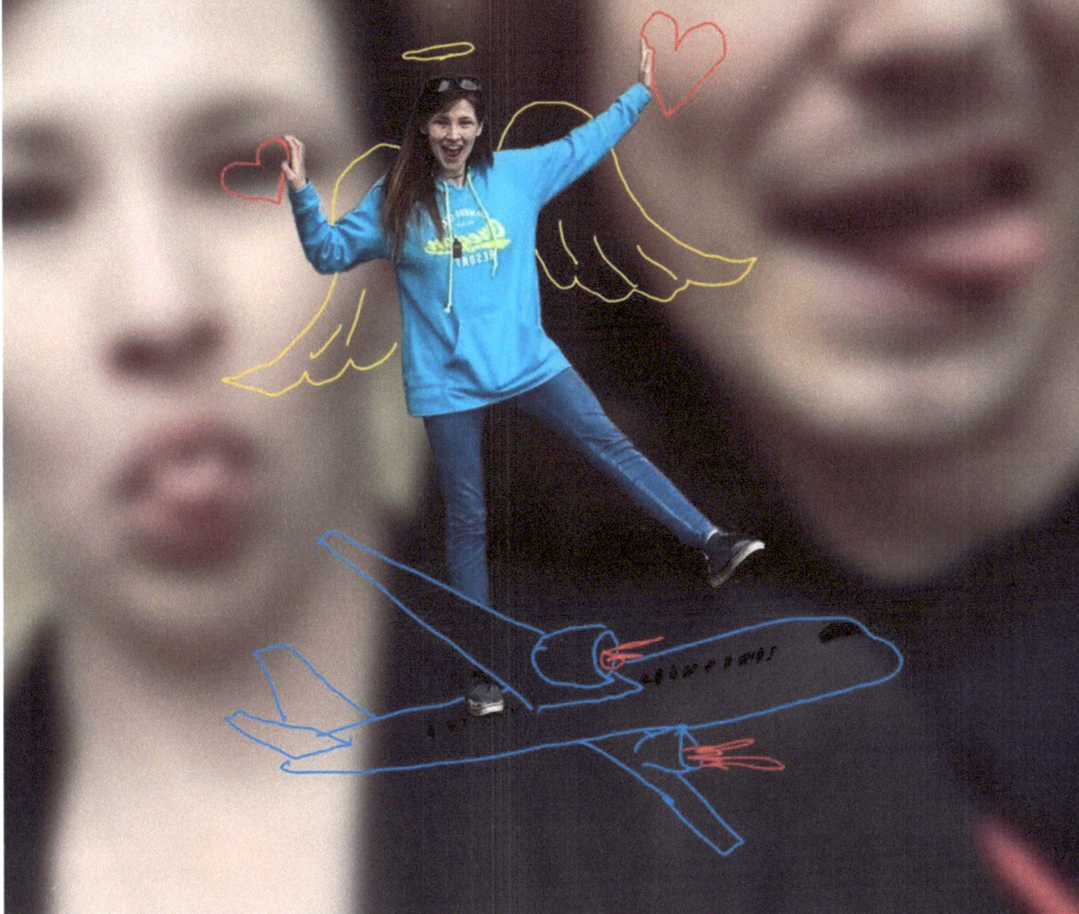
Dedicated to Spencer Warner

You see the sides of me
depicted in these pictures and
so much more, and you show love,
respect and appreciation for my
multifaceted nature. I love you.
Thank you.

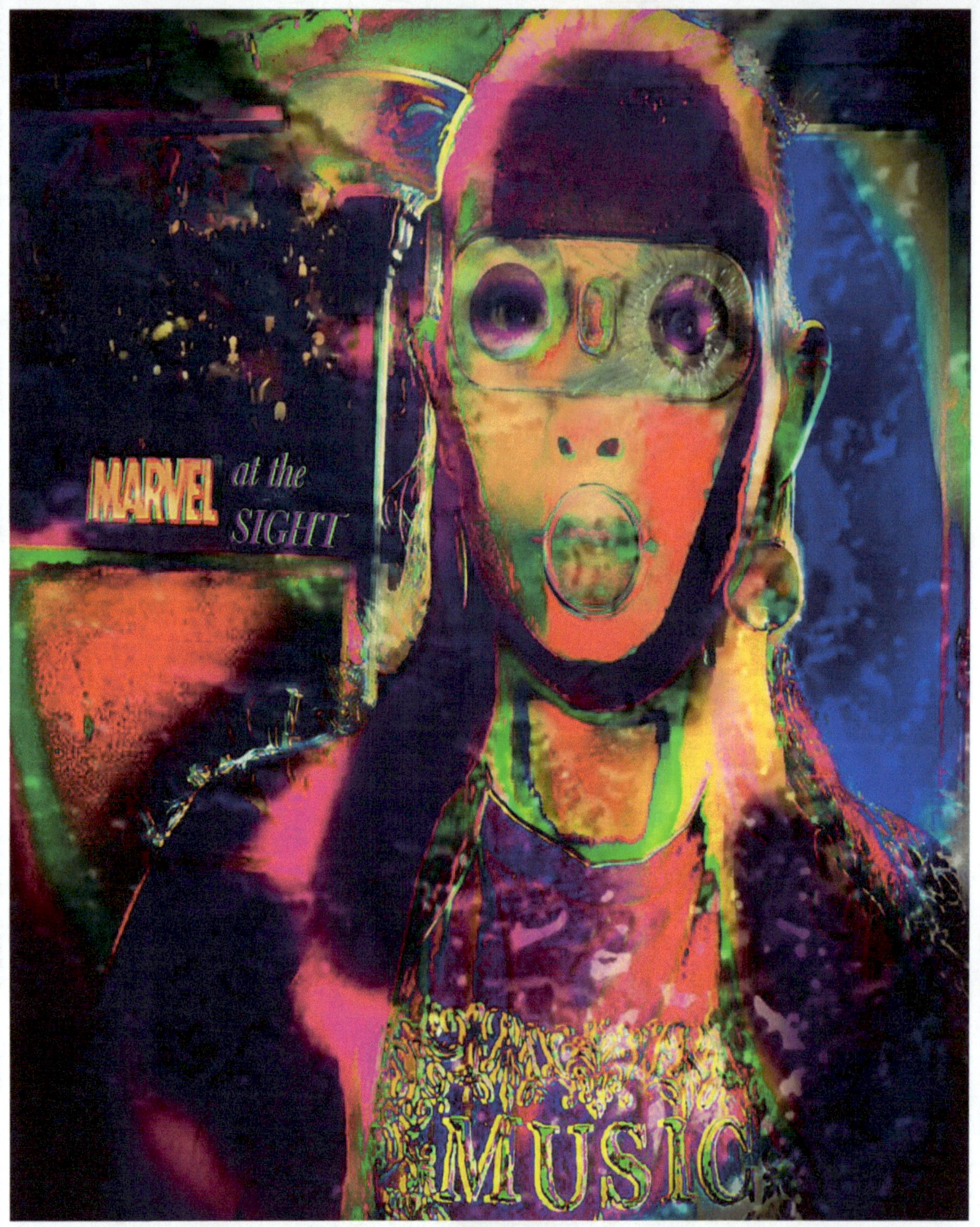
MARVEL at the
SIGHT
MUSIC

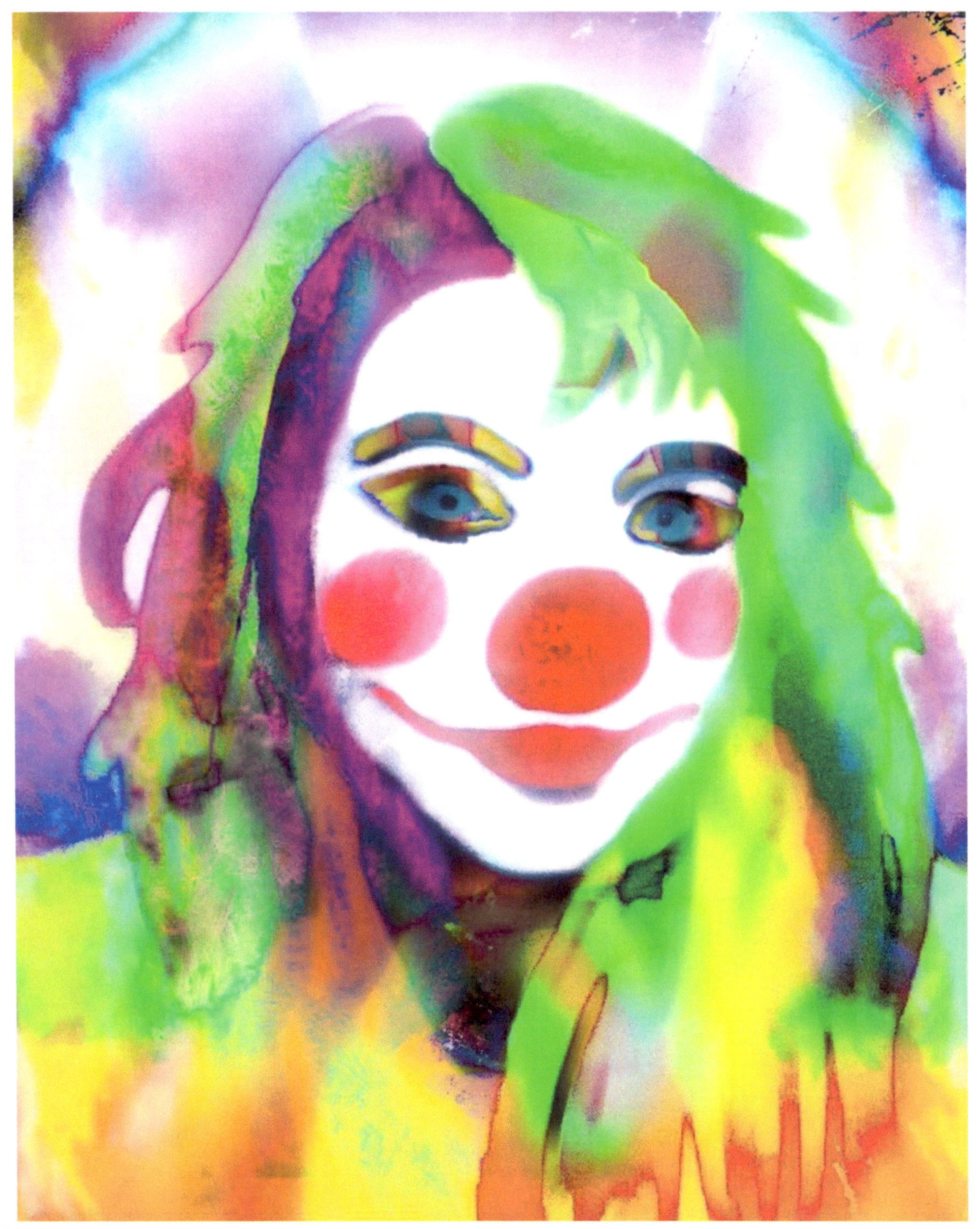

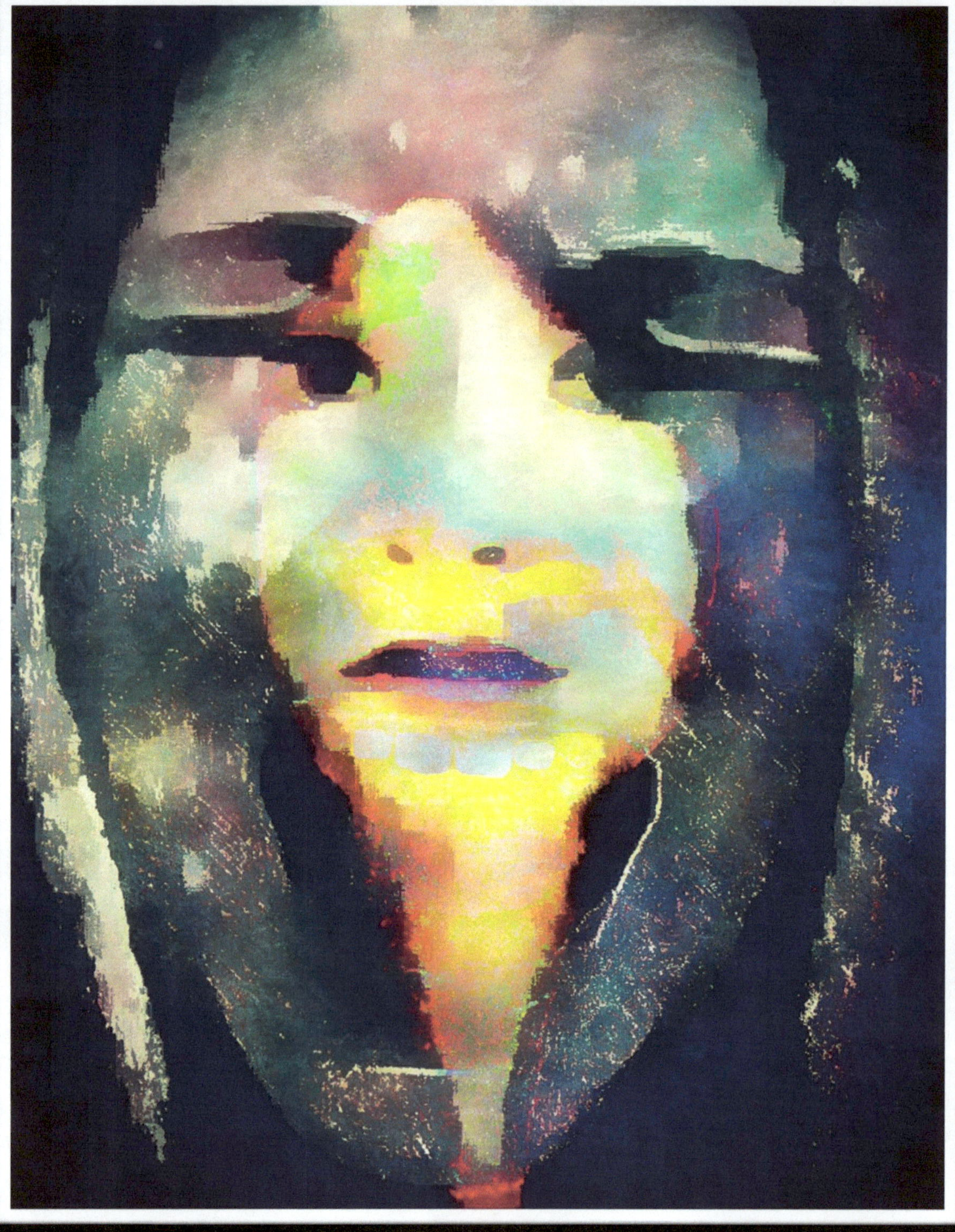

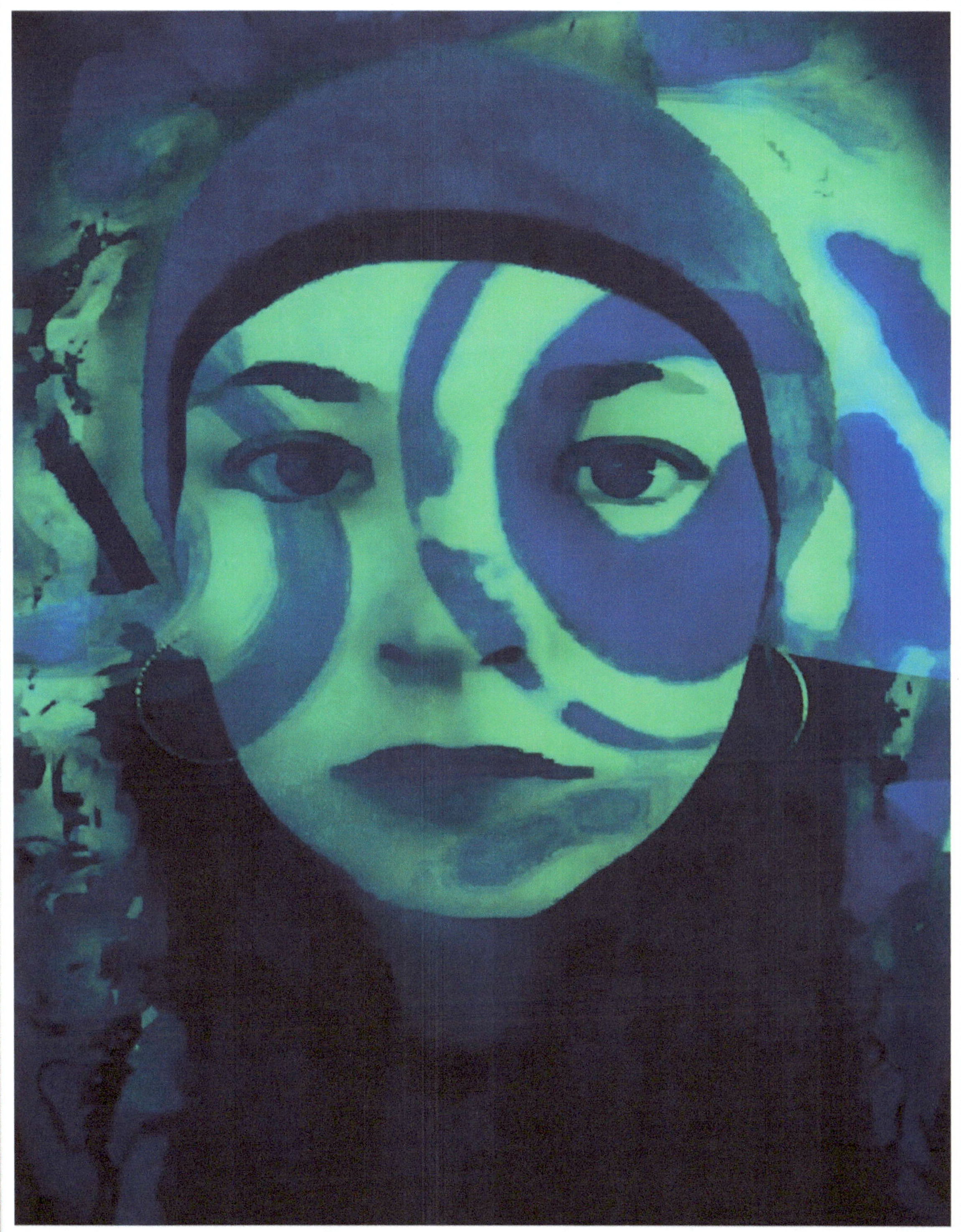

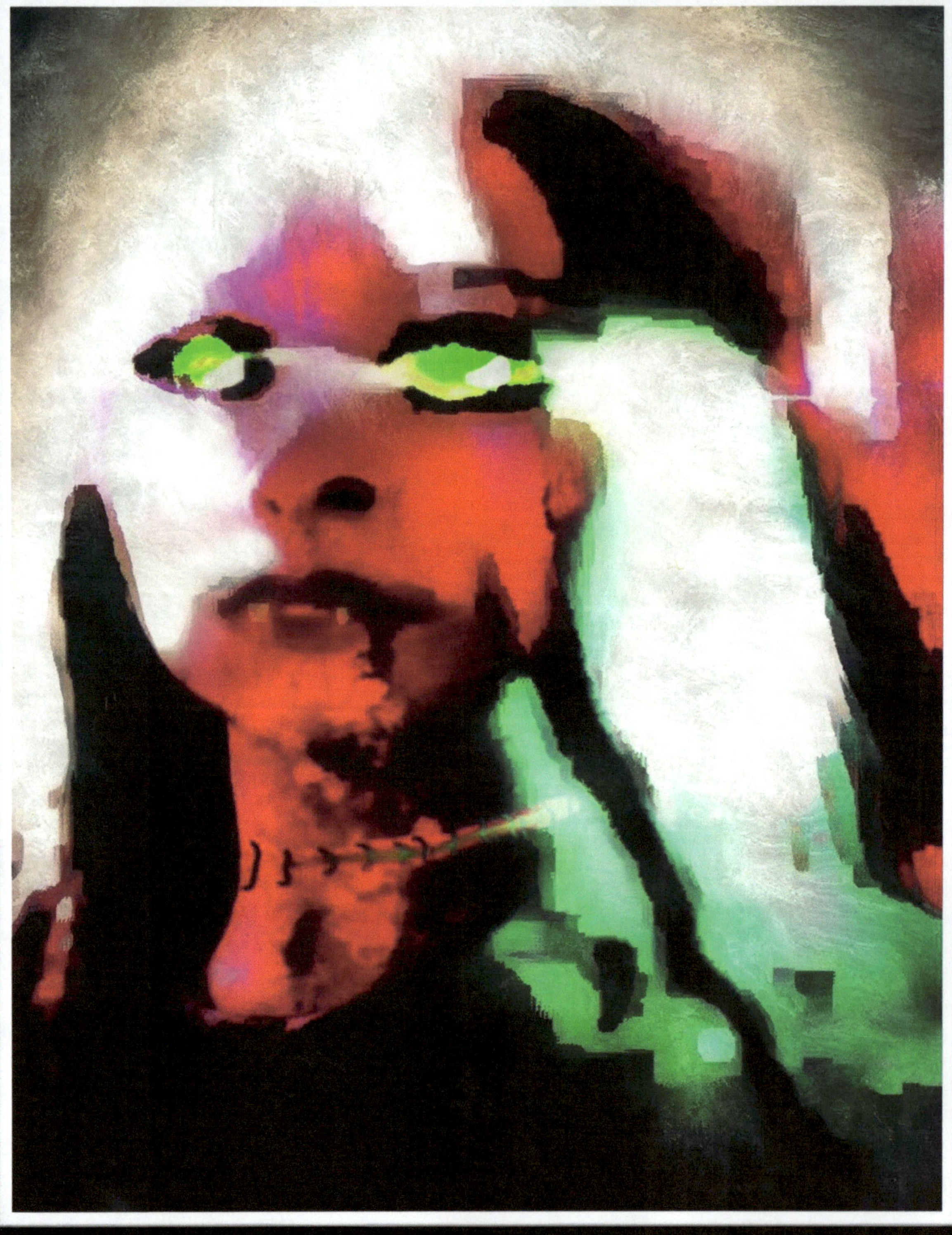

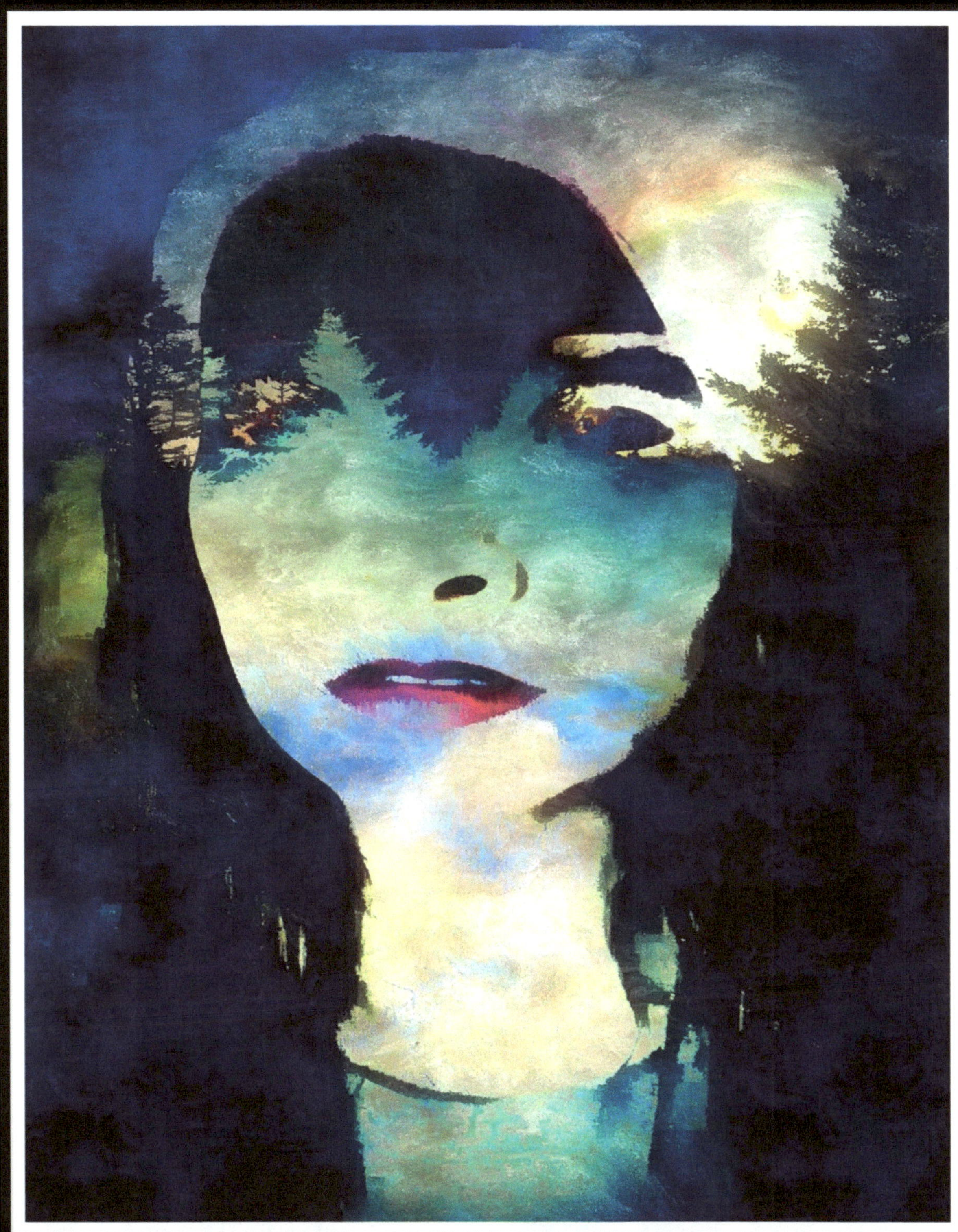

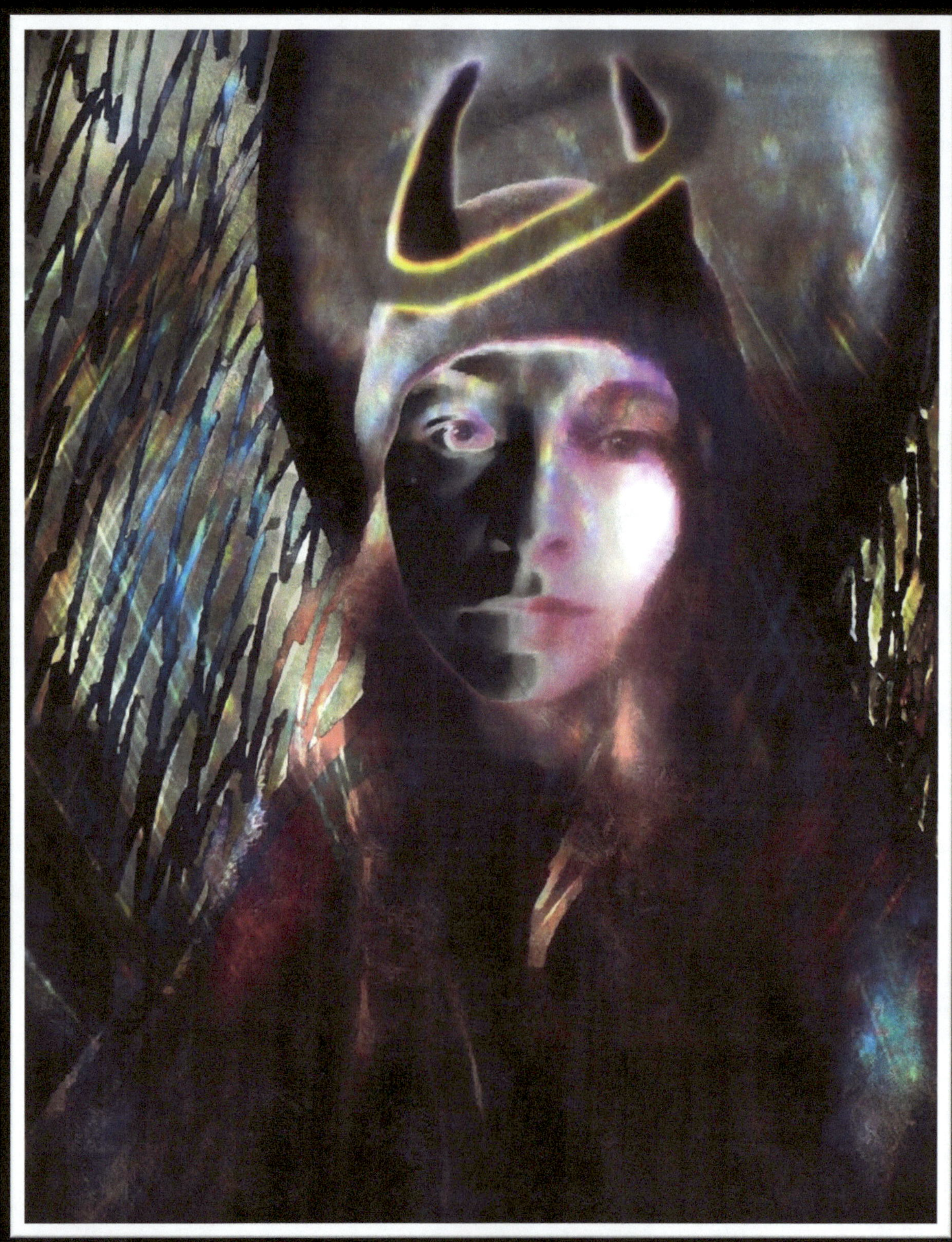
SHATTERED PSYCHE Vol 1(7)

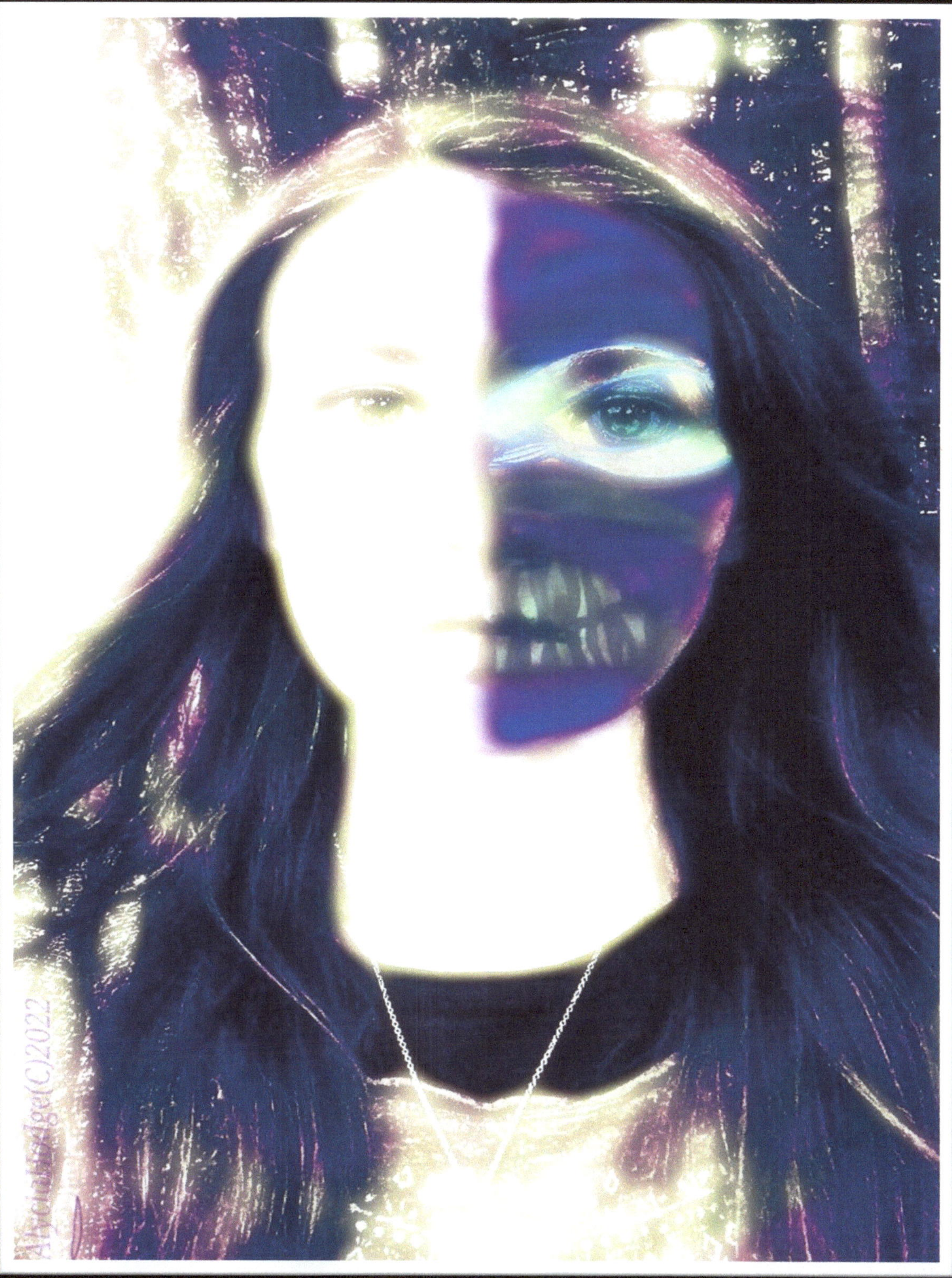

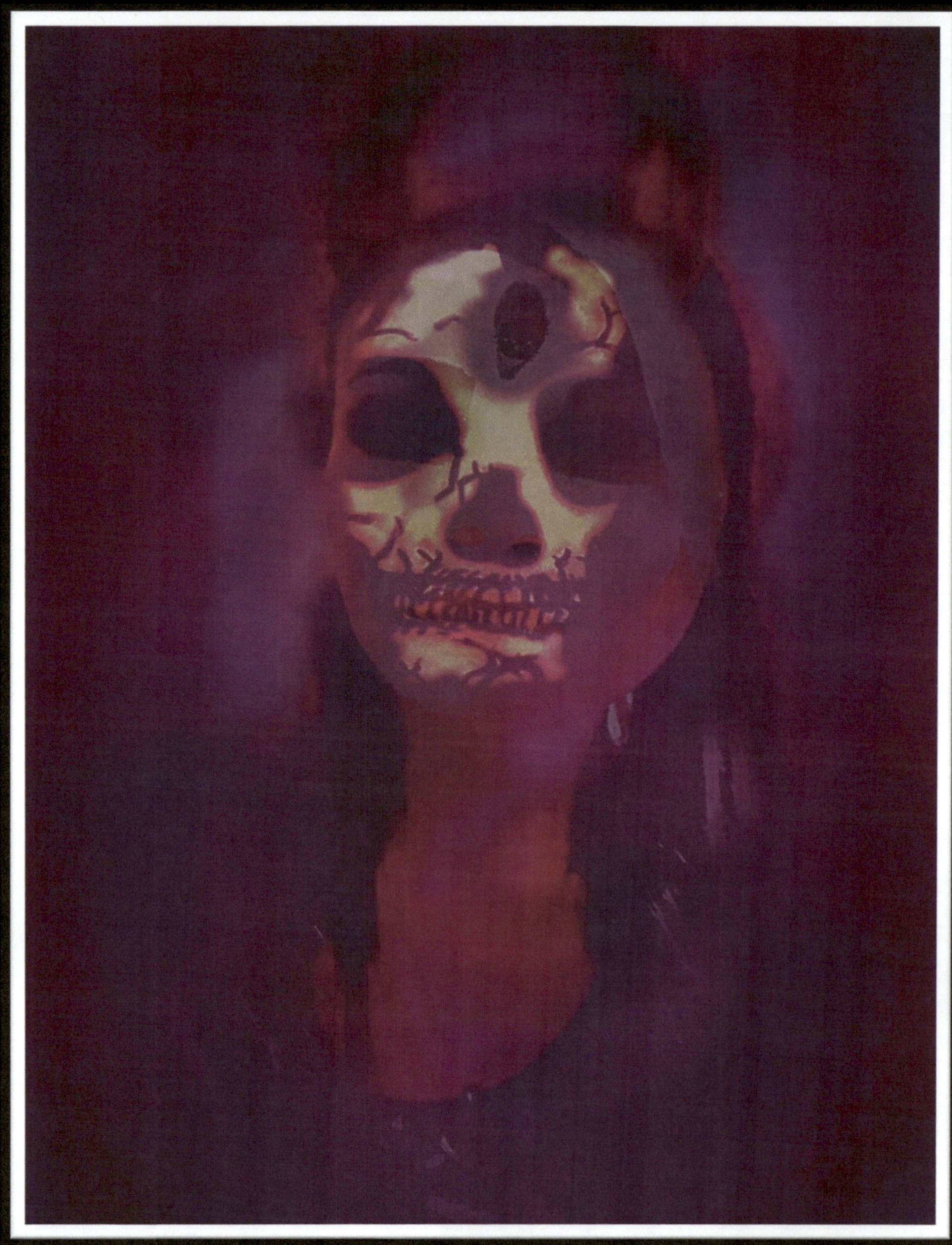

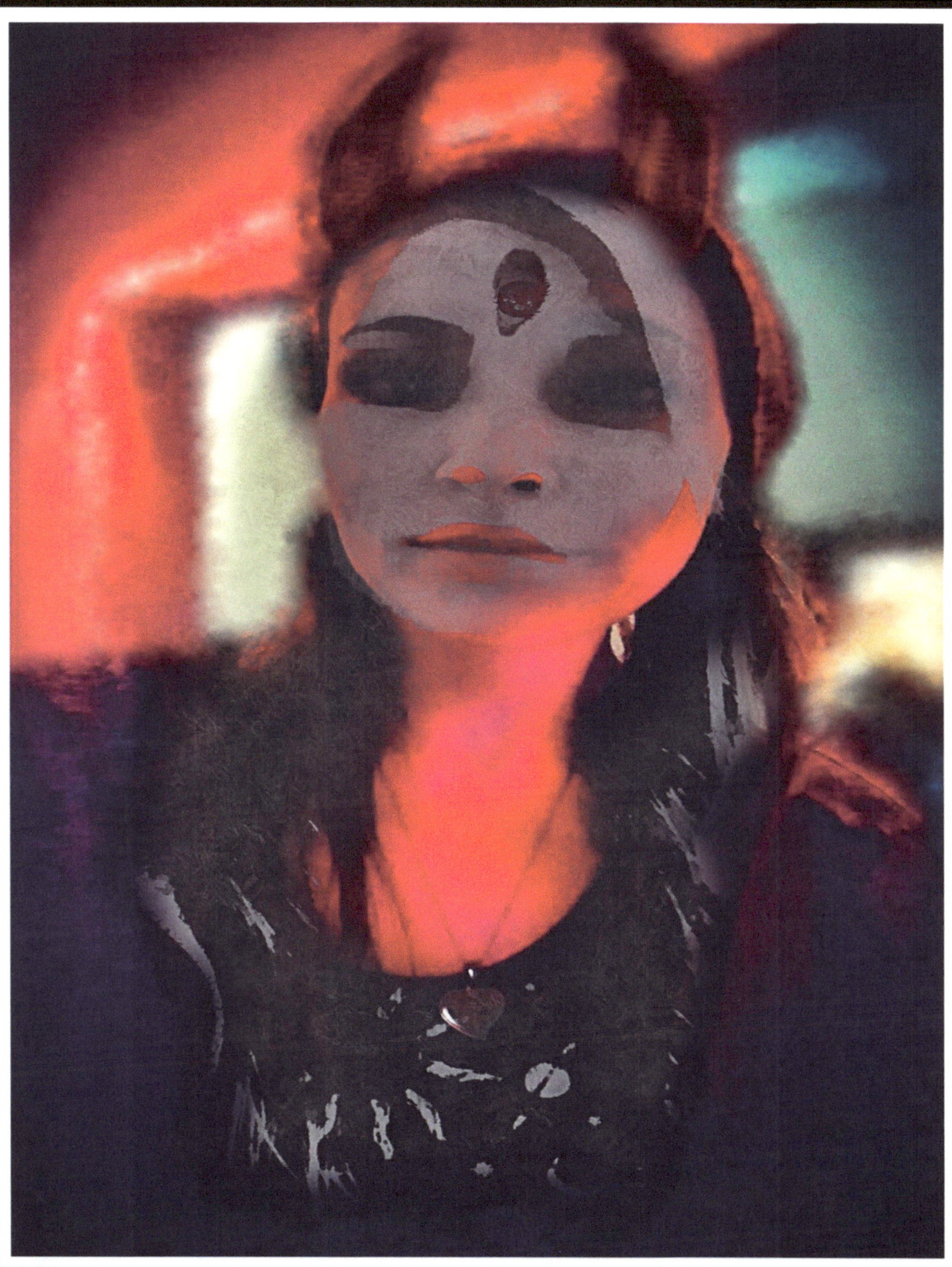

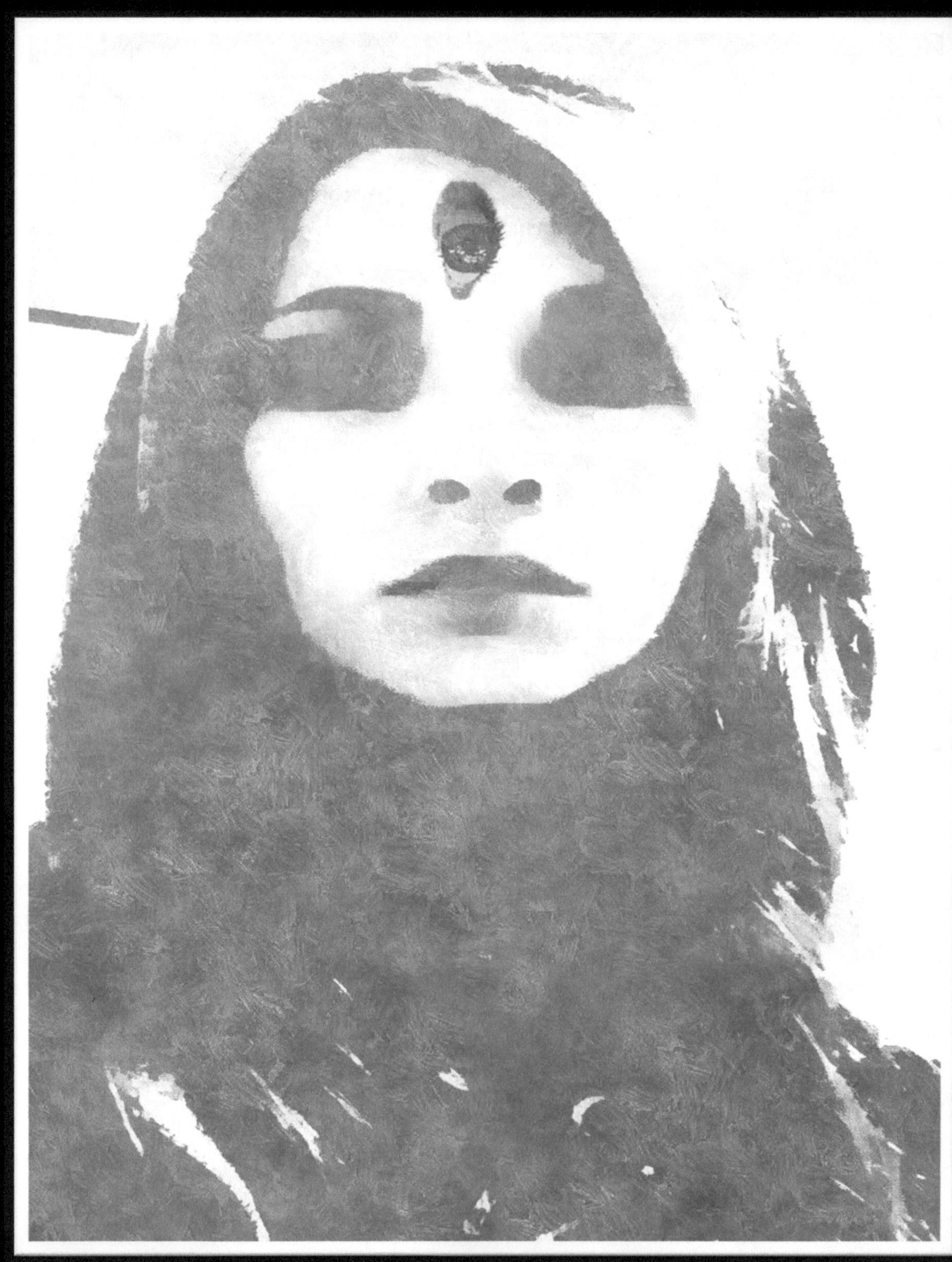

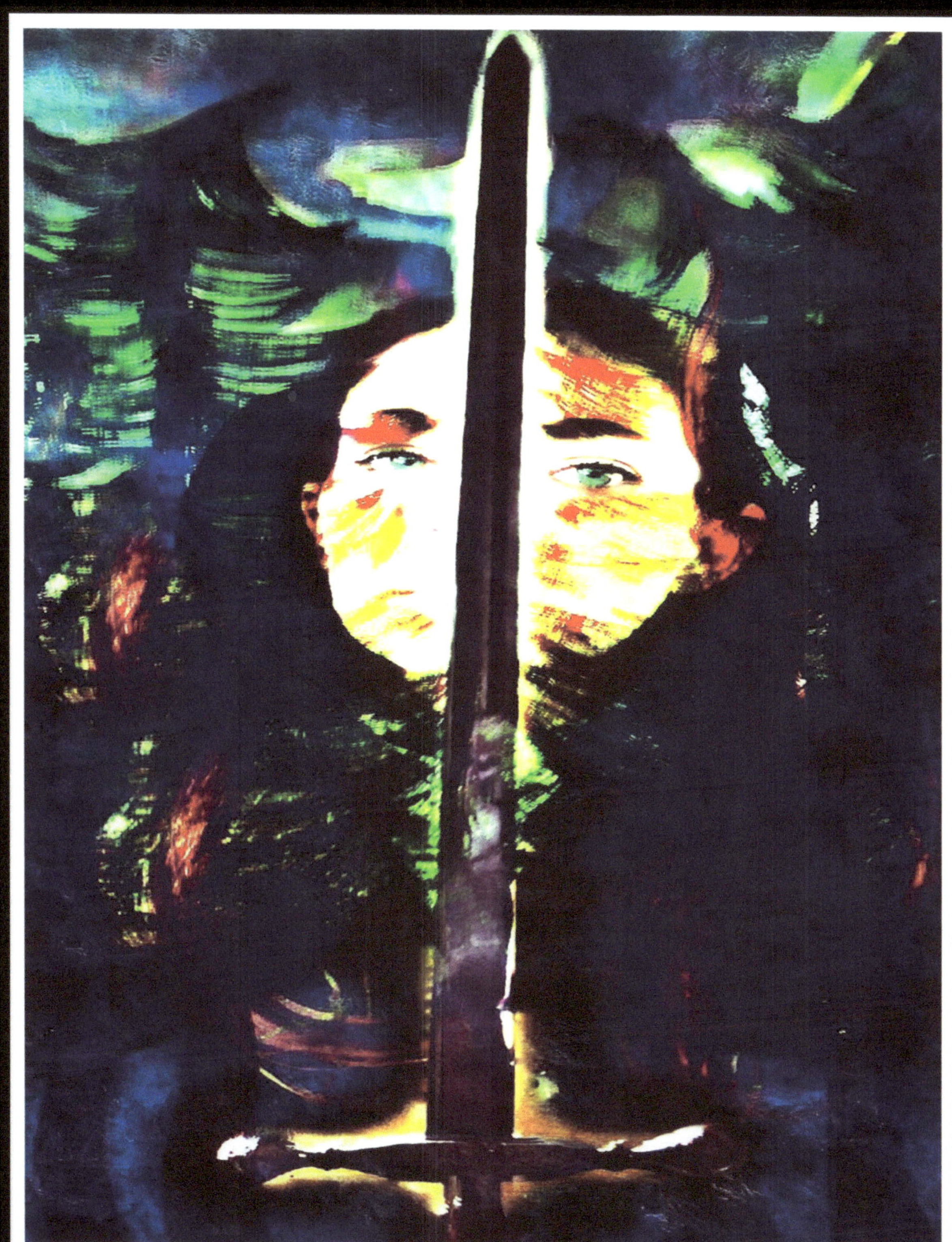

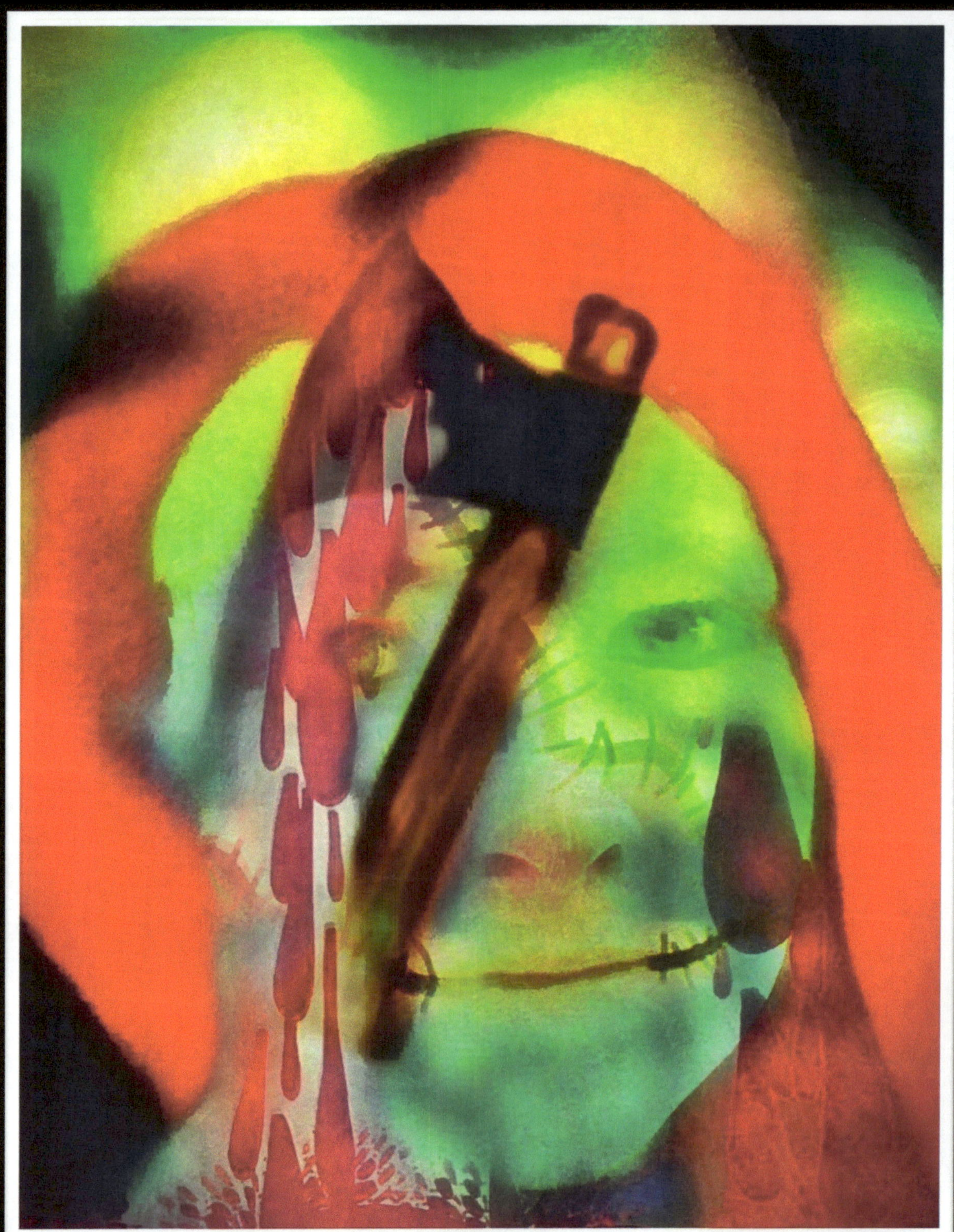

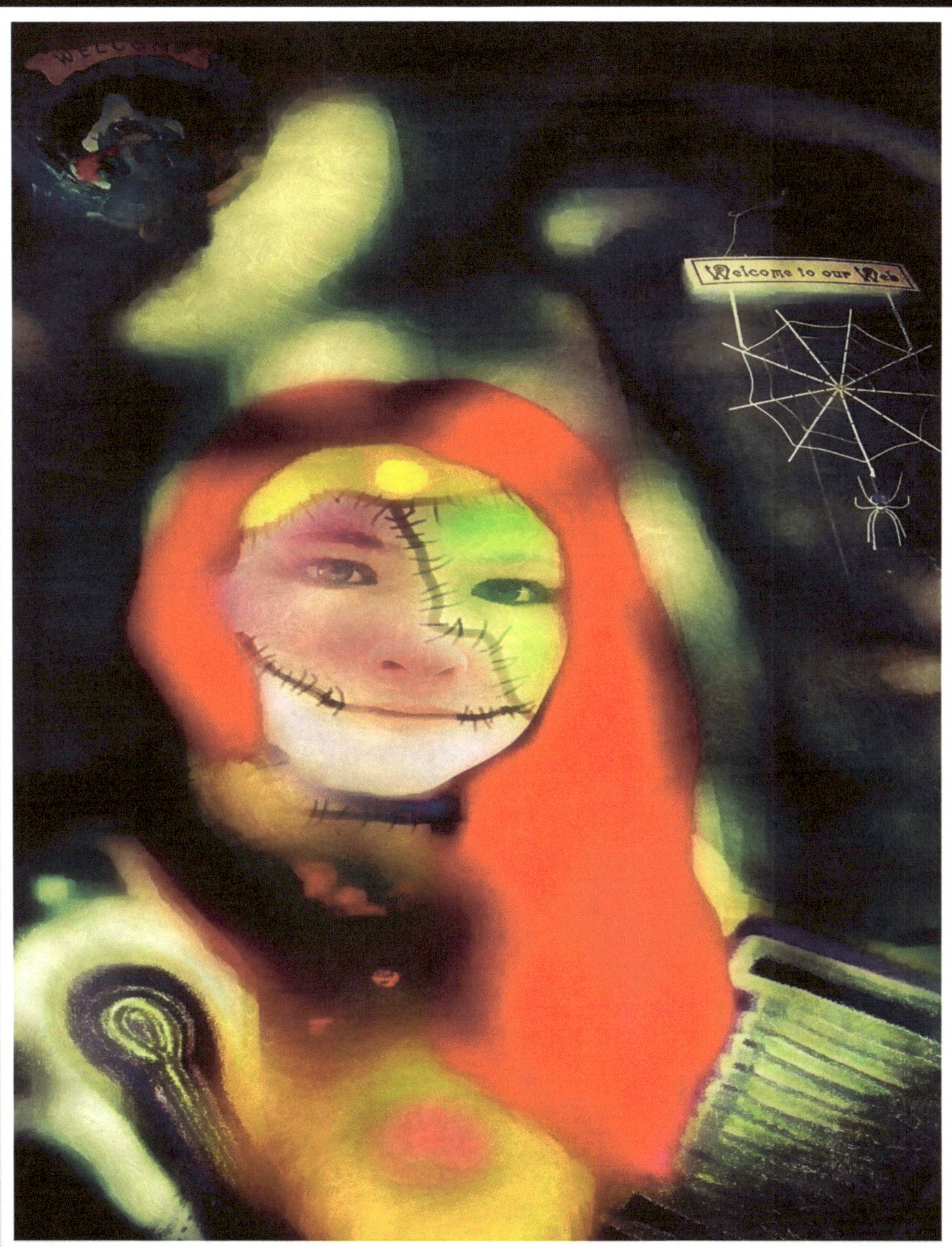
WELCOME
Welcome to our Web

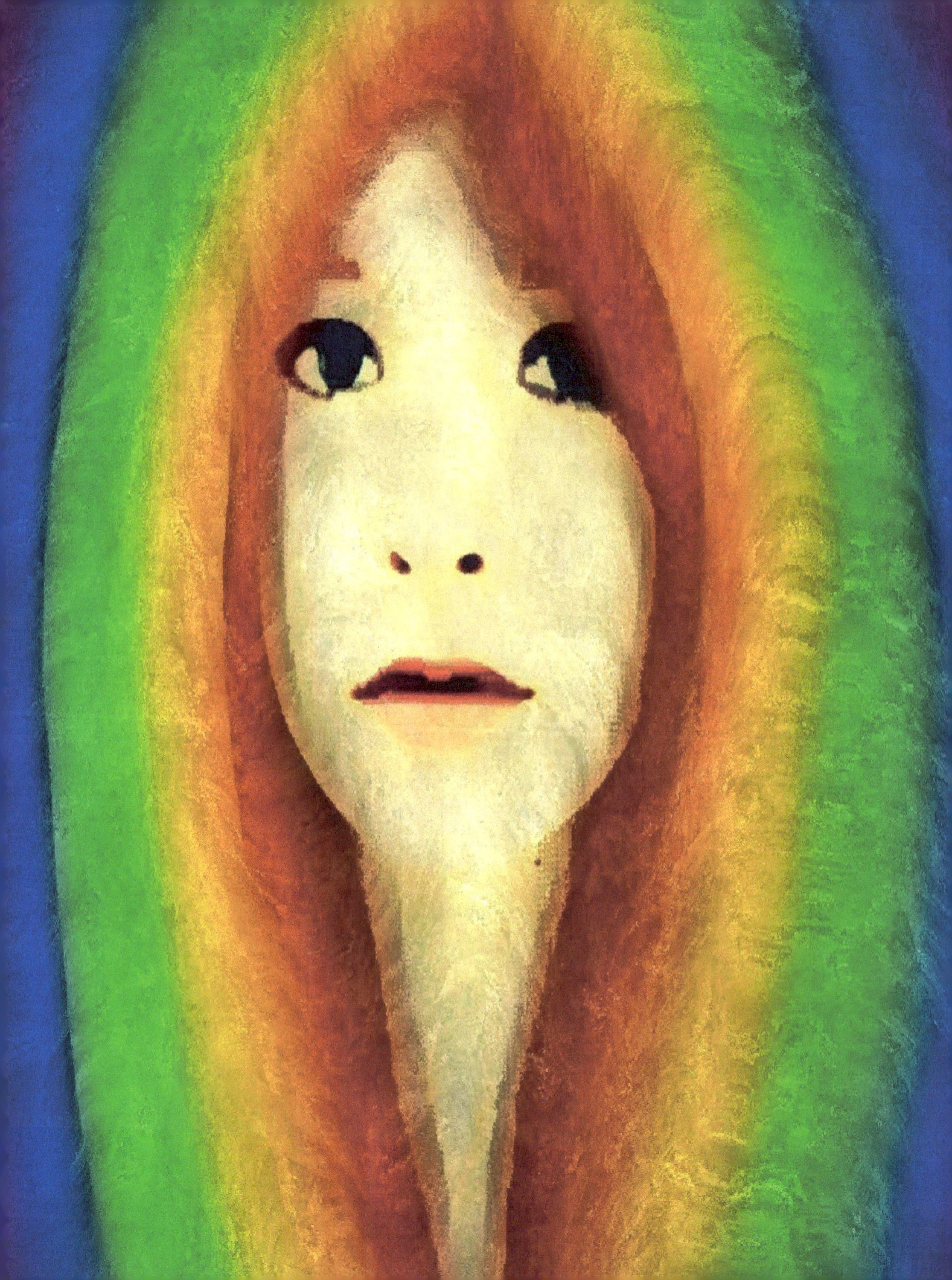

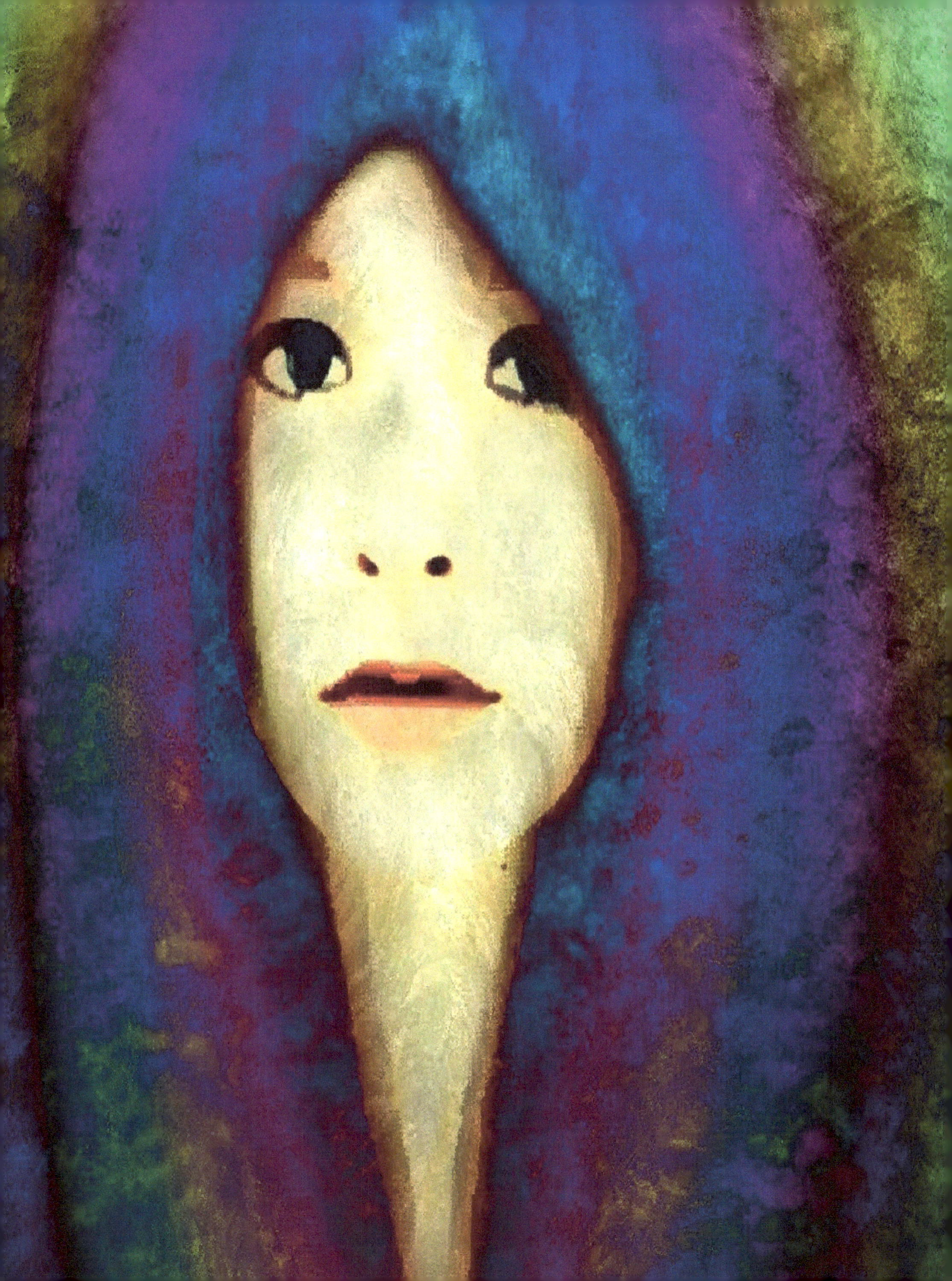

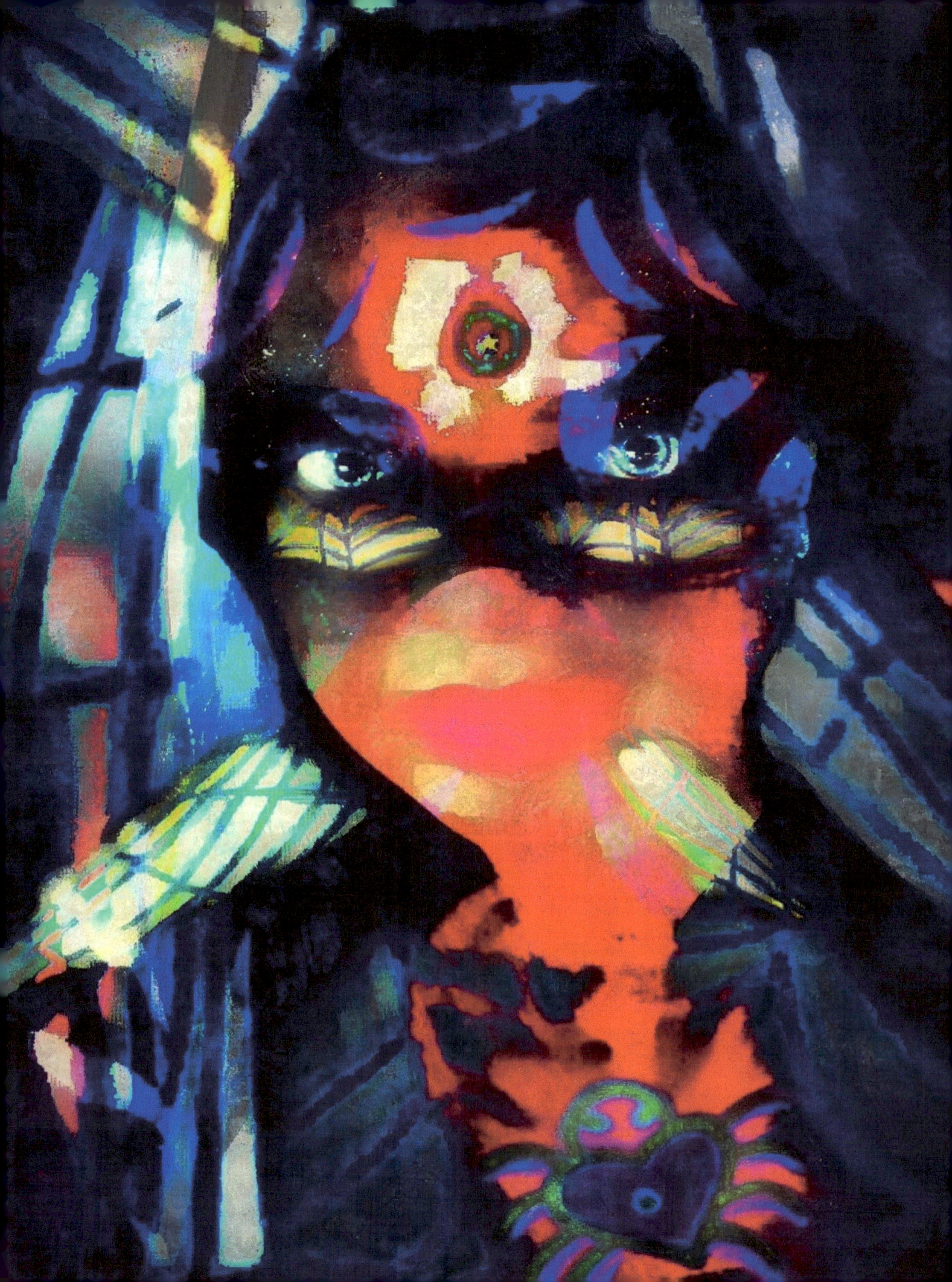

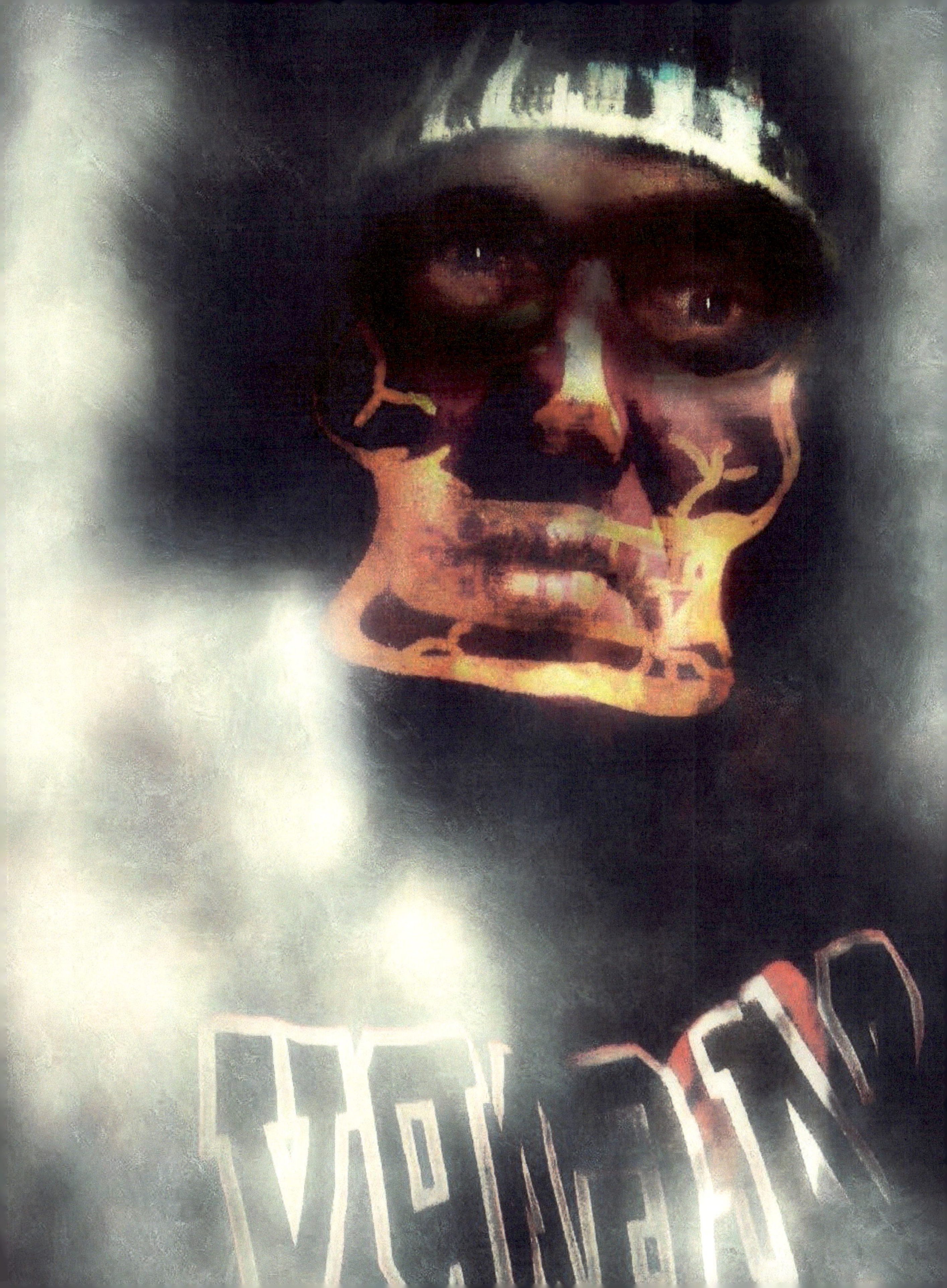
UNDERGROUND

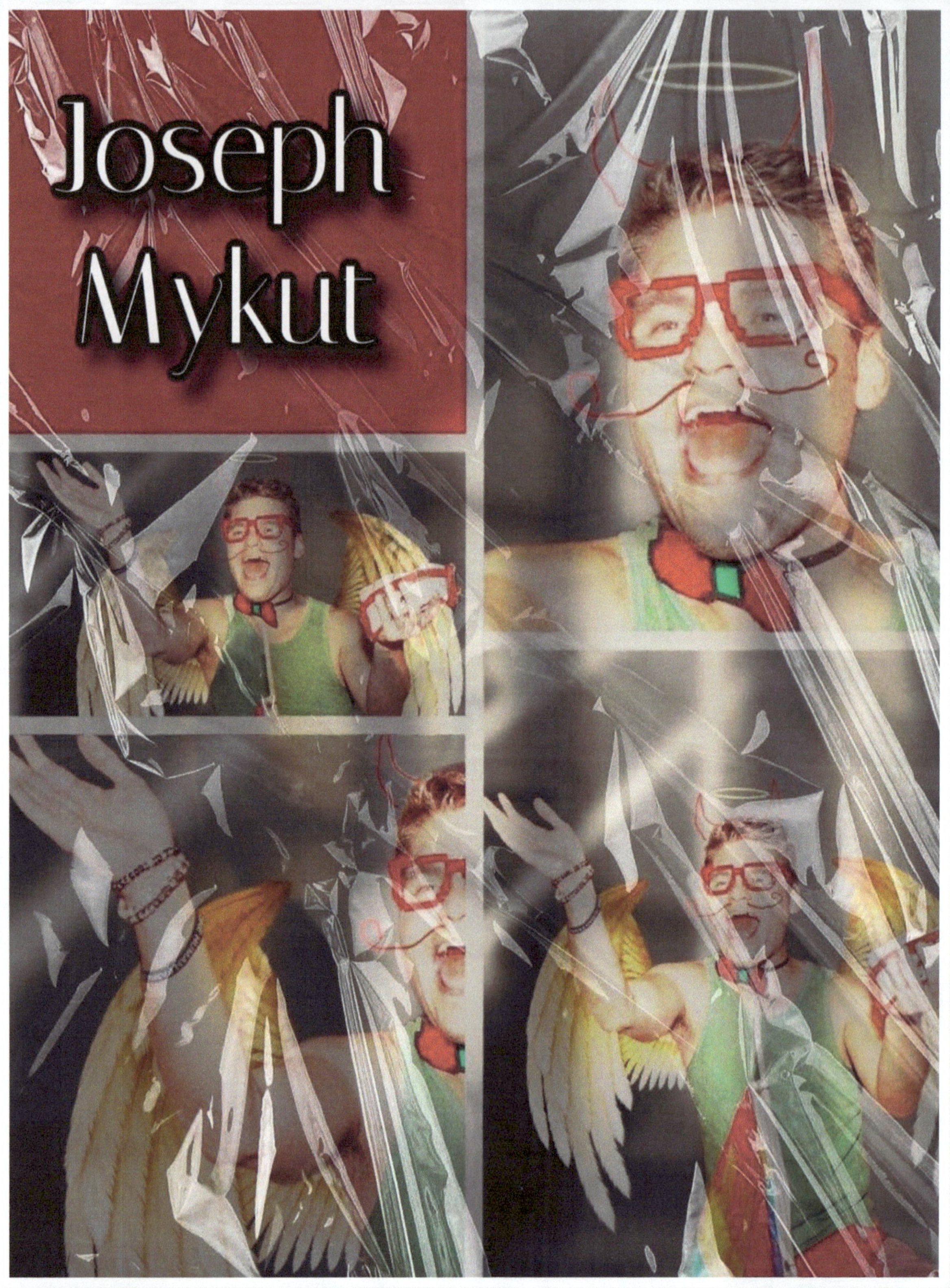
Joseph
Mykut

About the Artist

Joseph Mykut is an internationally published, author, photographer, and artist. Their work can be found in the 3 Amigos Ink and Splatter Anthologies as well as their children's book, "Beautiful Boy." Joseph pulls their inspiration from everyday life, finding the extraordinary in the ordinary. Their work is hugely influenced by nature and the outdoors as well as the worlds beyond those we easily perceive with our senses. Joseph is a shaman in training as they believe a shaman always to be.

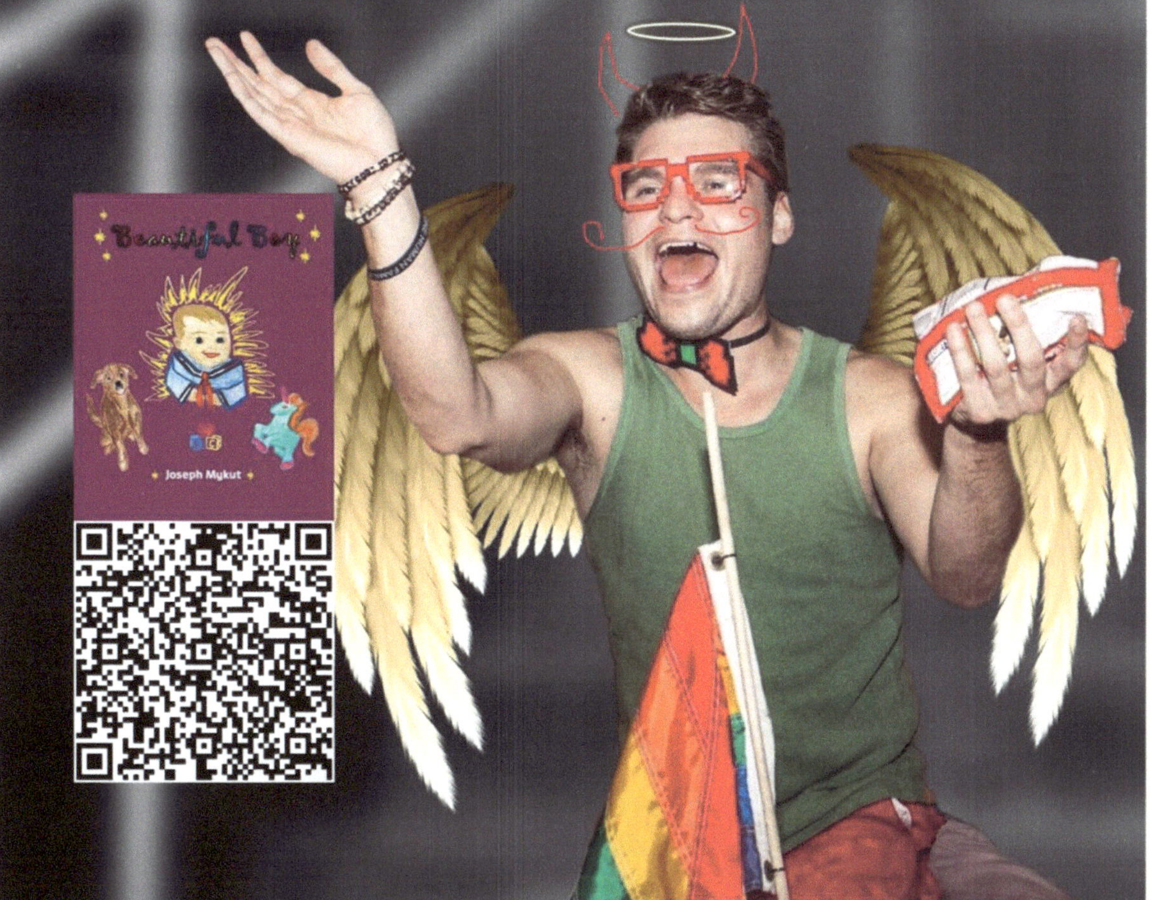

About the Collection

The world around us is alive. There is living art everywhere, from the curvature of architecture, to the subtle beauty of arbitrary items scattered among us and around us daily. I hope to capture and share exactly what my mind's eye sees. The beings, shapes, and art that is formed in the seemingly mundane. Much like pareidolia and apophenia, if you look for the connections and the patterns, then beauty, love, life, and art will present itself to you.

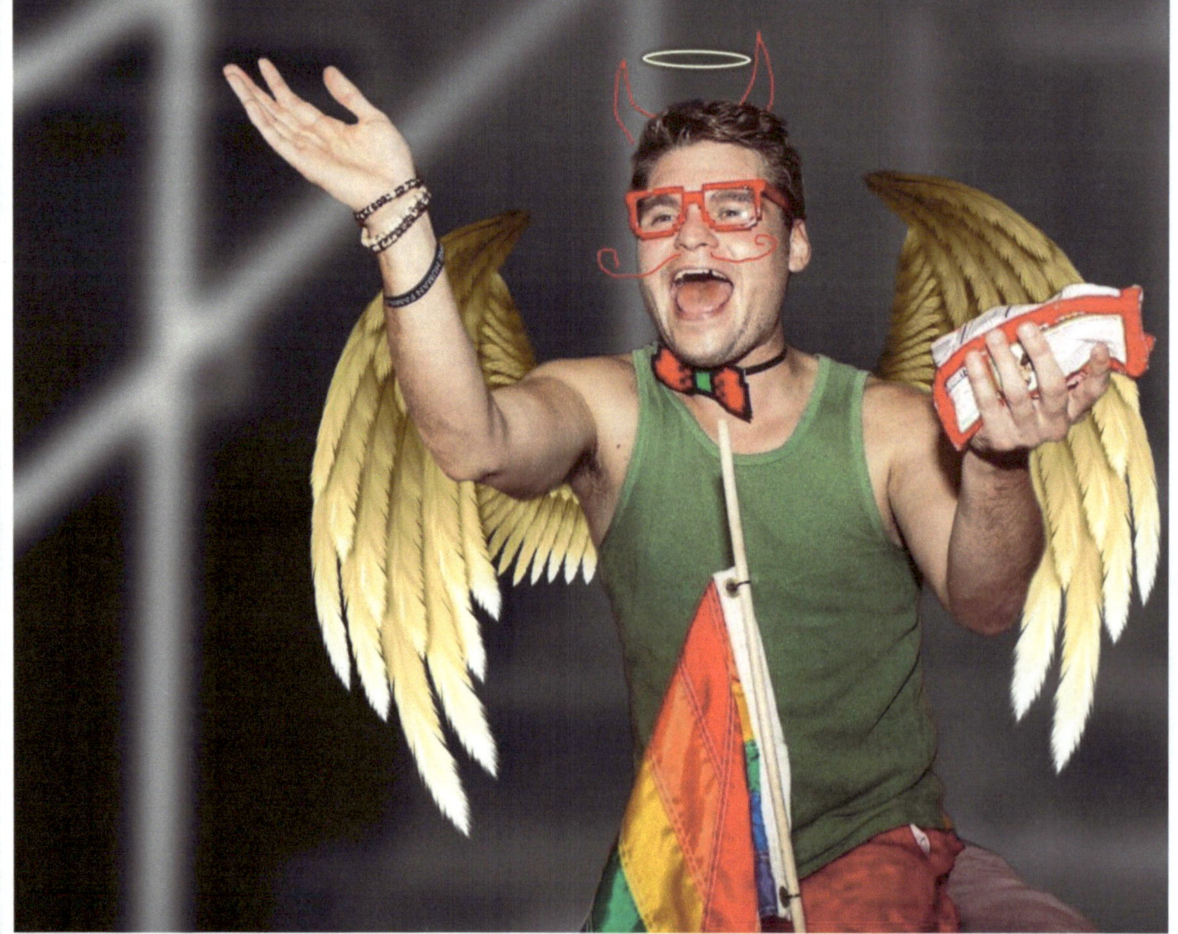

Dedication

I dedicate my works within this anthology to my beloved dog, Yogi. He blurs the line between human and animal, having shown me some of the greatest examples of love, friendship and companionship. I hope to be half the person he seems to believe me to be. He is the kindest and sweetest dog I could have ever asked to spend a portion of my life with. Humanity can take a page from the book of dog law because there we will find unconditional love nearly beyond our understanding. Thank you Yogi for making my life experience better for having you be a part of it. I cherish everyday I have you with me. You navigated the roughest of days and the greatest of days right by my side with patience beyond my deserving. For you I am grateful.

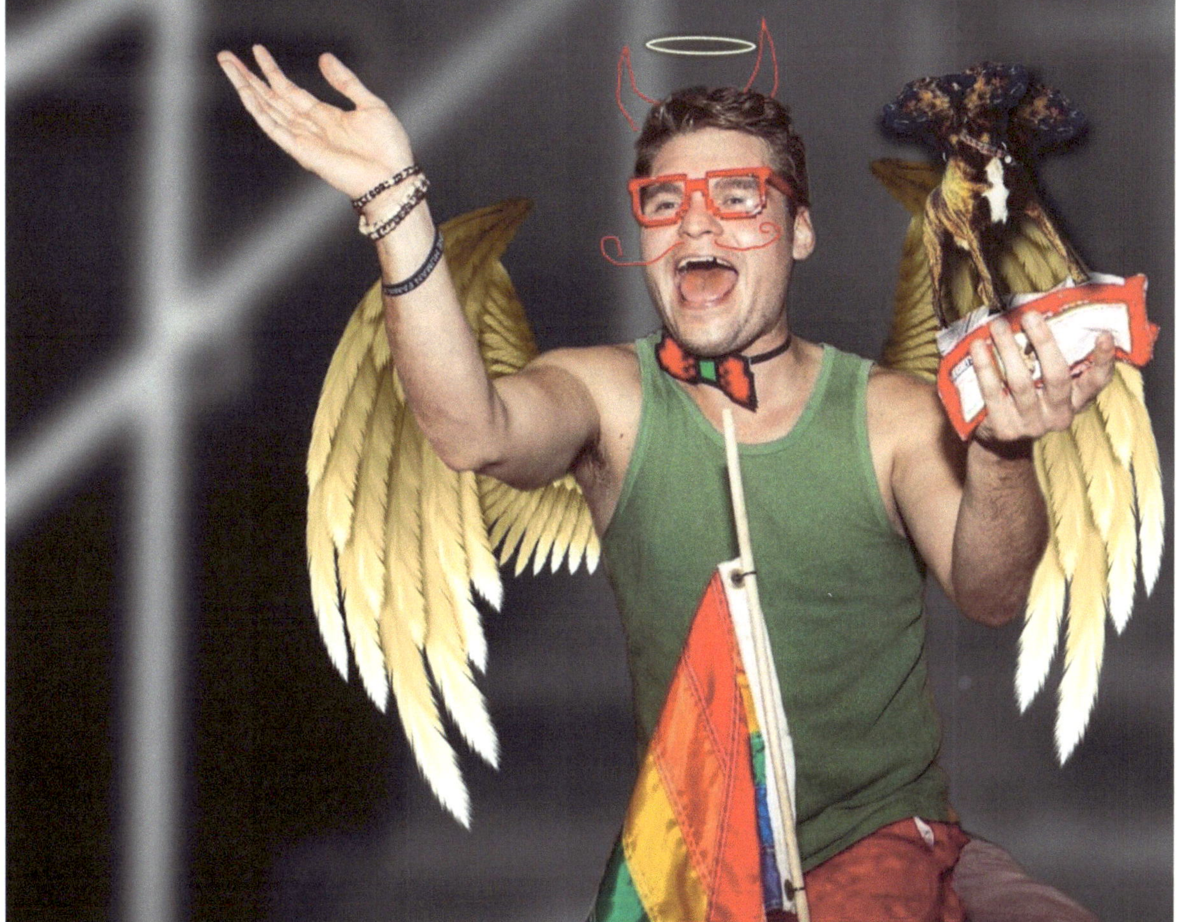

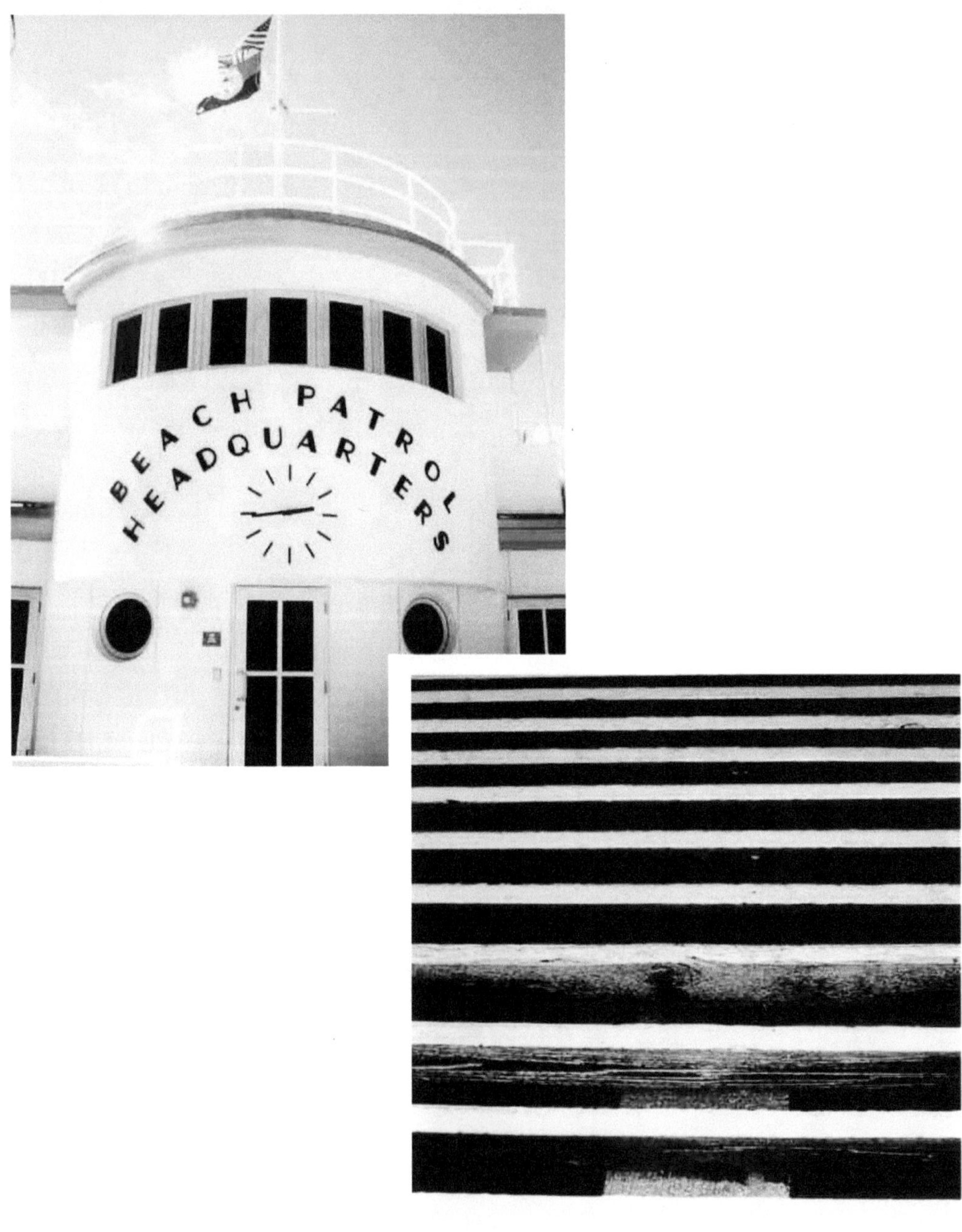

BEACH PATROL
HEADQUARTERS

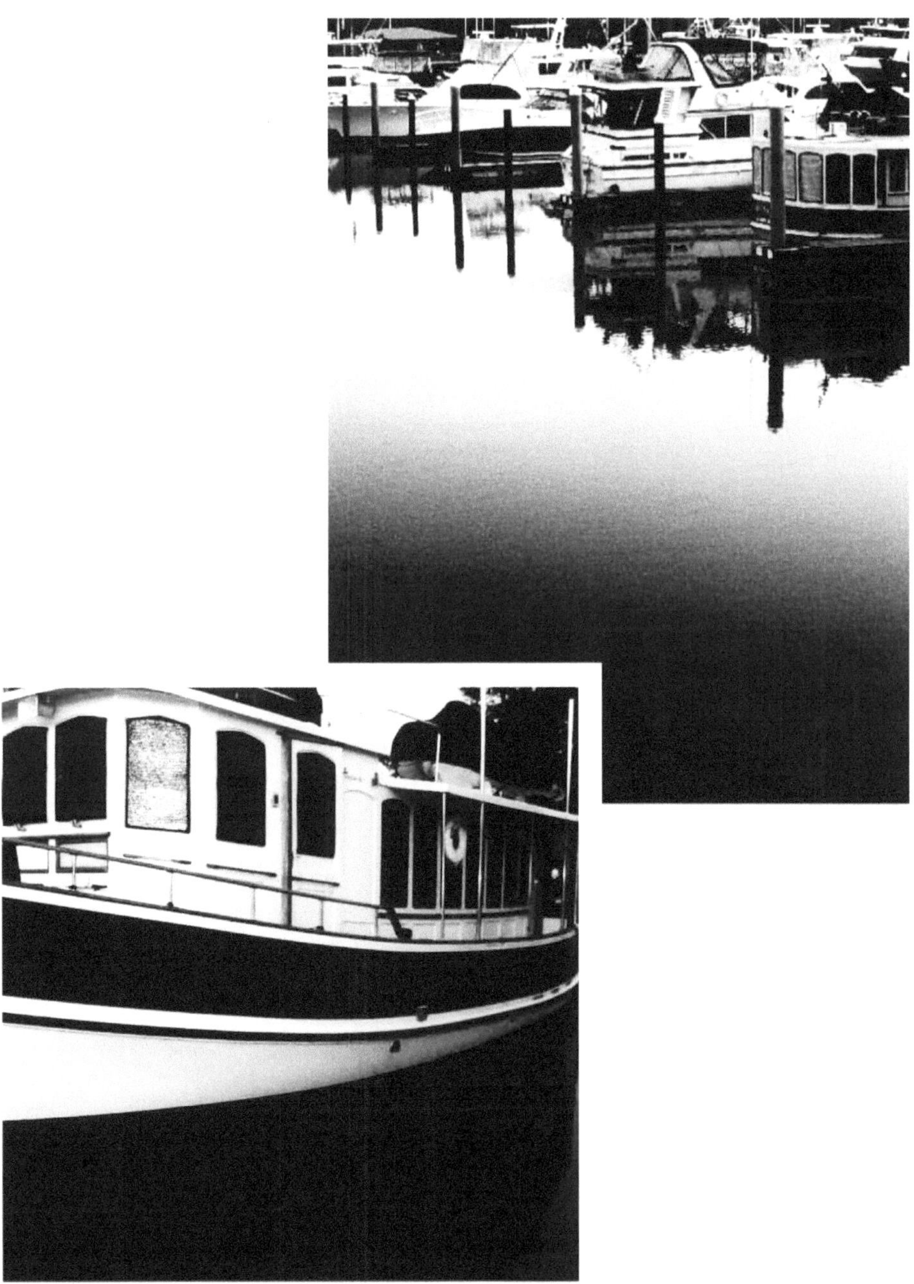

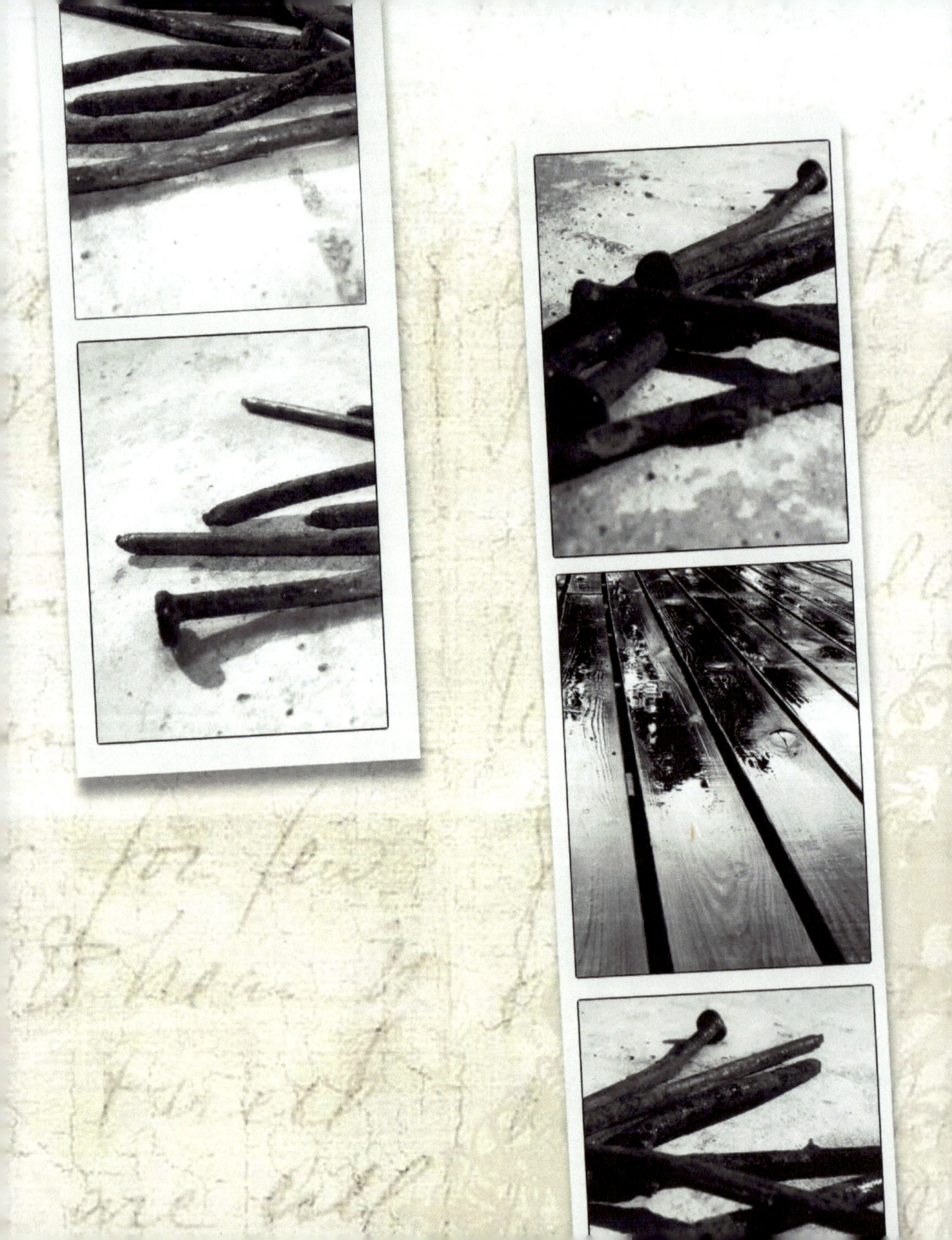

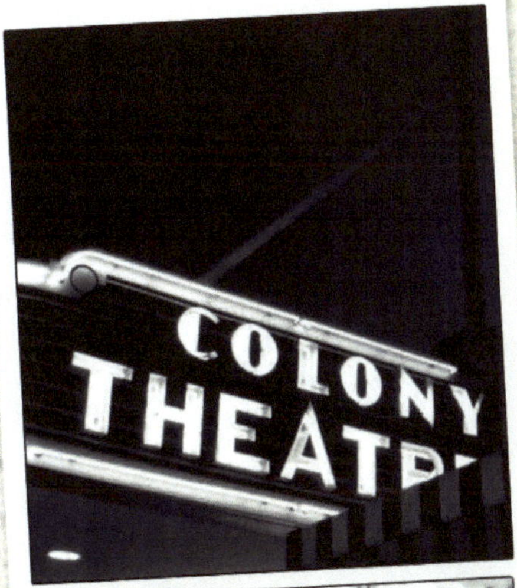

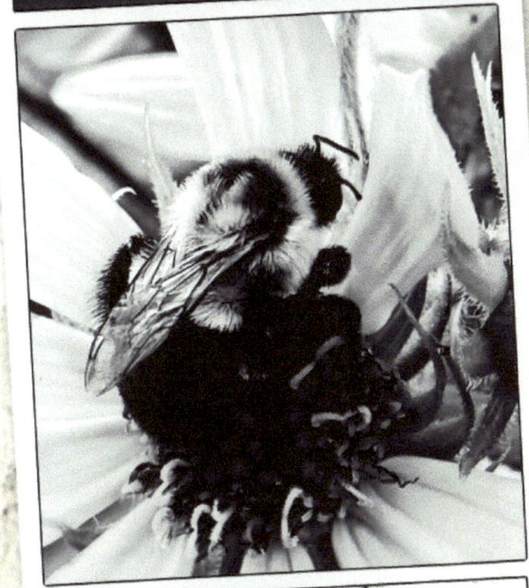

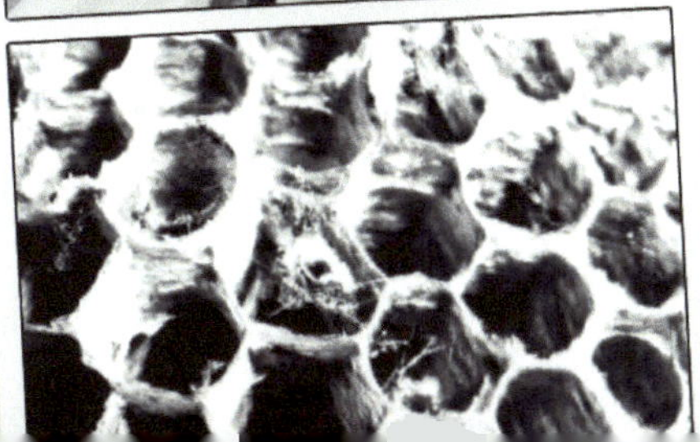

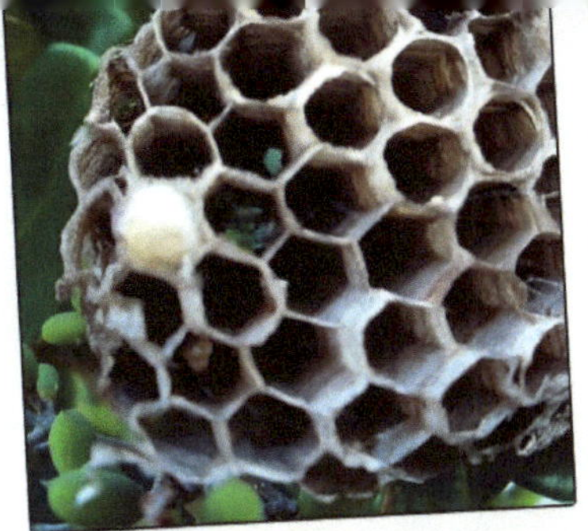
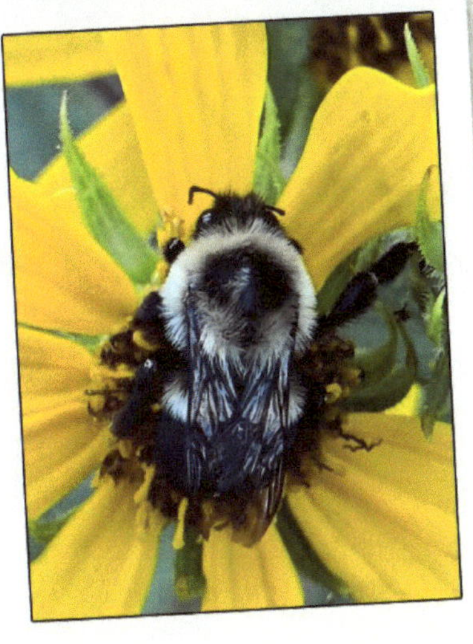

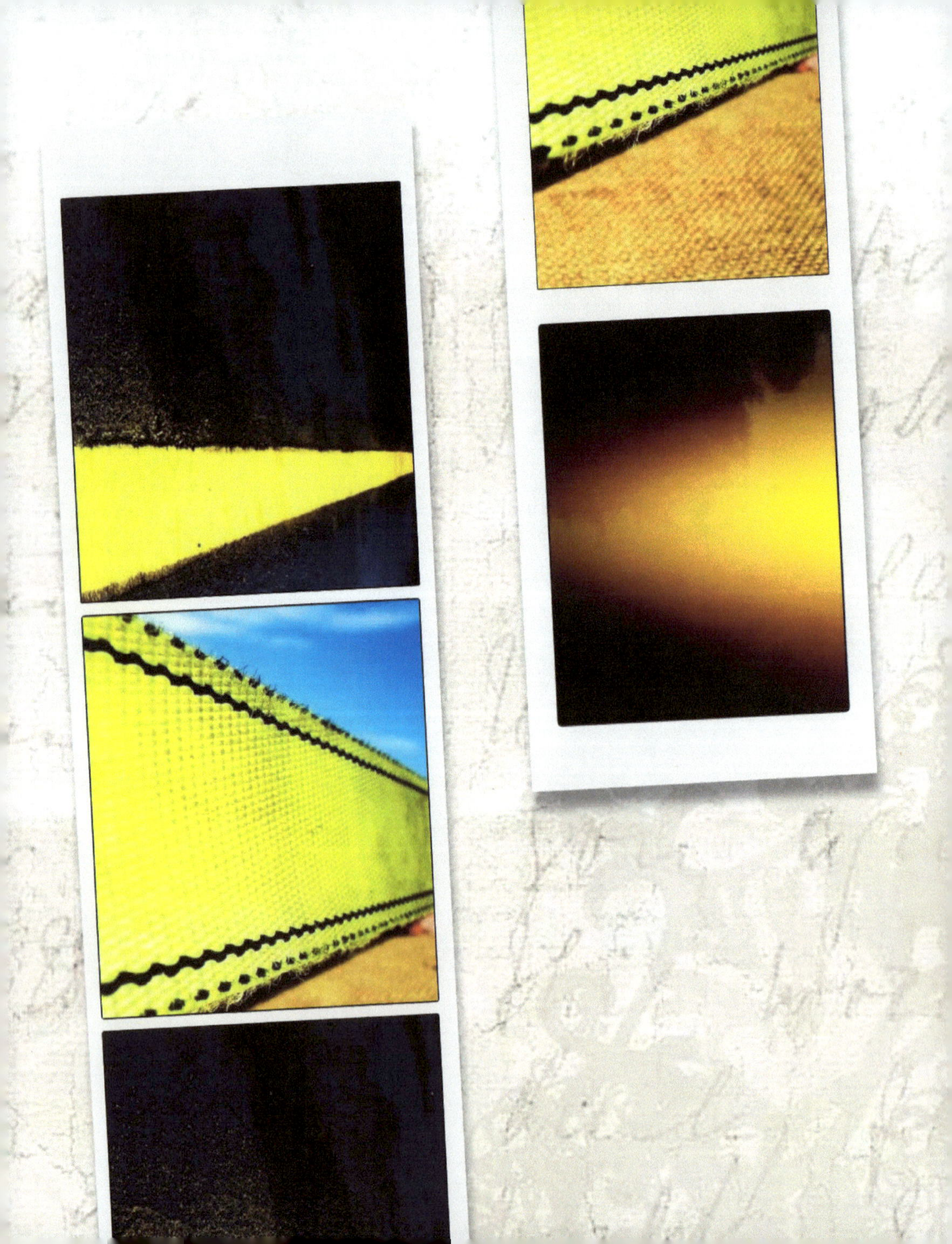

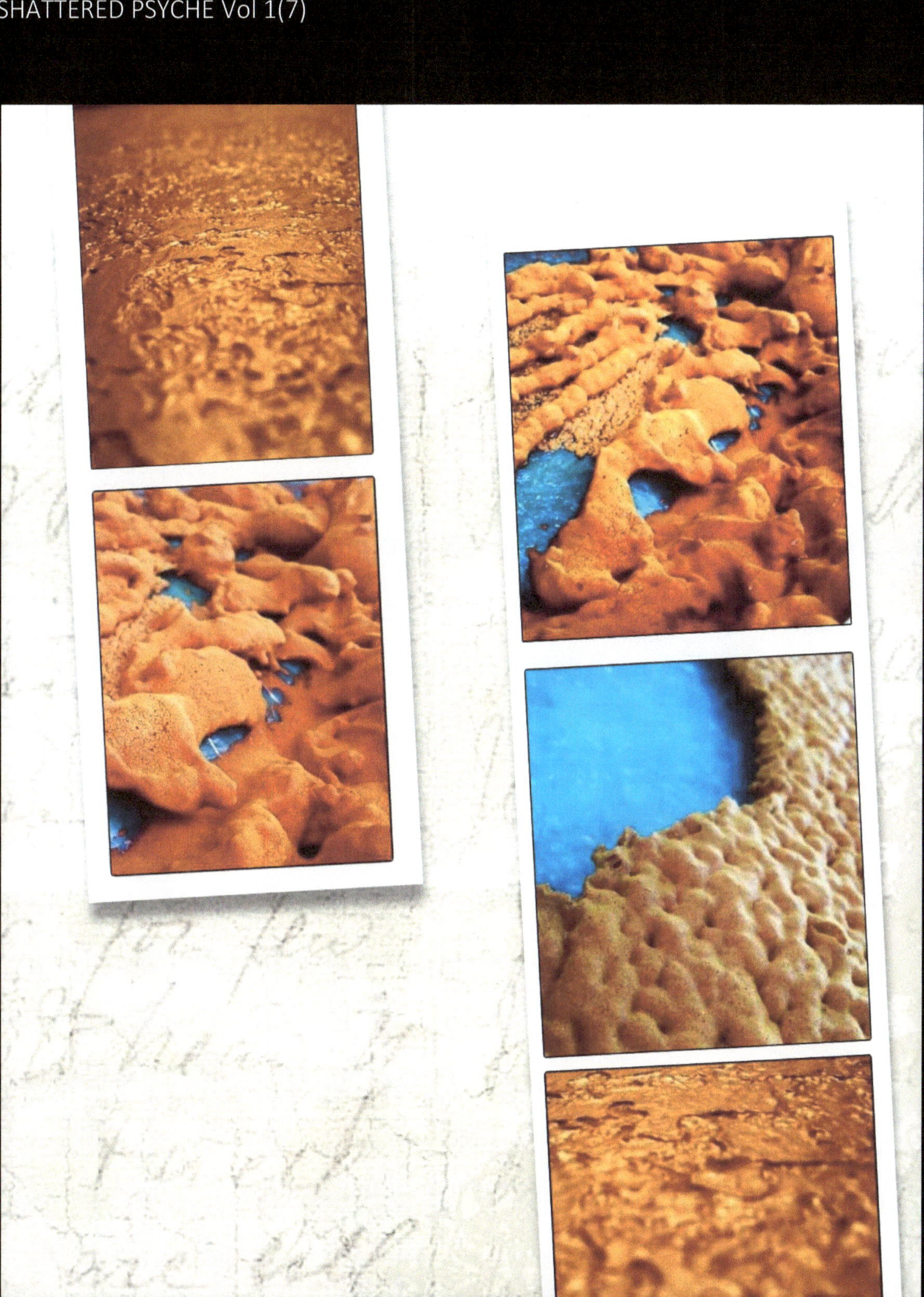

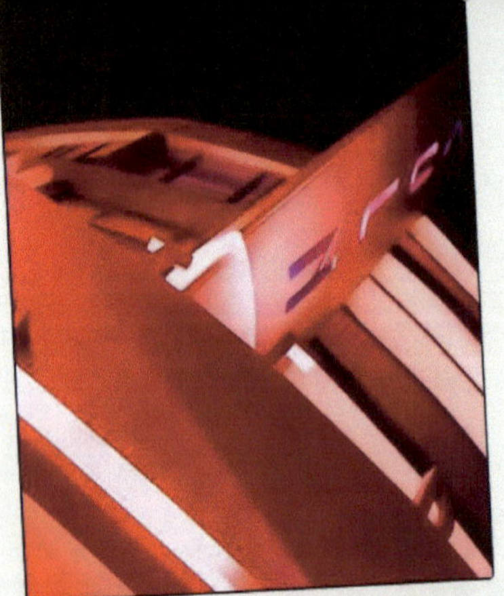

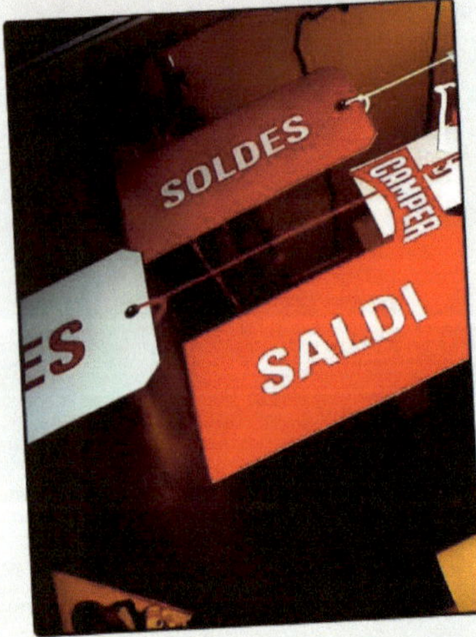
SOLDES
CAMPER
SALDI
ES

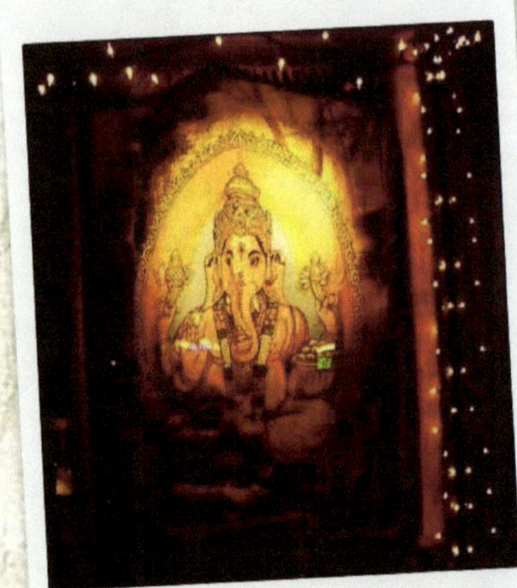

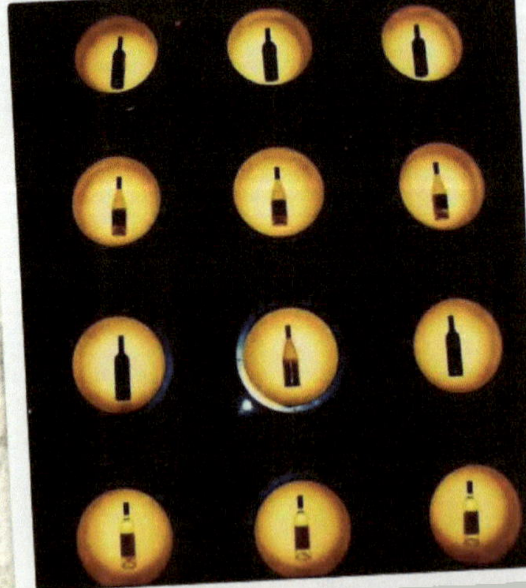

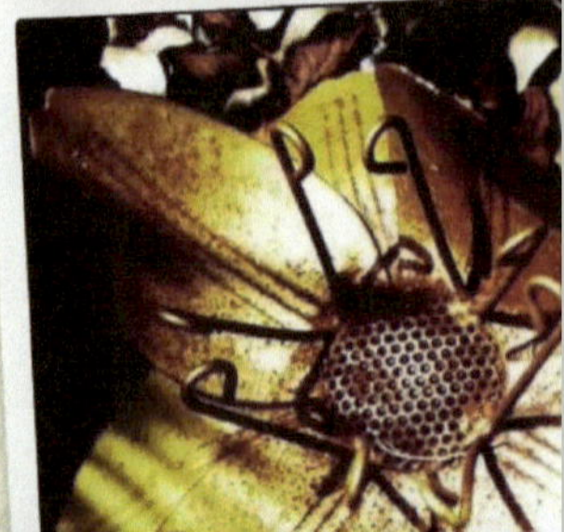

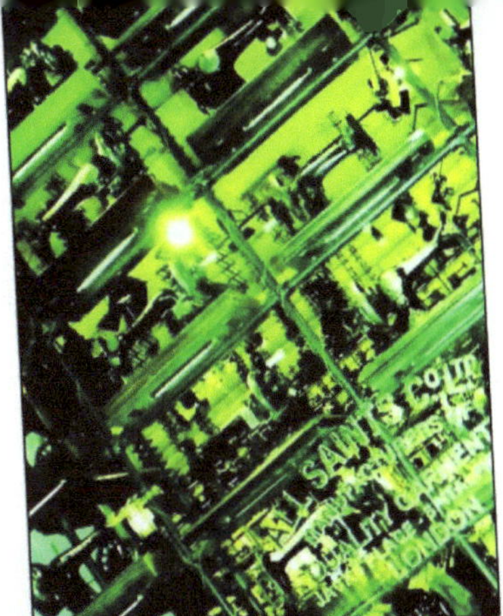
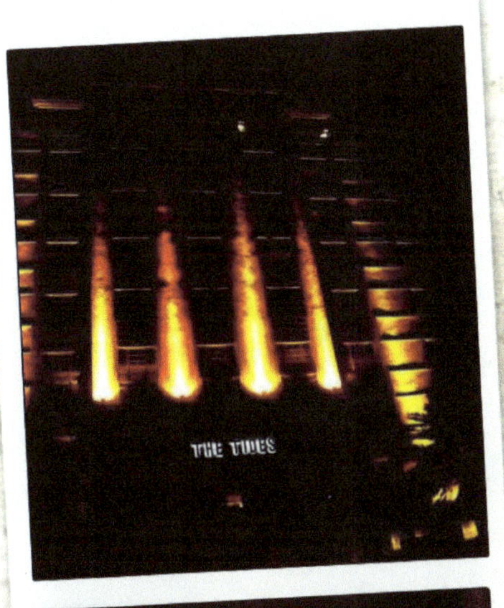

THE TIDES

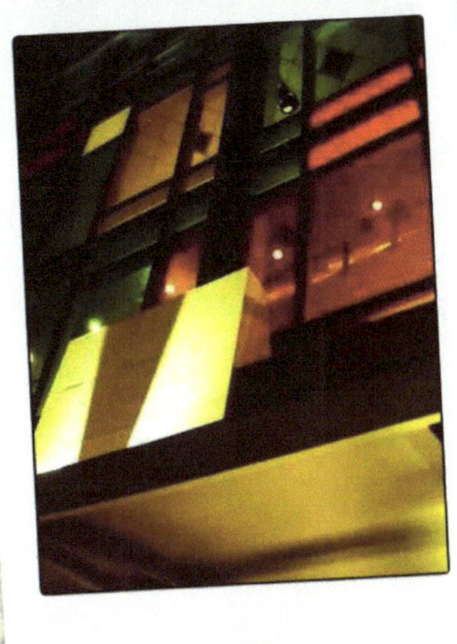
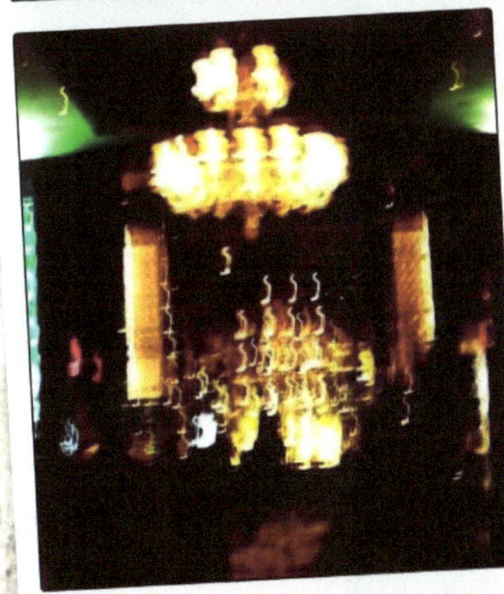
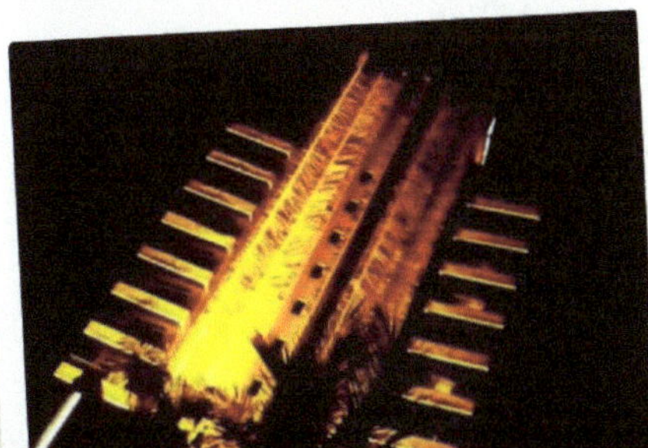

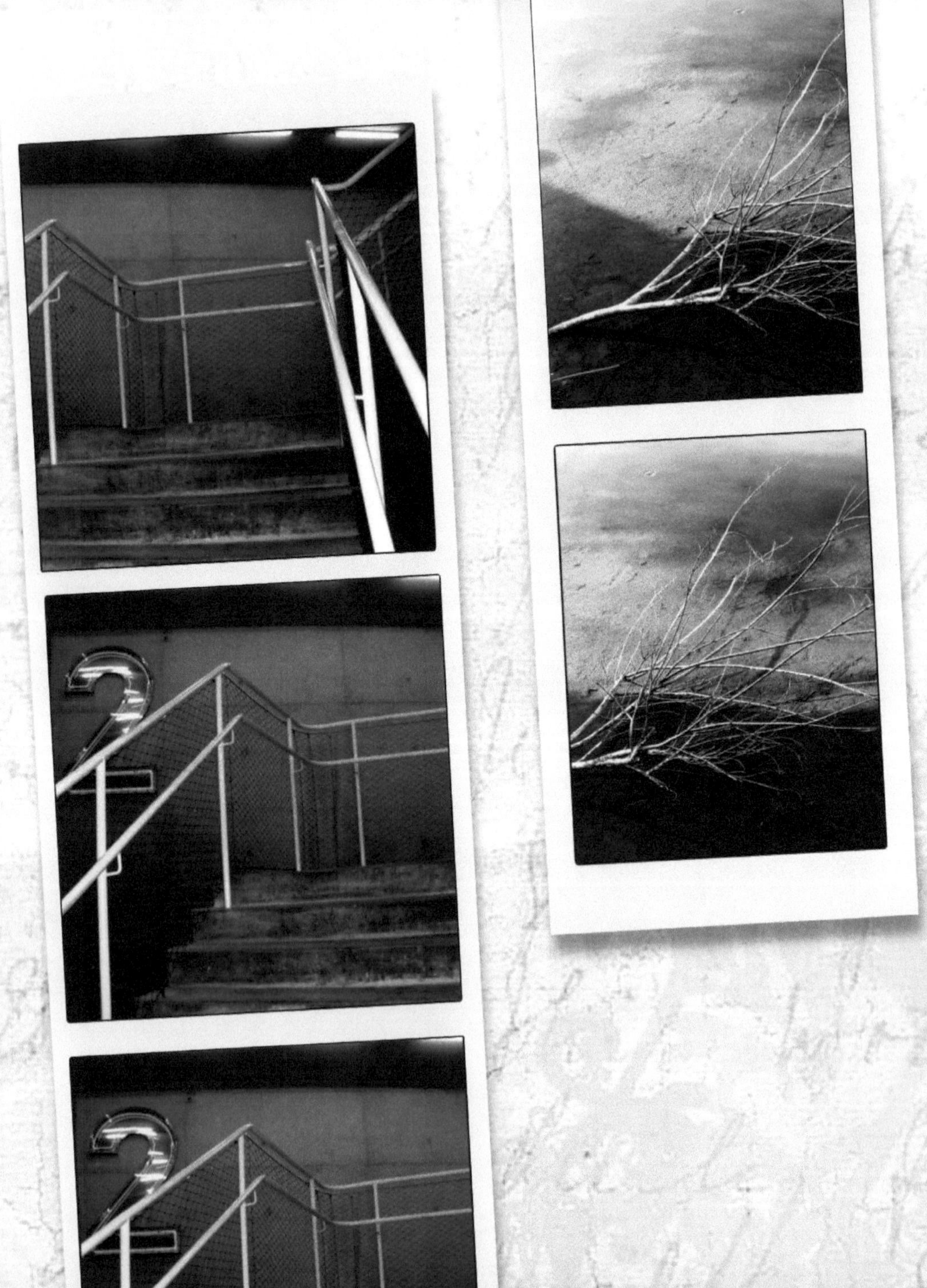

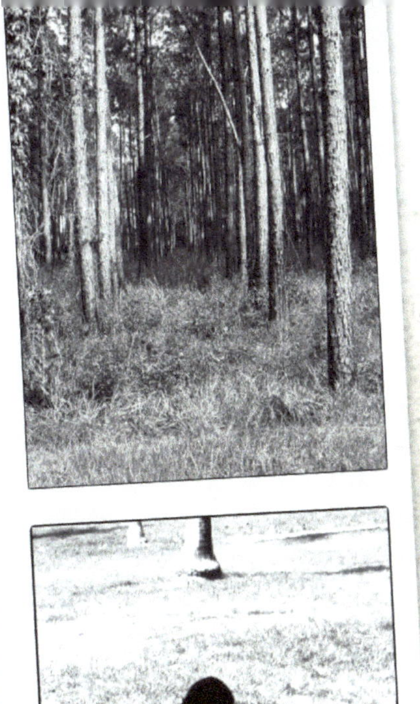

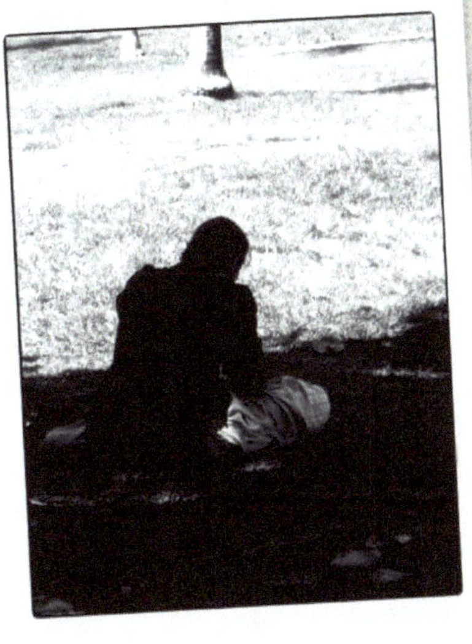

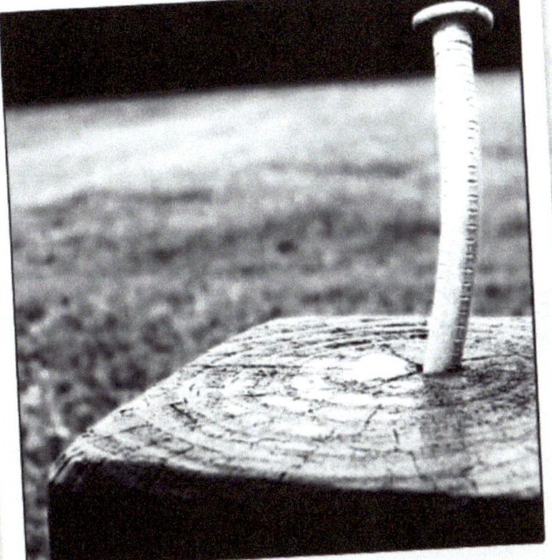

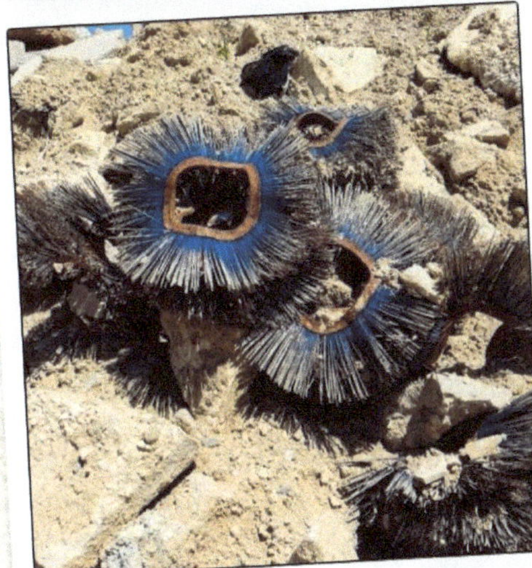

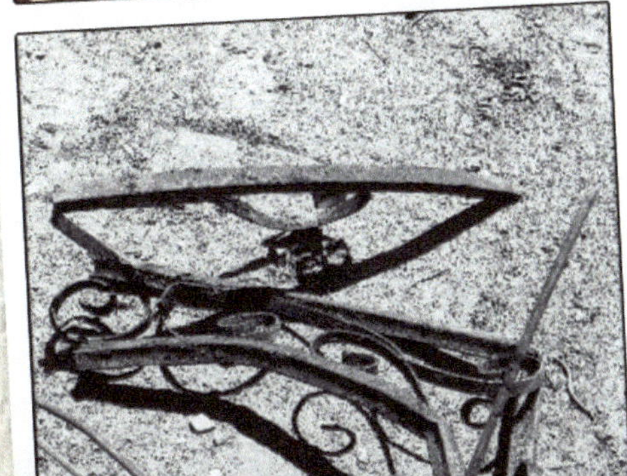

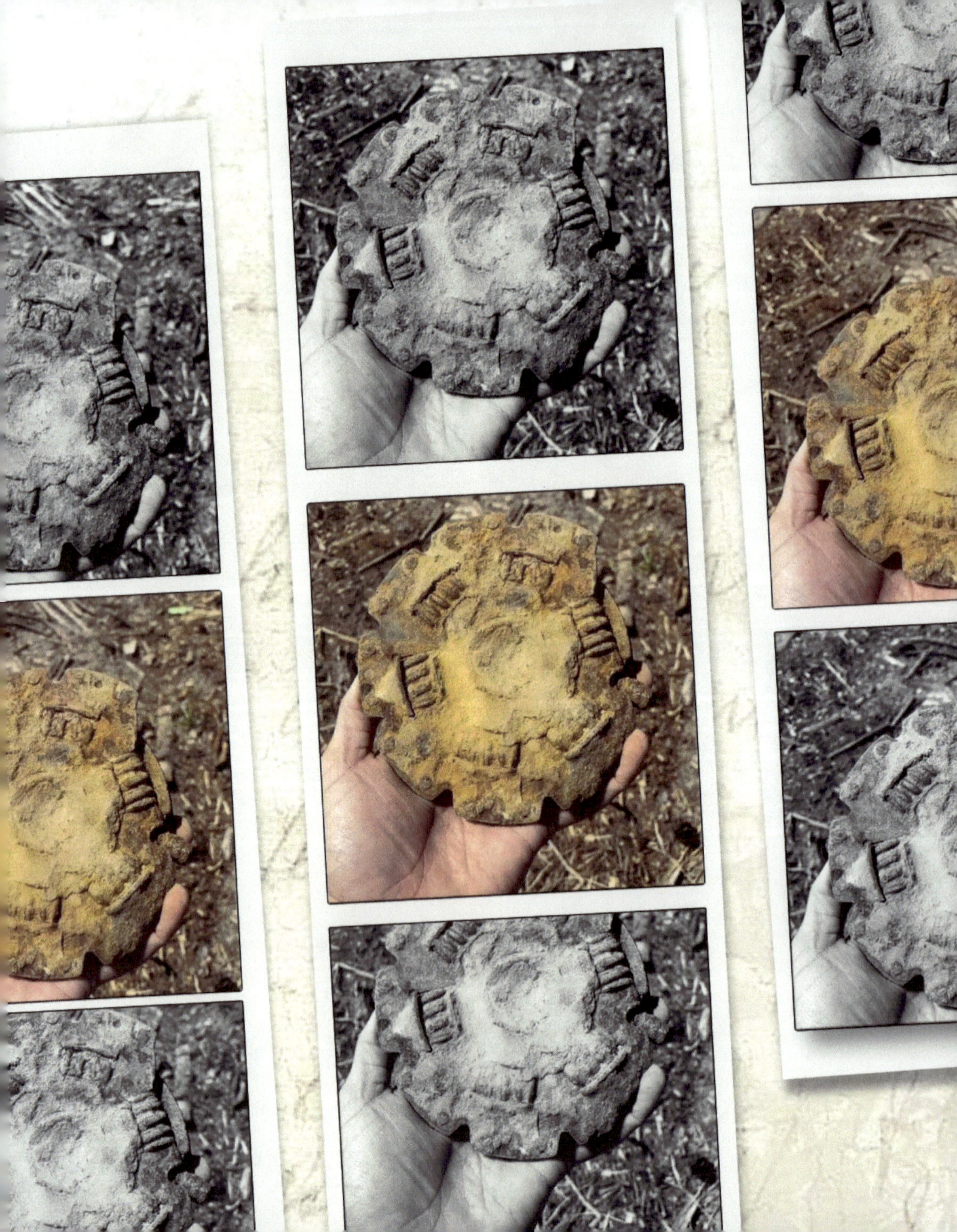

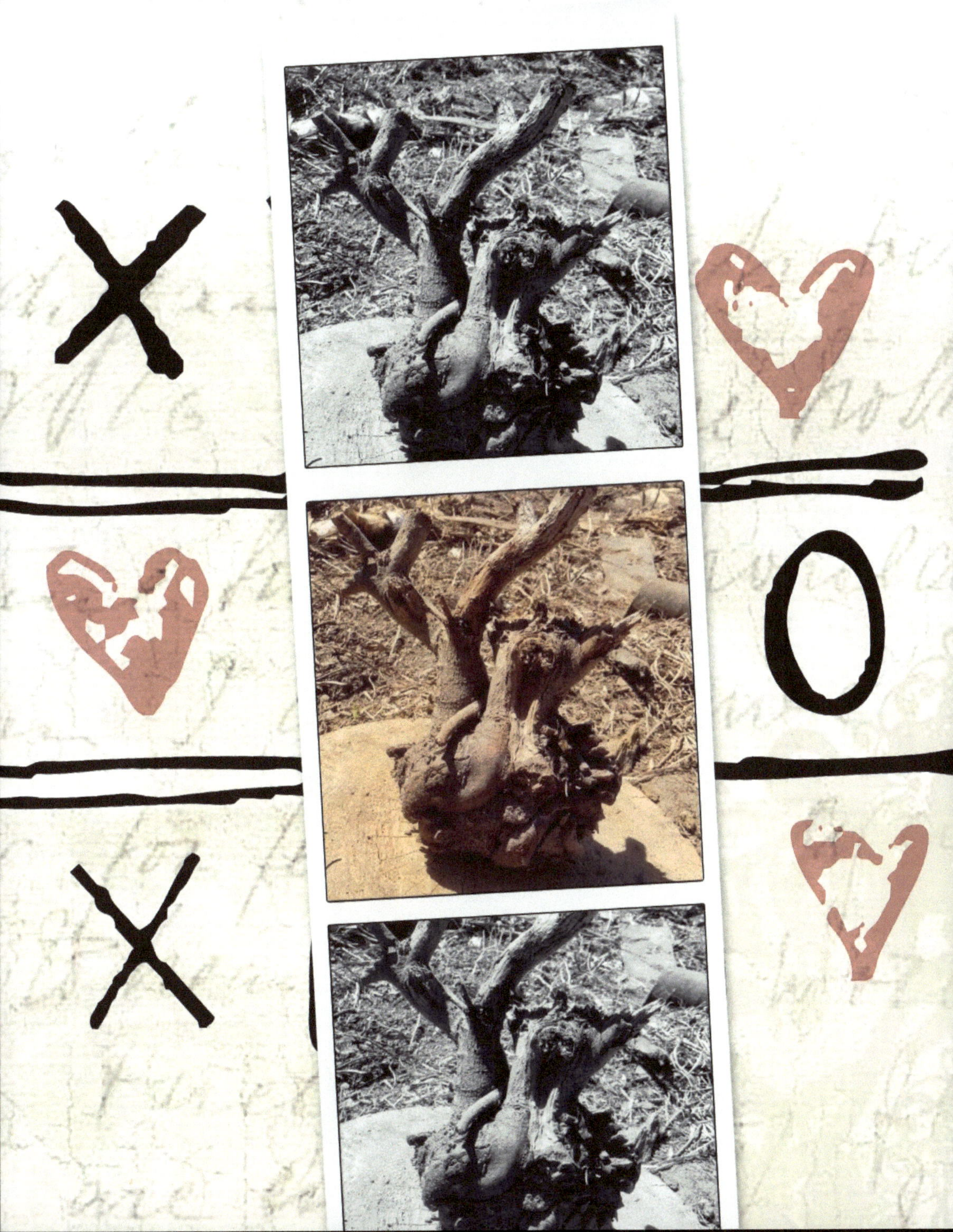

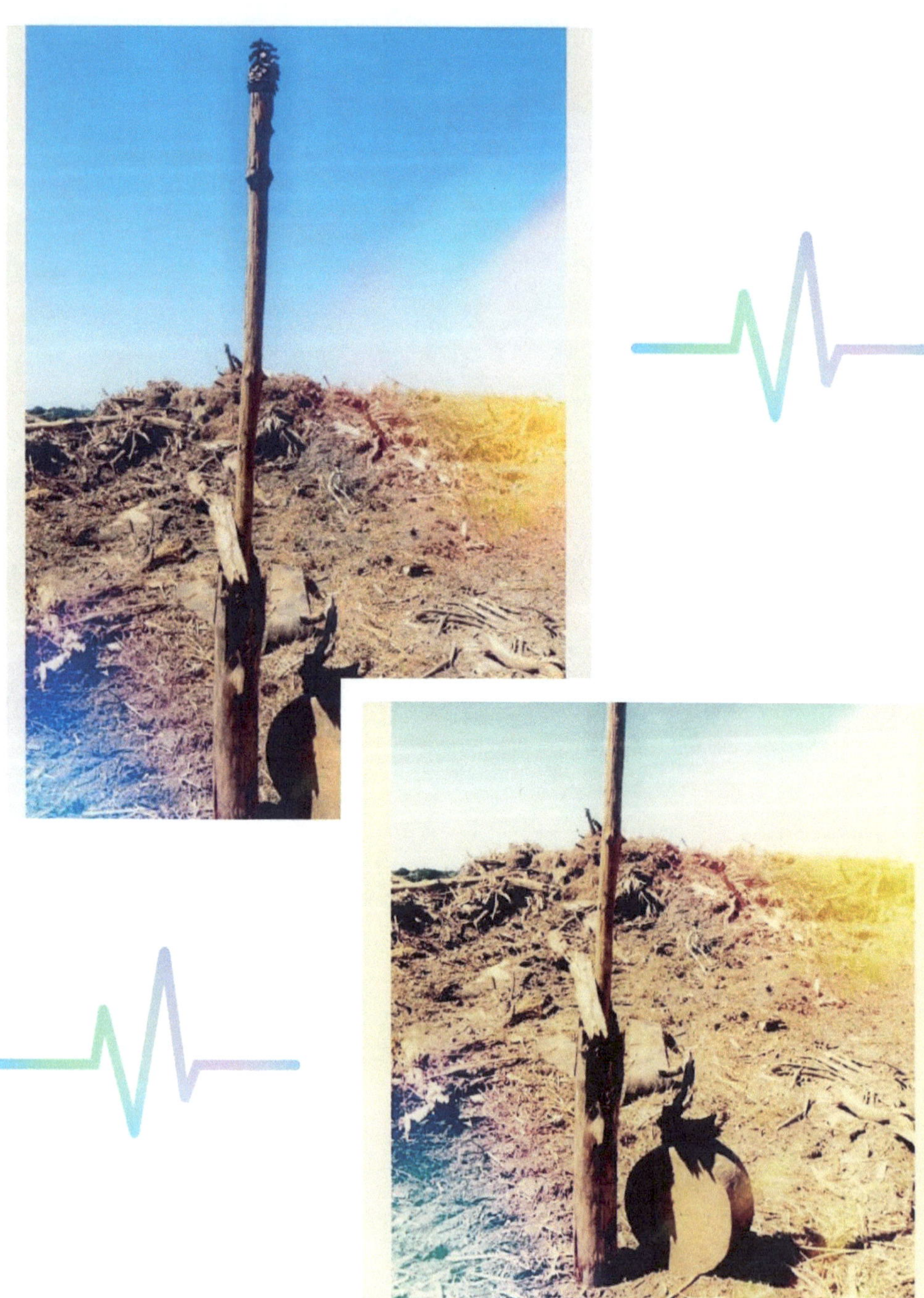

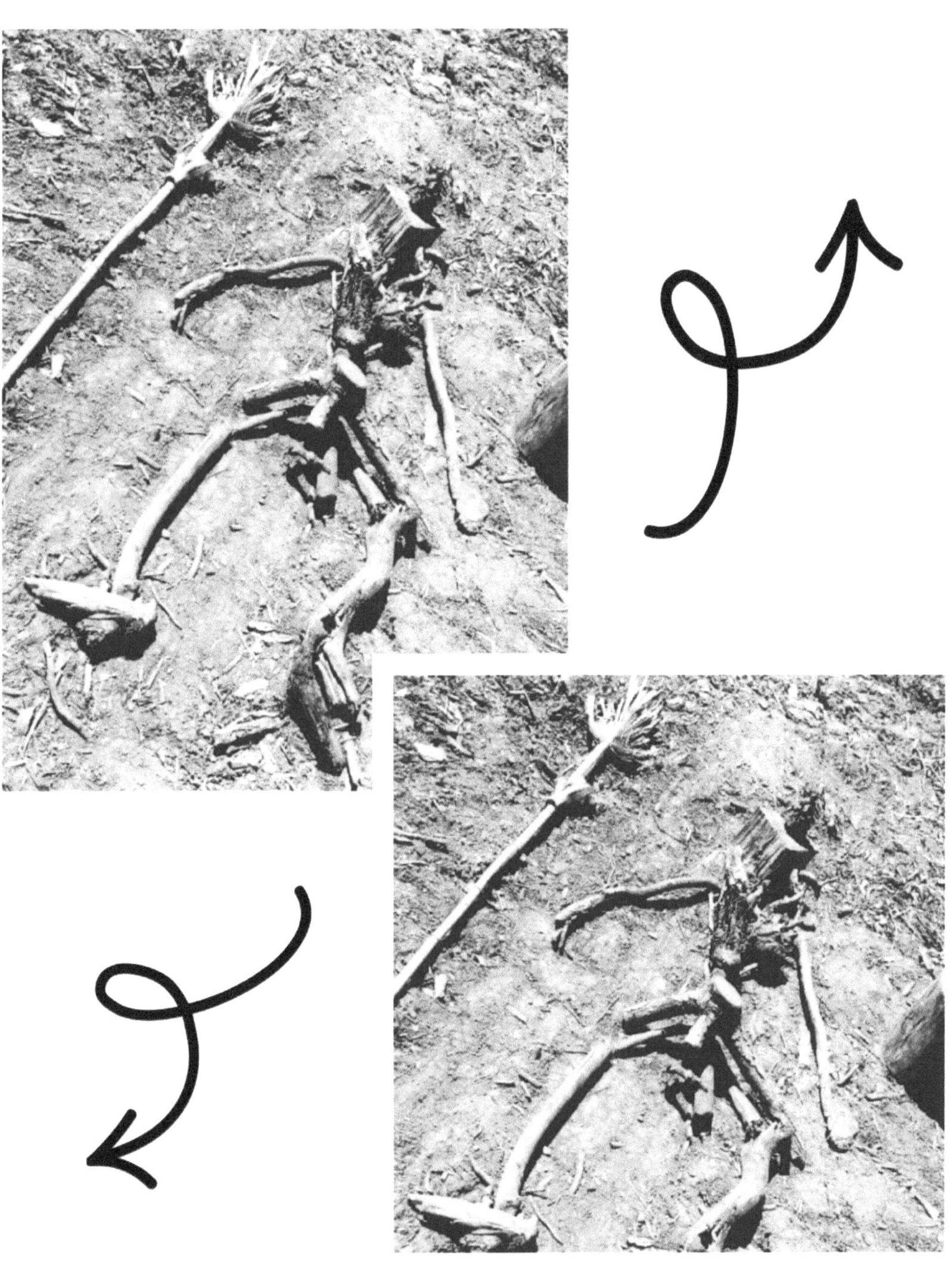

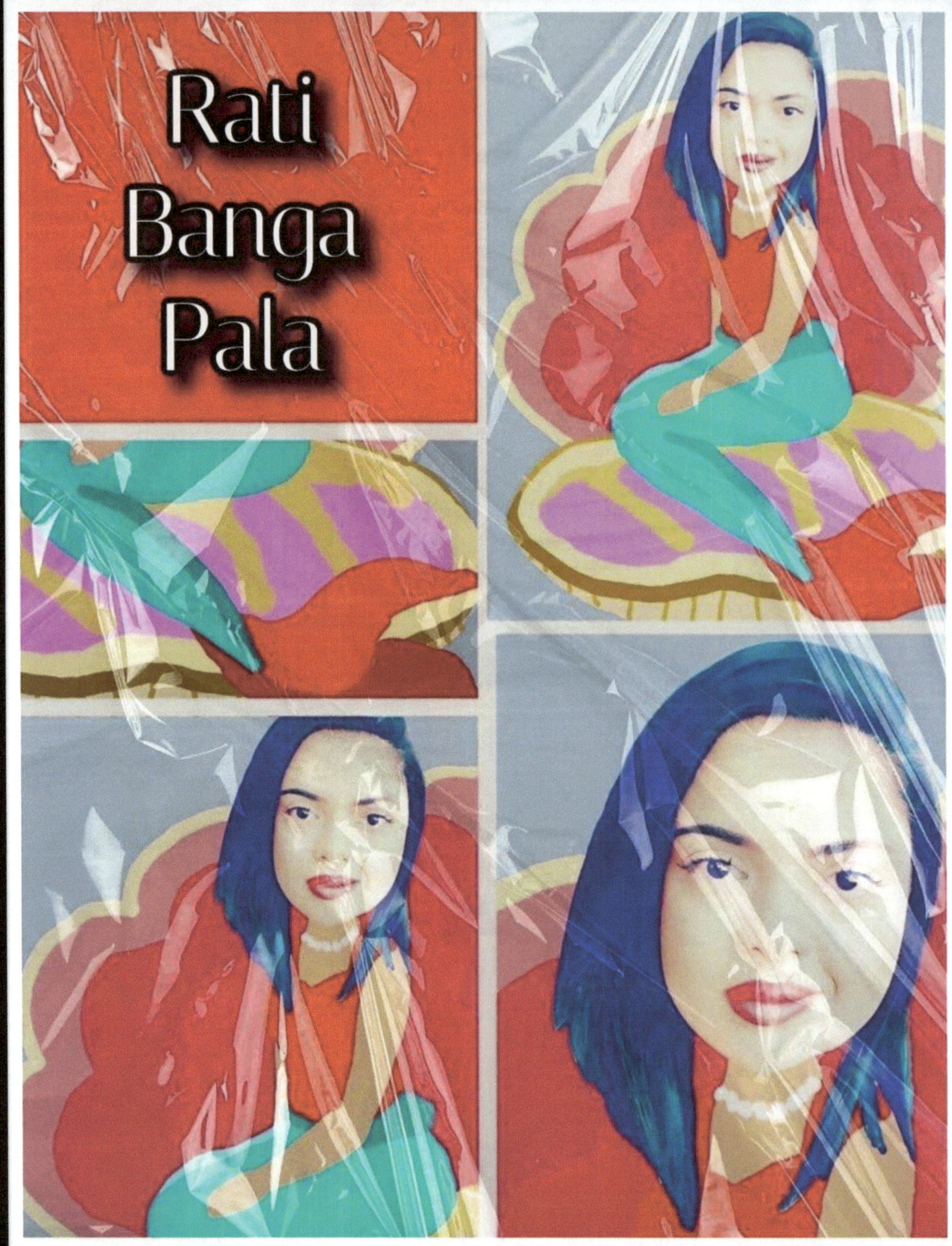
Rati
Banga
Pala

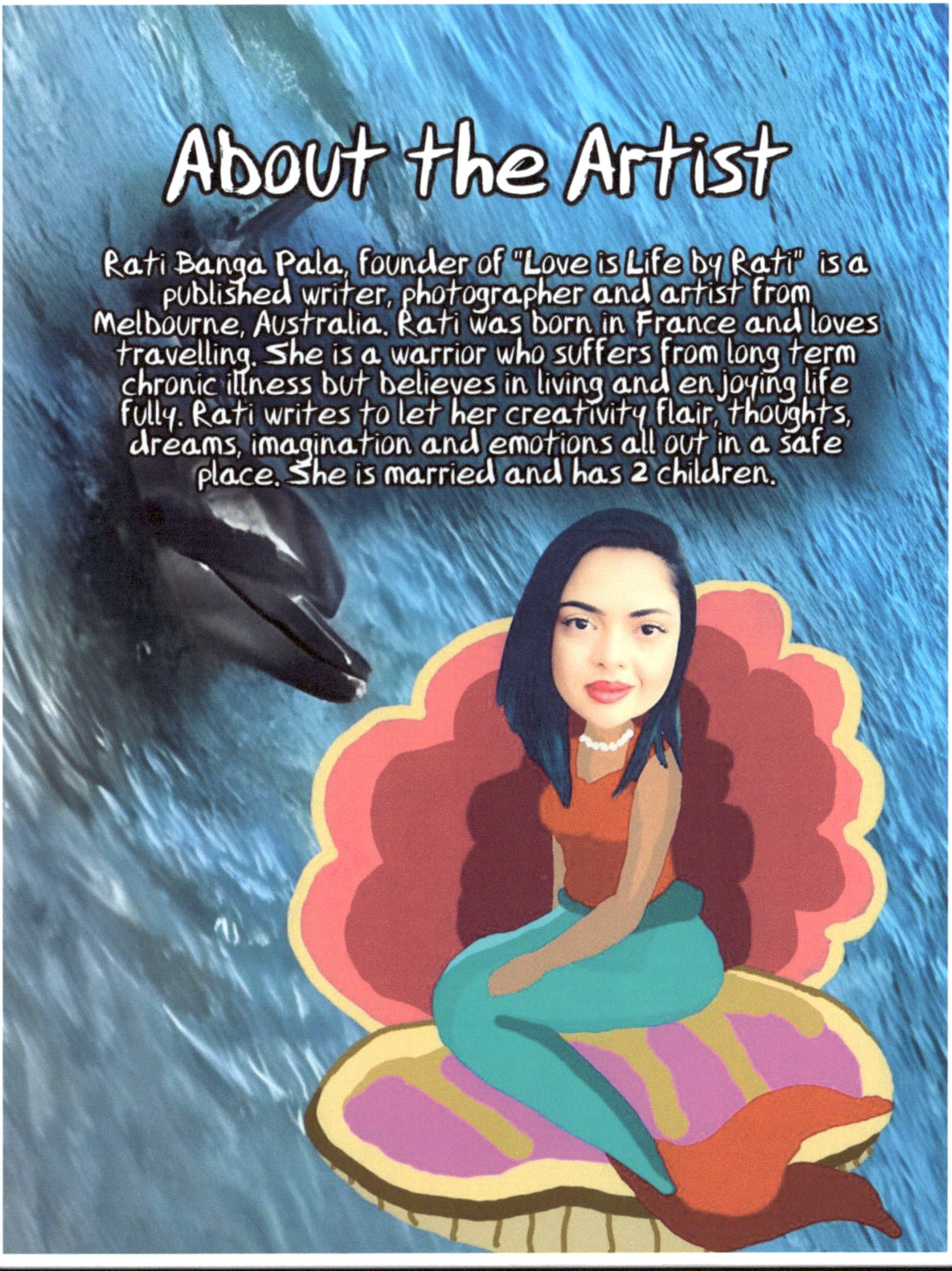

About the Artist

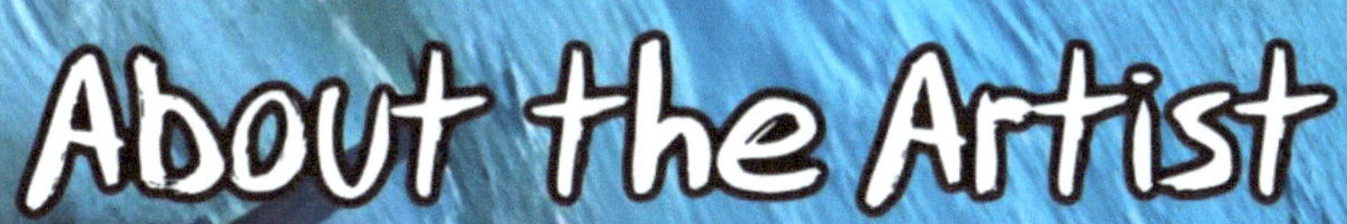

Rati Banga Pala, founder of "Love is Life by Rati" is a published writer, photographer and artist from Melbourne, Australia. Rati was born in France and loves travelling. She is a warrior who suffers from long term chronic illness but believes in living and enjoying life fully. Rati writes to let her creativity flair, thoughts, dreams, imagination and emotions all out in a safe place. She is married and has 2 children.

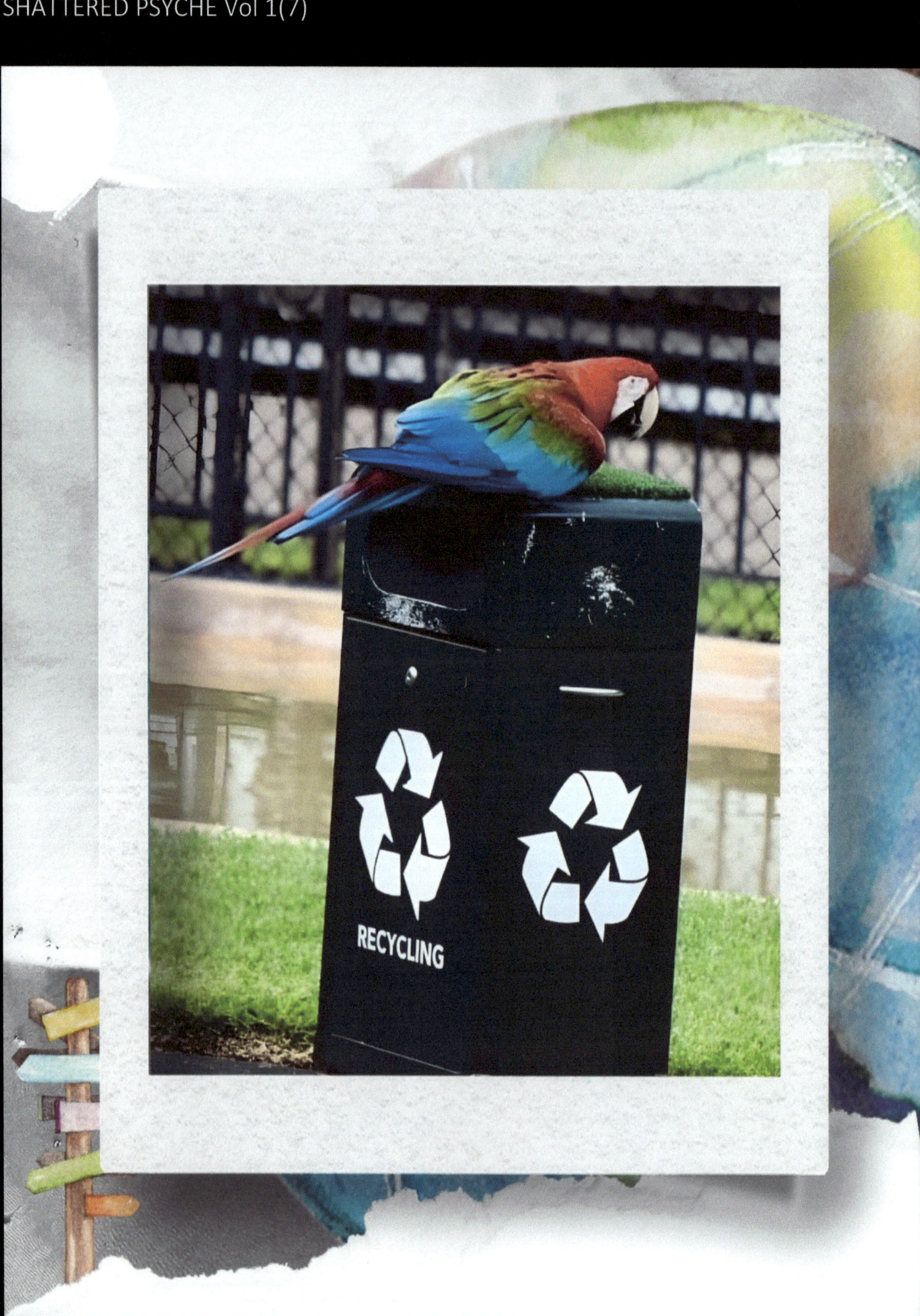
RECYCLING

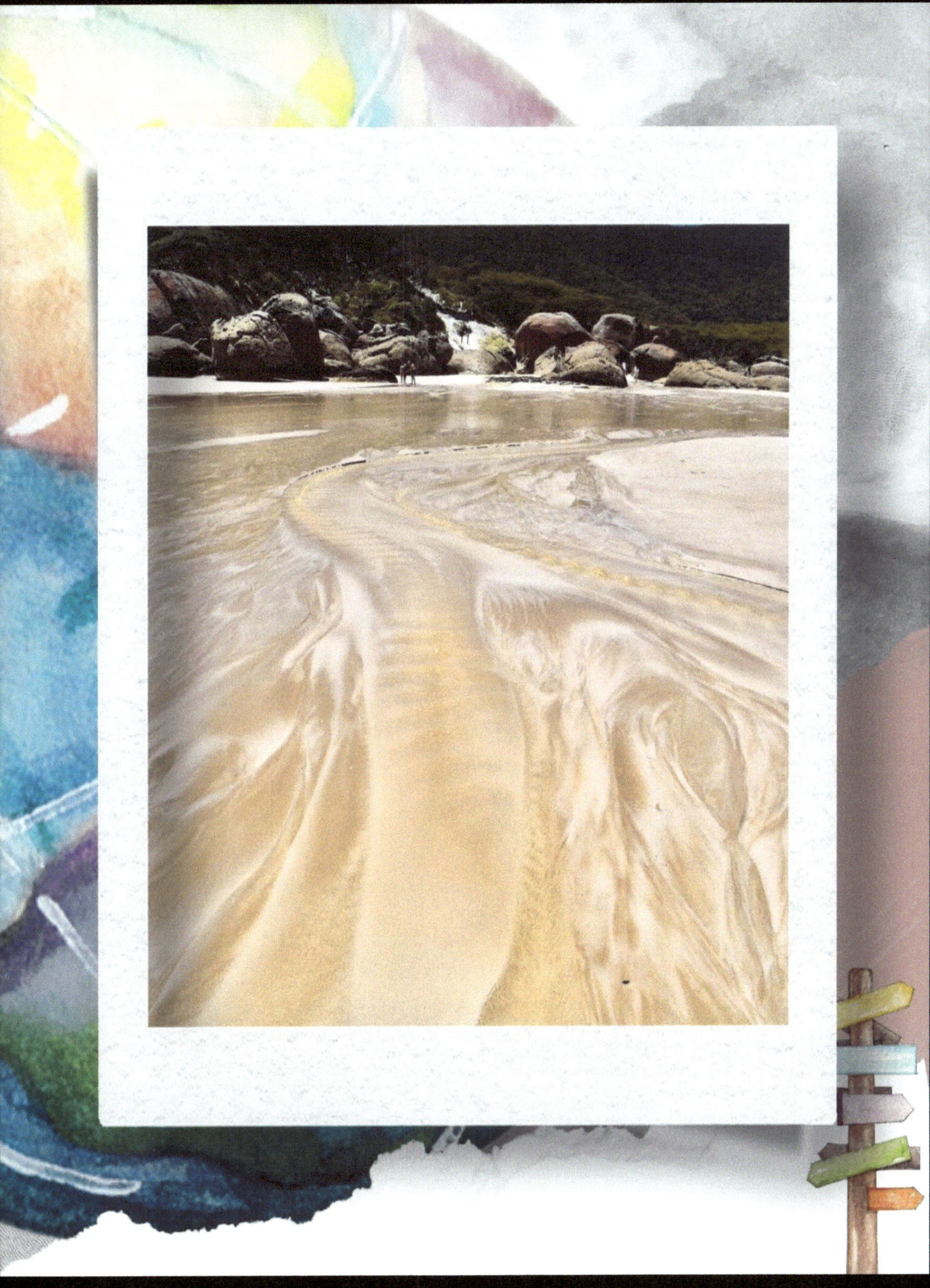

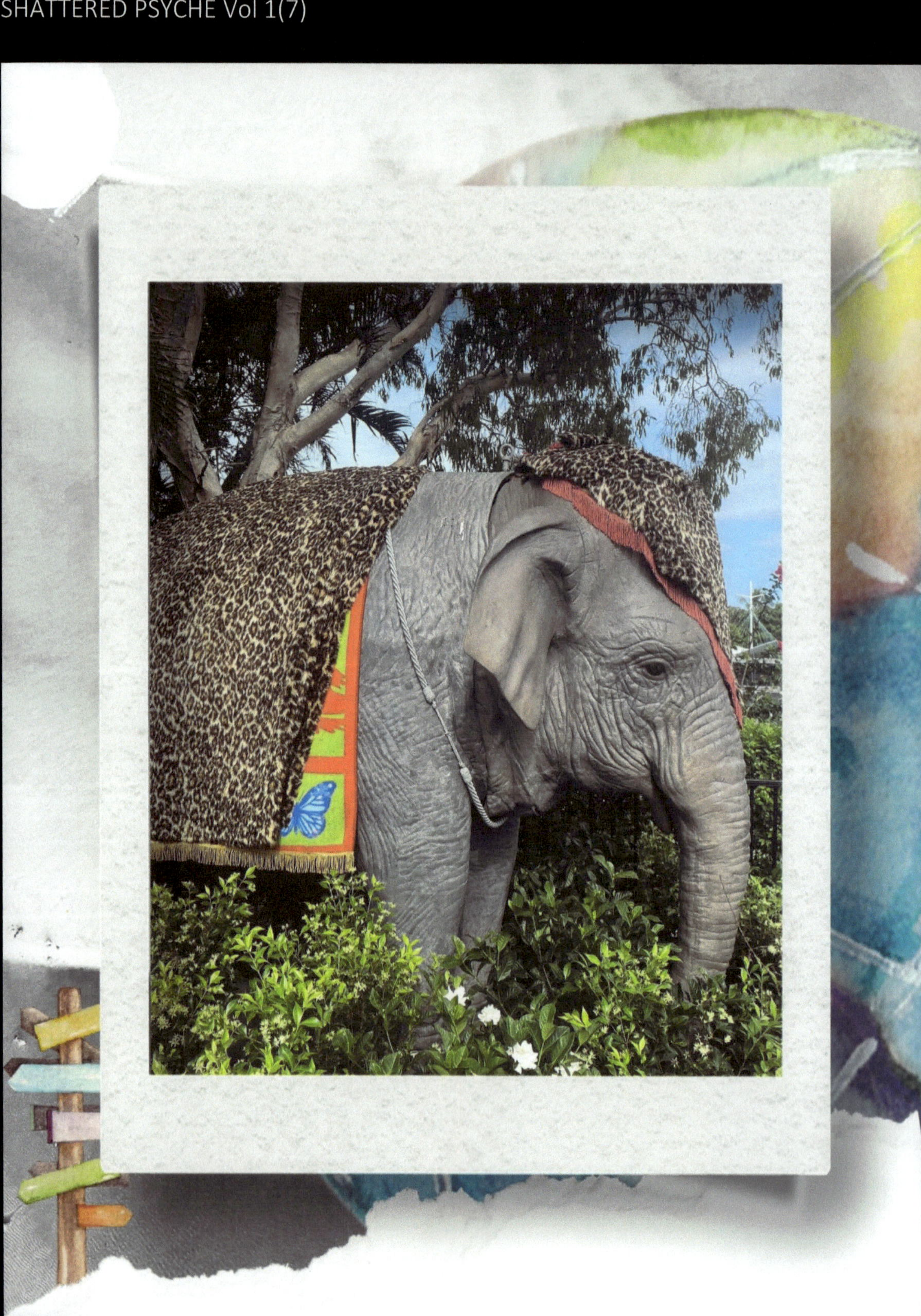

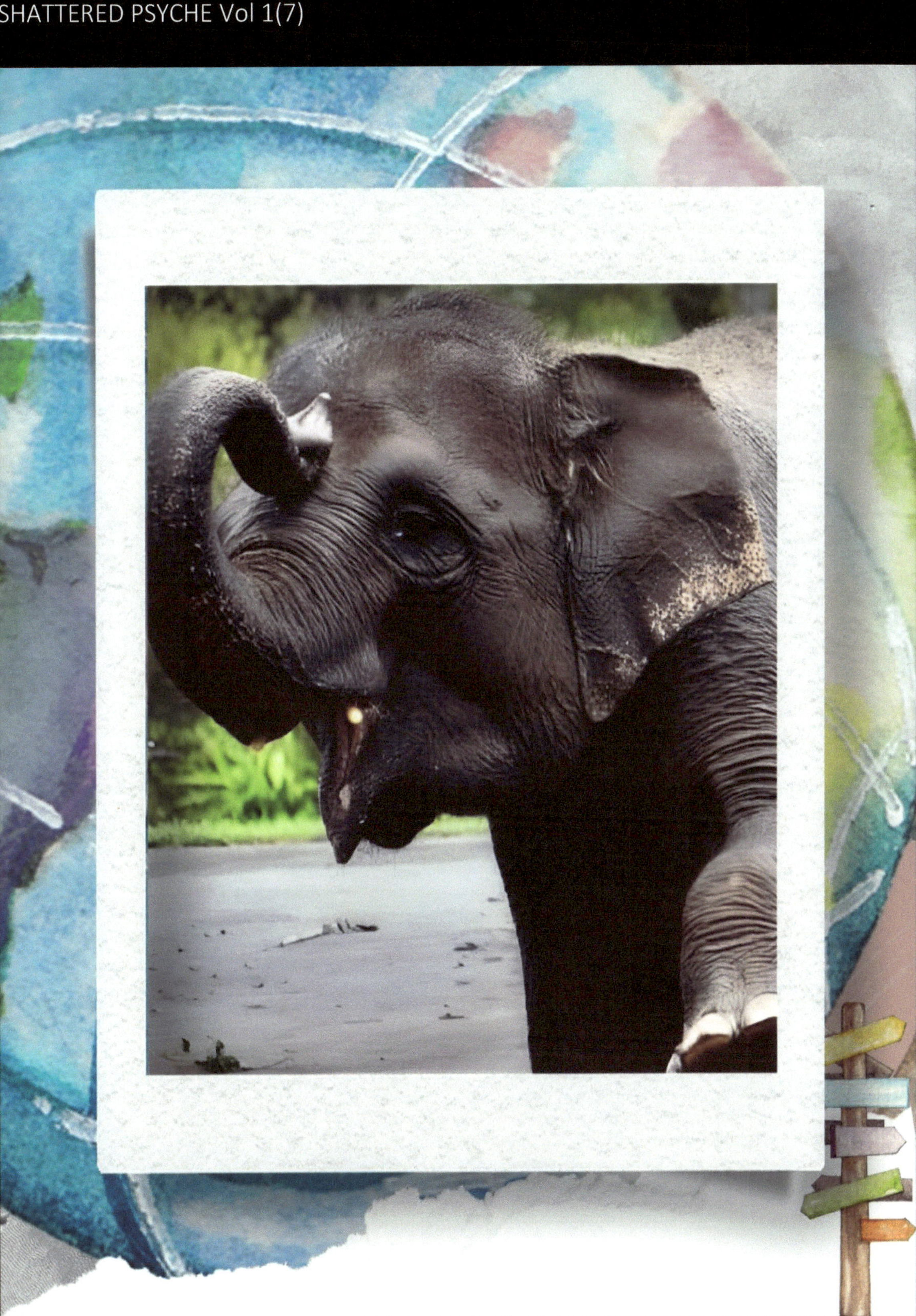

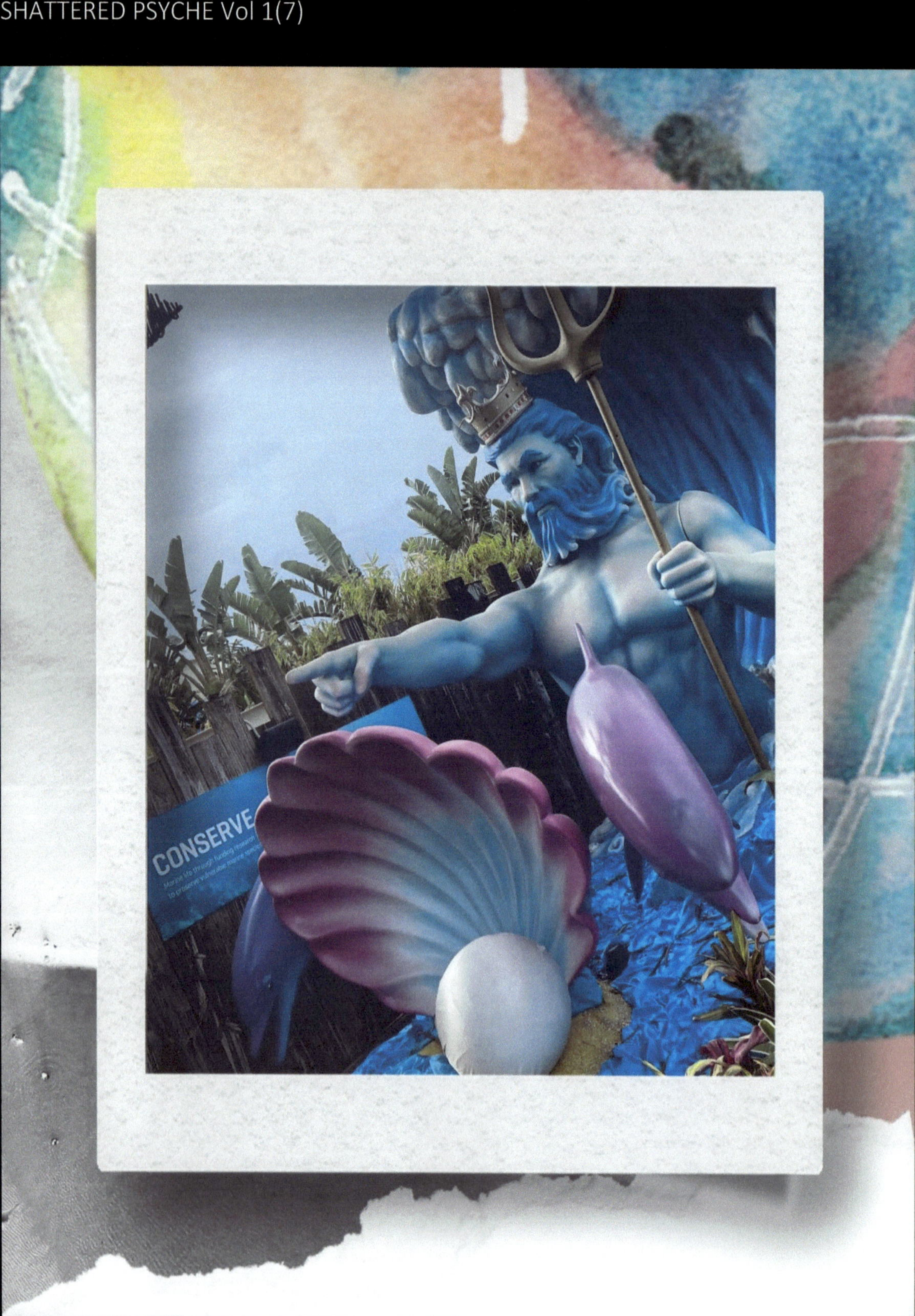
CONSERVE

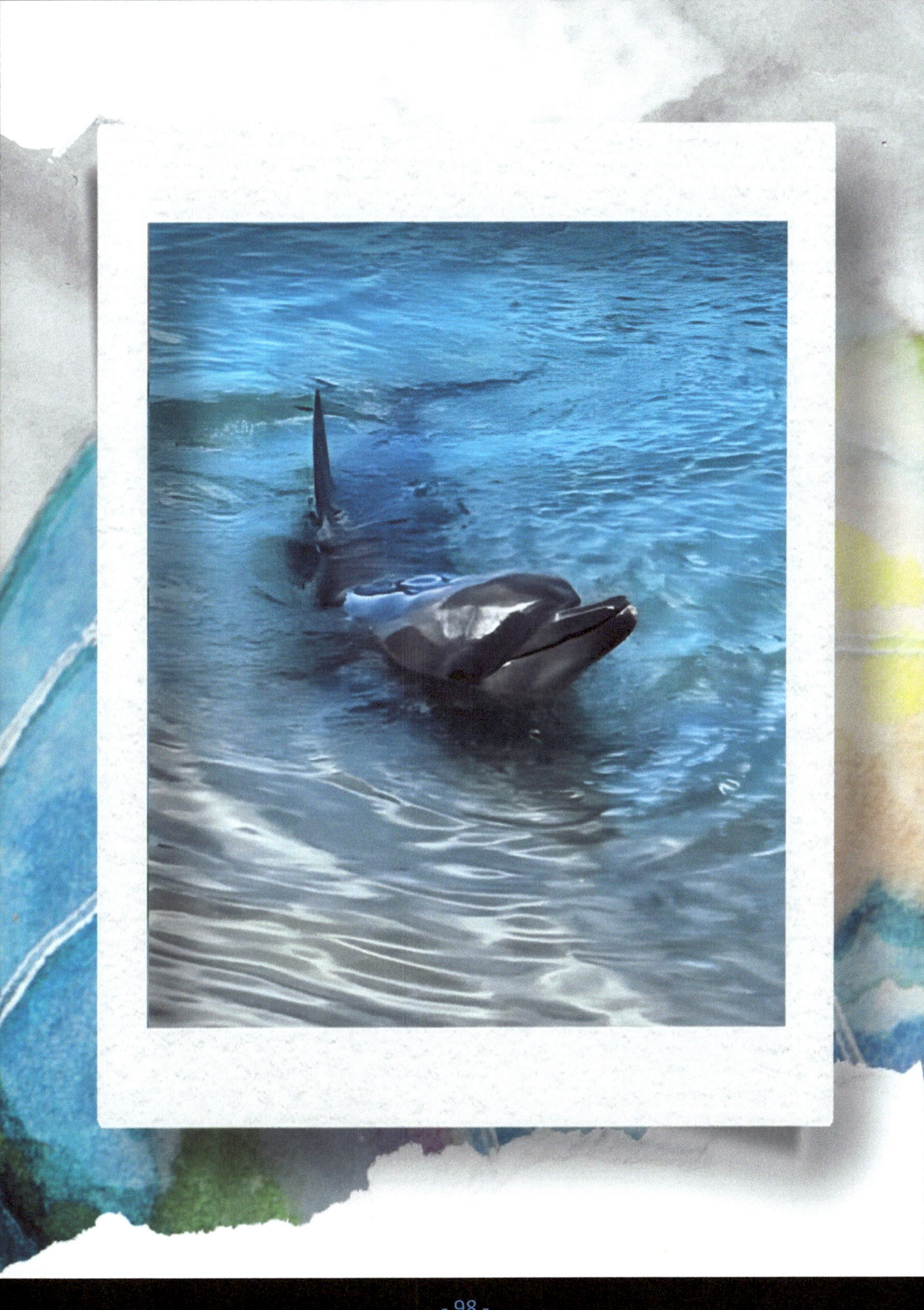

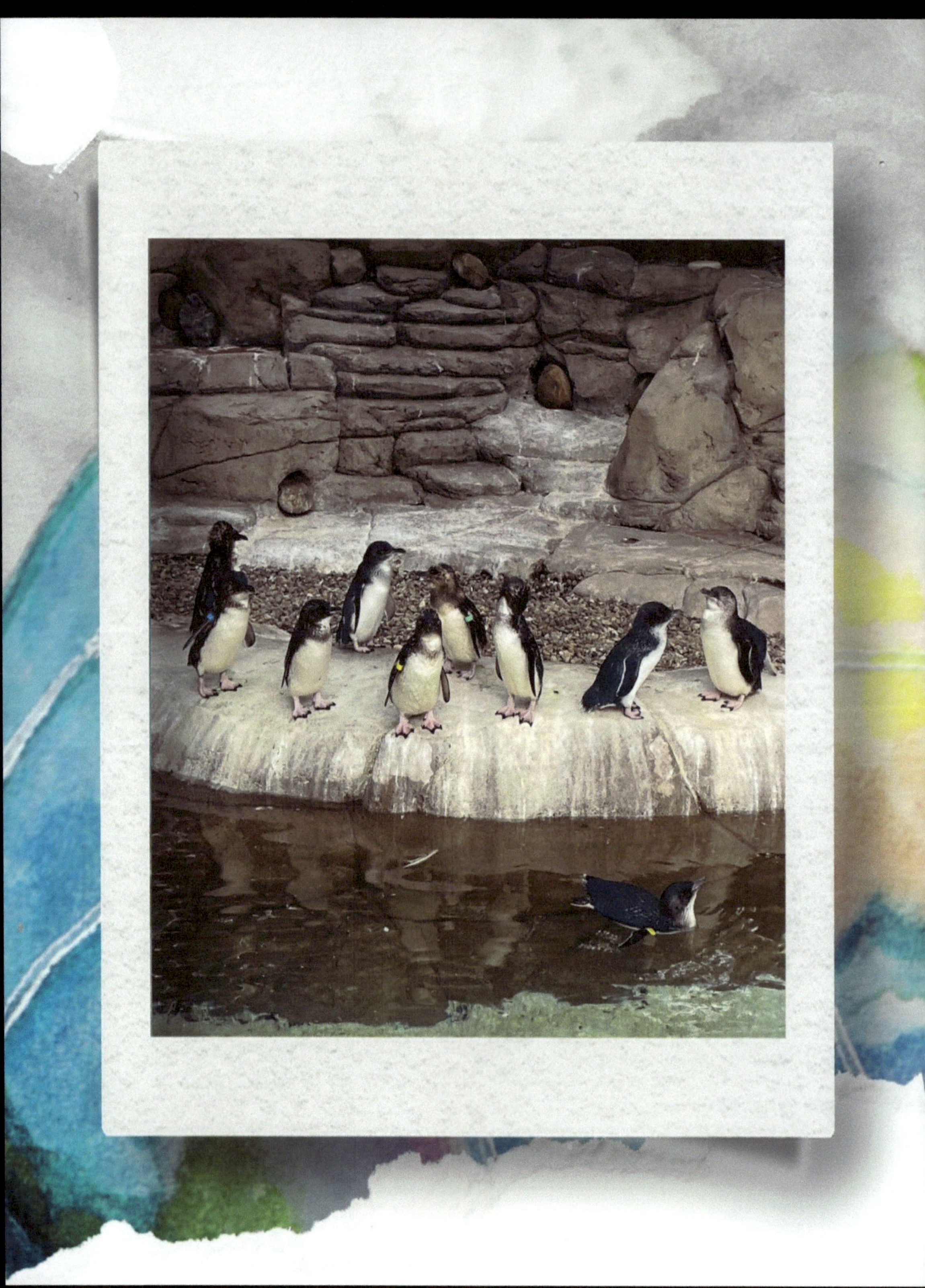

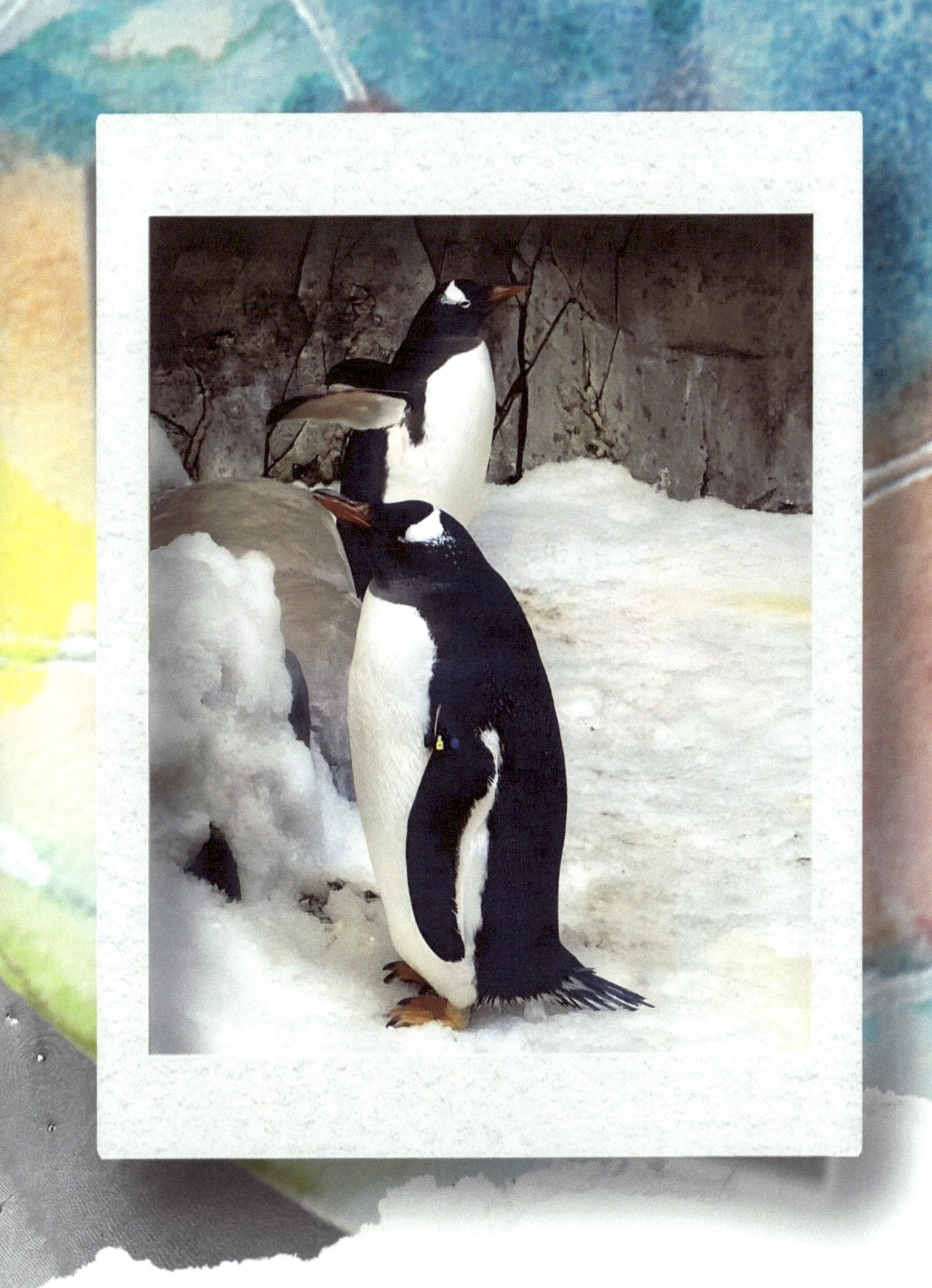

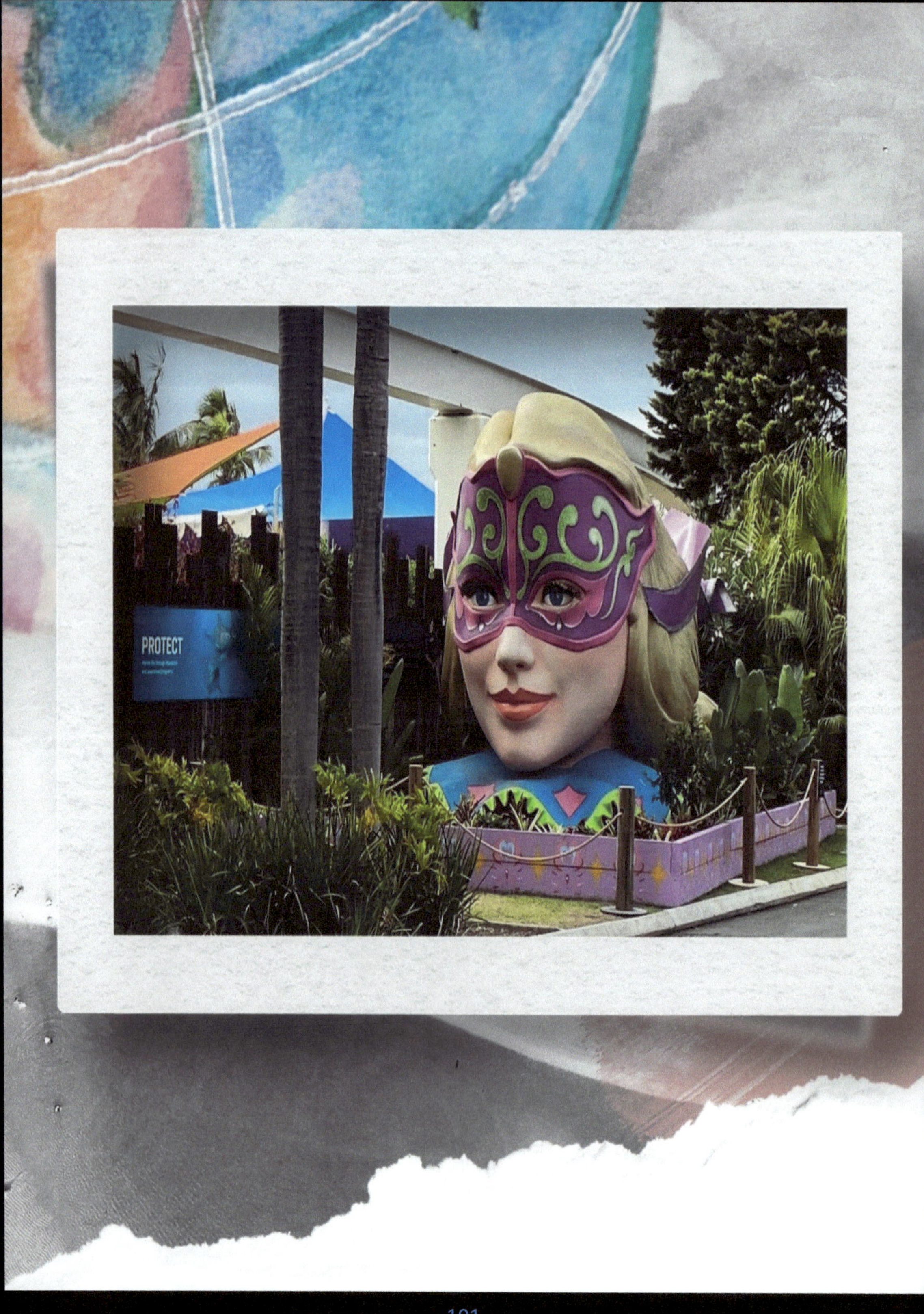
PROTECT

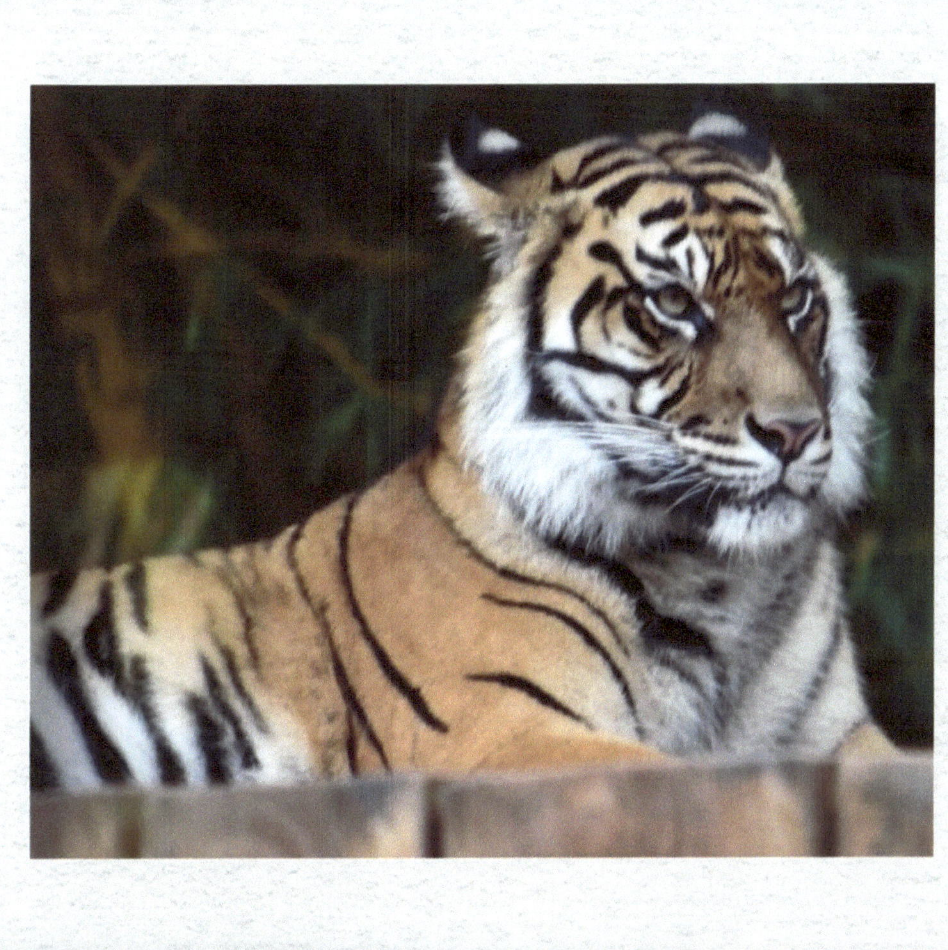

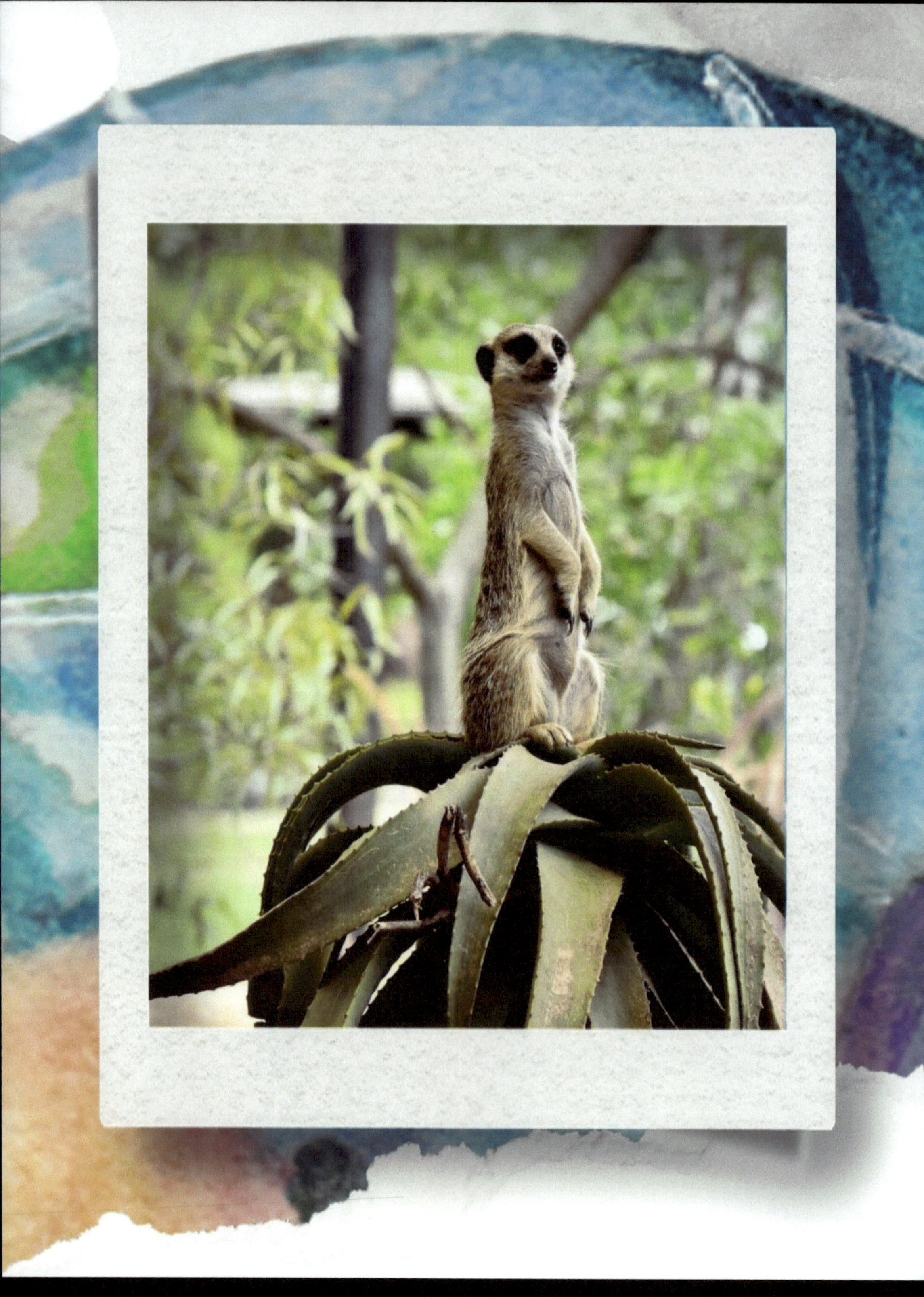

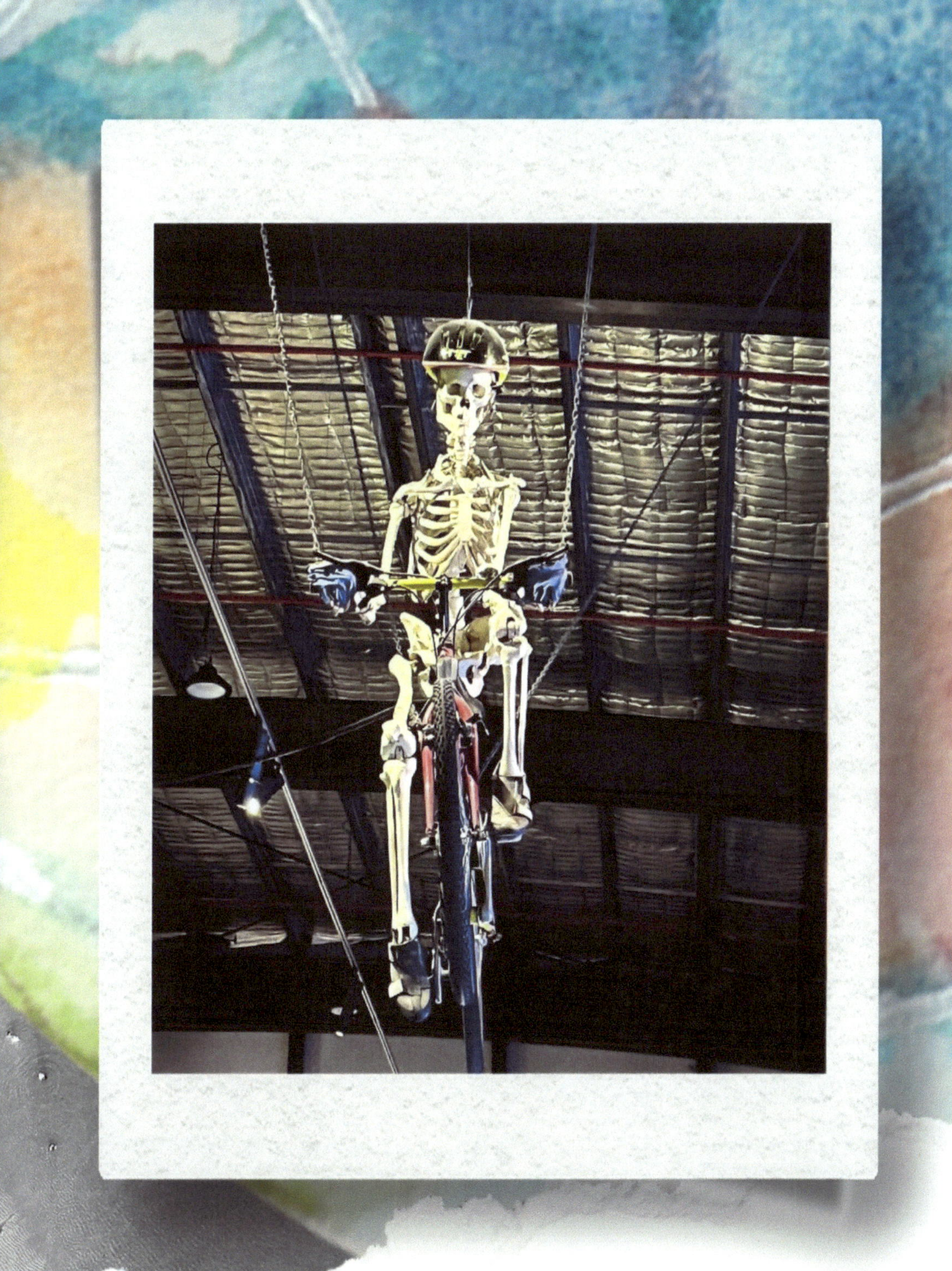

More from
I Ain't Your Marionette

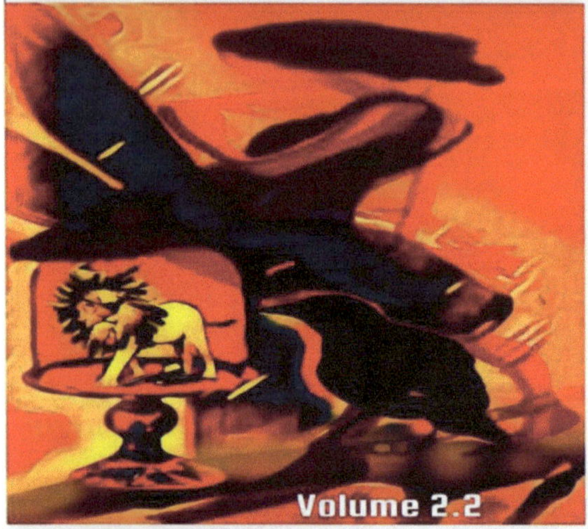

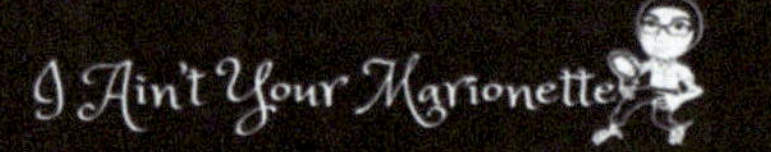

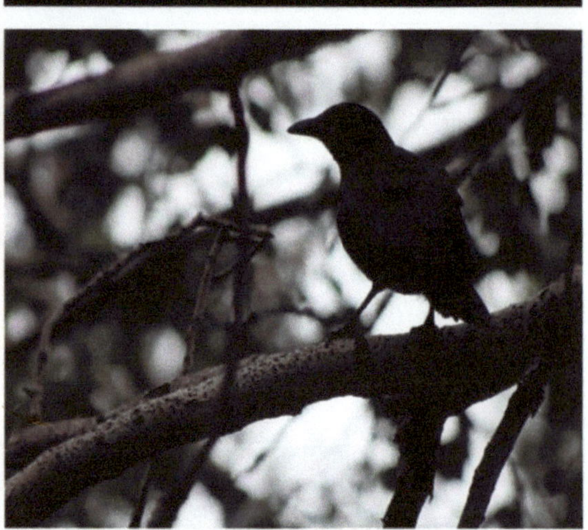

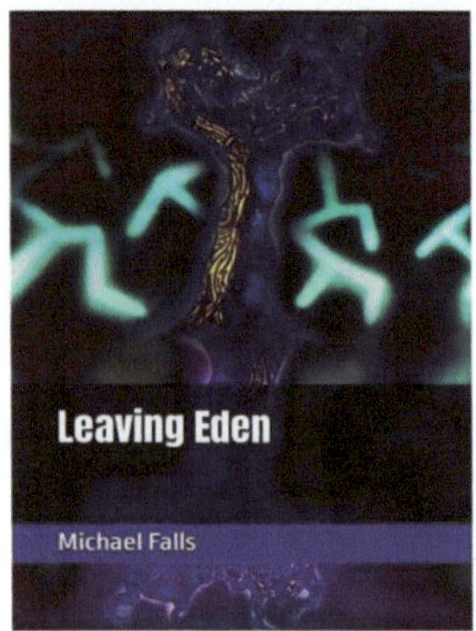

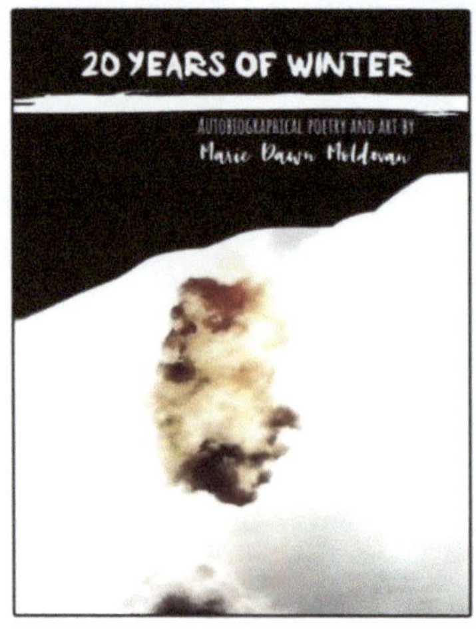

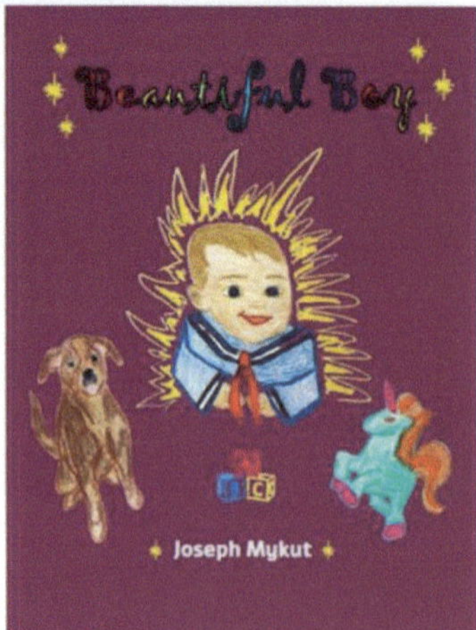

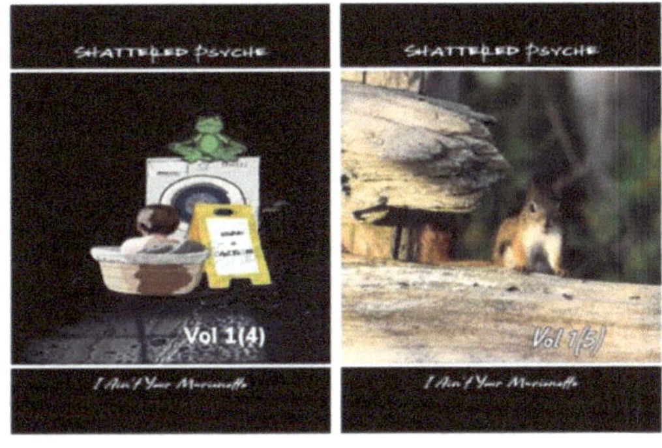
SHATTERED PSYCHE
Vol 1(4)
I Ain't Your Marionette
SHATTERED PSYCHE
Vol 1(5)
I Ain't Your Marionette

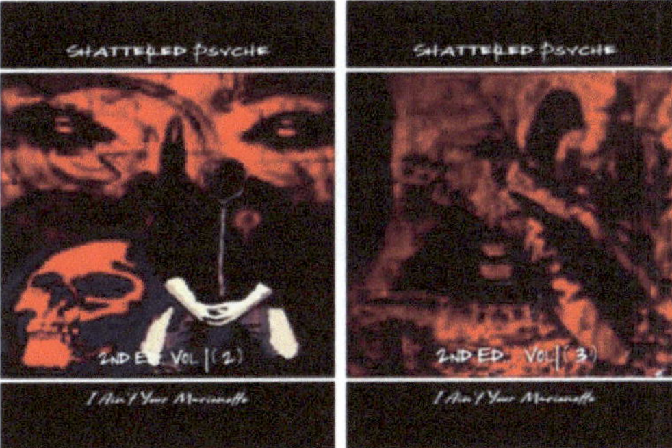
SHATTERED PSYCHE
2ND ED, VOL 1(2)
I Ain't Your Marionette
SHATTERED PSYCHE
2ND ED. VOL 1(3)
I Ain't Your Marionette

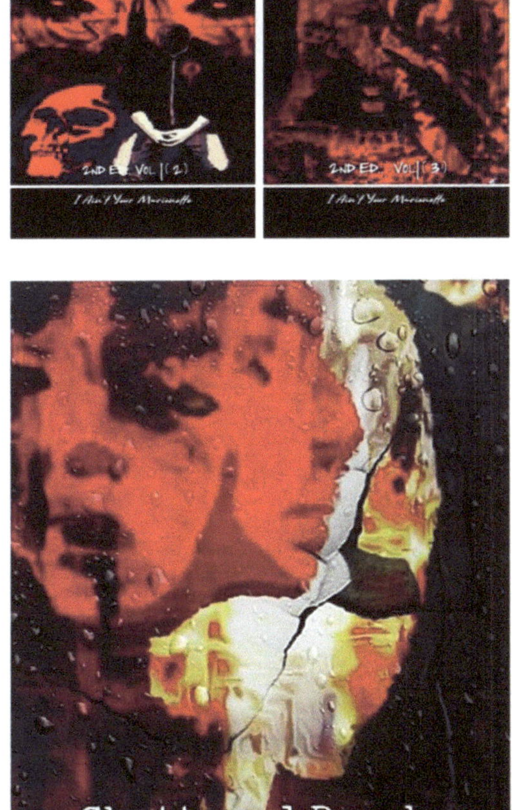
Shattered Psyche
2nd Ed., Vol 1(1)

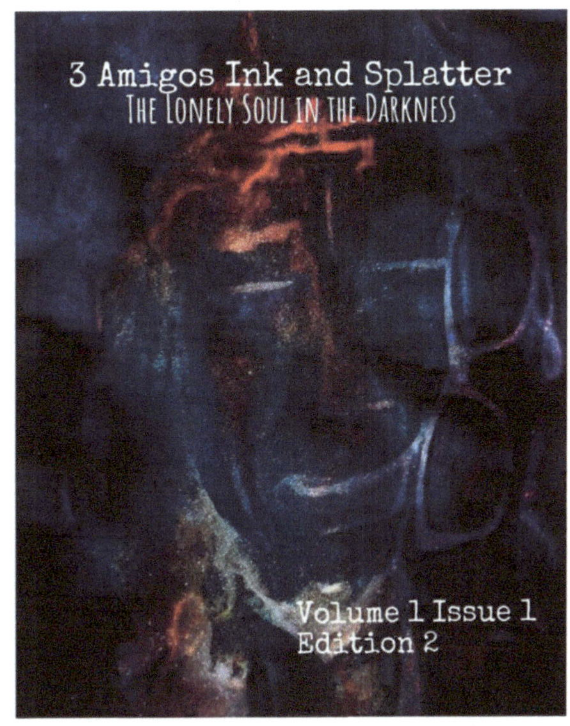
3 Amigos Ink and Splatter
THE LONELY SOUL IN THE DARKNESS
Volume 1 Issue 1
Edition 2

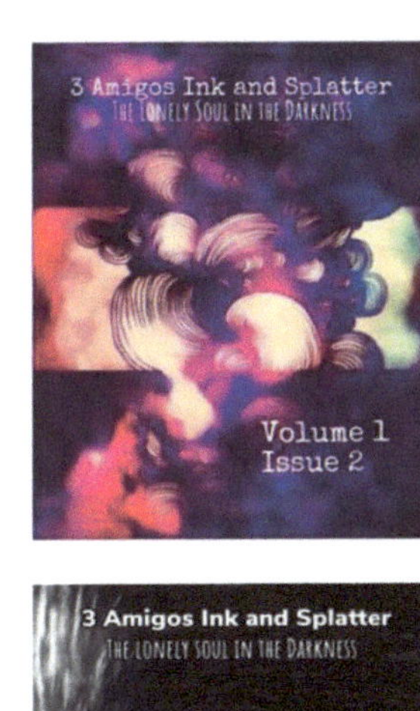
3 Amigos Ink and Splatter
THE LONELY SOUL IN THE DARKNESS
Volume 1
Issue 2

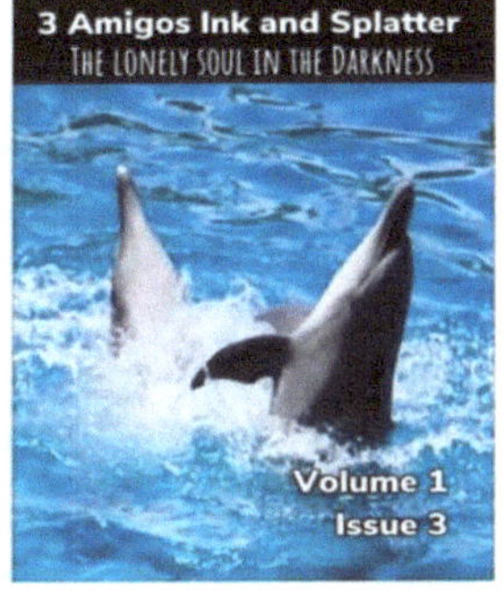
3 Amigos Ink and Splatter
THE LONELY SOUL IN THE DARKNESS
Volume 1
Issue 3

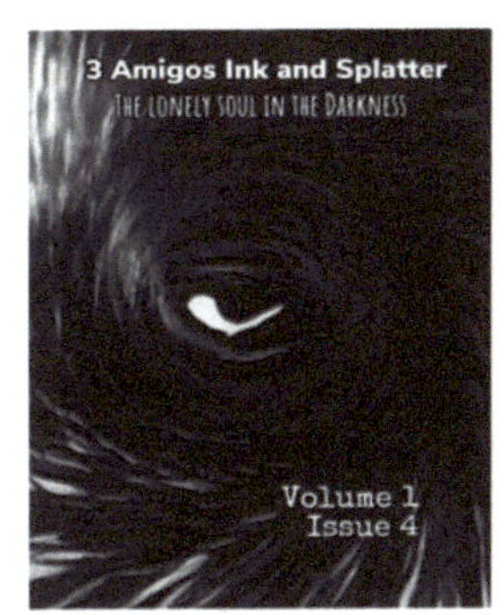
3 Amigos Ink and Splatter
THE LONELY SOUL IN THE DARKNESS
Volume 1
Issue 4

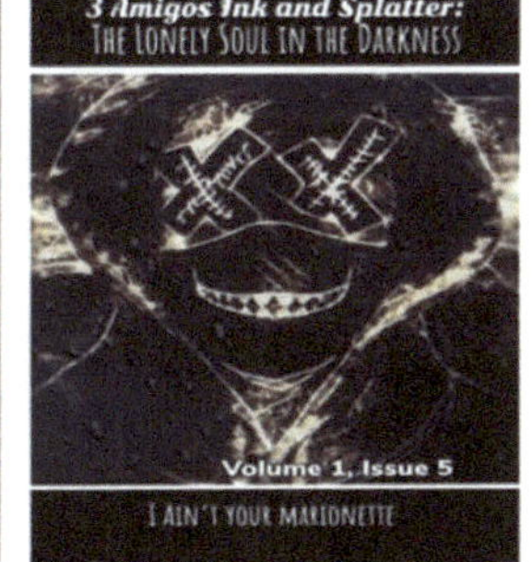
3 Amigos Ink and Splatter:
THE LONELY SOUL IN THE DARKNESS
Volume 1, Issue 5
I AIN'T YOUR MARIONETTE

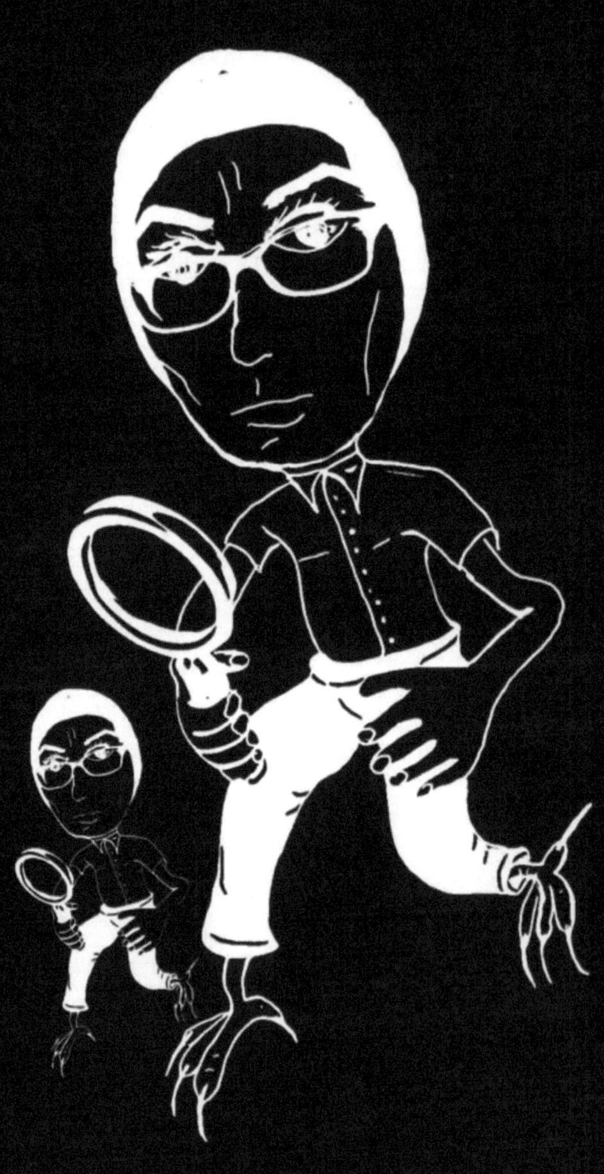

THANK YOU